# THE CORNISH VIKING

# The Cornish Viking

## Volume 1: From Rat Race to Tide Race

Christopher Marrow

Waterside Productions

ISBN-13: 978-1-958848-82-1 print edition
ISBN-13: 978-1-958848-83-8 e-book edition

Waterside Productions
2055 Oxford Ave
Cardiff, CA 92007
www.waterside.com

*This book is dedicated to my one-in-a-million wife who came with me to do strange things in strange places, and to my family who came along for the ride. It also thanks the wonderful people of Orkney who welcomed me with such warmth and friendship.*

# TABLE OF CONTENTS

# MAPS

# PREFACE

D ialect or not dialect? That is the question!

Dost thoo ken whit hid means if thoo reads the like o' this?
(Do you know what it means if you read something like
this?)

As I write I find myself in a quandary. Much of the part of my
life covered by this book takes place in Orkney and Shetland. If
I show speech in the King's English the stories I will recount will
lose a great deal of authenticity. On the other hand, most people
will not be familiar with many aspects of the accent and dialect of
Orkney and Shetland and readers may find it very hard to understand. Before I reach passages where quotations will feature, I think
it best to acquaint the reader with some of the basics.

Most will be aware of the Scots use of the word 'bairn' for a child,
and also their use of the word 'wee' for small. Thus, a small child in
Scotland becomes a 'wee bairn'. However, although the Orcadians
and Shetlanders still talk about 'bairns', the universally used word
for small is 'peedie', or sometimes 'peerie', and therefore the 'wee
bairn' becomes a 'peedie bairn'. Peedie is a word that is thrown
into many sentences and appears frequently. To quote something
that was once said to me, "The poor peedie bairn wis tekked tae
hospital in Aberdeen fer it wis bloodless!" You will doubtless be able
to interpret that as, "The poor little child was taken to hospital in
Aberdeen because it was bloodless." I cite this as a linguistic example, rather than a medical diagnosis, of course!

Some pronunciations that I will use phonetically may require some explanation as well. The Orkney dialect will use 'thoo' instead of 'you' and 'hid' instead of 'it'. Thus the Orcadian for, "You know, I've never seen anything like it," becomes. "Thoo kens, Ah've ne'er seen the like o' hid!" It is very widely recognised that to ken something is the Scots way of saying that they know something.

Where understanding risks being stretched to near breaking point I will add a translation afterwards, or make it clear what is meant from the context.

Happy translating!

The following is my next quandary. Inevitably the stories that follow involve people many of whom are either still alive or who are still remembered. Just changing their names would not in many cases disguise the person to whom I am referring. In such small communities any characteristic is enough to identify people and they may not want some quirk or some escapade from their younger years to be broadcast to friends, acquaintances or to a new generation. On the other hand, they might be quite proud to have been involved in some prank or humorous incident. This poses a problem – how to describe an incident without embarrassing those concerned?

I have tried to avoid embarrassing people by creating fictitious names in many instances and at this juncture I would like to make it clear that everyone who appears has my undying good will. Thus, where there is doubt as to whether people would want to have a new generation reminded of escapades from years past, that is where I have either missed out names or changed them. They were, almost to a person, friendly people and showed kindness that was worthy of appreciation and admiration. True they were often eccentric, but I say that as a compliment. It is therefore my sincere wish that people take pride in having been involved in the stories that follow. With the old way of life seemingly dying out, I hope that anyone who has been recognised will see themselves as beacons of a disappearing culture and that I for one am pleased to record episodes that are increasingly being replaced by an anodyne and homogenised world. "The old order changeth, yielding place to new!" (Alfred, Lord Tennyson.)

It is true that life has led me into unexpected and little-known places doing unexpected things, to the extent that fitting the story of my life into a single book has proved impossible. This book takes us via New Zealand and London to Orkney and Shetland and the stories revolve around wild weather, racing tides and the glorious eccentricities of people in that distant corner of the UK. It also recounts stories from a way of life that is rapidly disappearing and many aspects of it have already receded into history.

Later my life as described in future books will change entirely as I head to the South Pacific and the results of a famous mutiny are involved, and then on to living in a war zone in Africa. Humour changes to pathos, poverty and danger. In subsequent books I hope to recount how I explored a river route that had been closed for a generation, go down a river to a remote part of Nicaragua in a canoe and then run the fleet of ships on Lake Malawi from the gloriously named Monkey Bay. Be warned: the mood changes entirely from book to book.

# WHERE IT ALL BEGAN:

I have always claimed to be Cornish, and there is certainly a good deal of Cornish ancestry in my background, but in these days of DNA testing it has become very clear that we are all mongrels. My maternal grandfather's family had come from the Redruth area, and he himself had ended up as an engineer in Devonport Dockyard. Mum met Dad when they played in the same hockey team at college in Plymouth, but when the second world war commenced, Dad had been called up to join the Somerset Light Infantry. This has always seemed somewhat contrary as he was a qualified pharmacist and physically as far from being a light infantryman as one could imagine. Clearly he was better suited to the medical corps, though, given their very high mortality rate during the war, perhaps the illogical choice was fortuitous. He ended up in Greece and Italy and Mum was left staying with her parents when I was born. However, the family home in Plymouth was badly damaged by bombing and they had to move in with a great aunt. Thus it came about that I was born in a remote cottage near the hamlet of Crowcombe in Somerset.

Once the war was over my Dad and paternal grandfather, also a pharmacist, bought a chemist's shop in the little town of Stratton in North Cornwall. My earliest memories are from Stratton. We stayed briefly in a house in the town and then moved into a cottage on a hill overlooking Stratton on one side and out to the Atlantic on the other. We could see from Trevose Head to Lundy Island, and on the horizon ships passed on their way to the Bristol Channel or the Irish Sea in one direction and to the seven seas in the other. West winds howled round the house in winter and it was even known for spume from the sea to reach us, but those southbound ships may have been headed for tropical climes and romantically named places - Cape Horn, the Caribbean, Africa.

How much has that view shaped my life? Those passing ships were a window into a big world beyond; exotic lands beckoned. A young boy's imagination was inspired.

And so I went to sea!

Not from Cornwall, however. Stratton was a dying town and increasingly becoming a dormitory for Bude, which had taken over as the main centre. Even so, as the old rhyme had it:

> *Bude was but a fuzzy down,*
> *When Stratton was the county town.*

However, the cattle market in Stratton closed and the writing was on the wall. Later Stratton Primary School, my alma mater, also closed. However, by then Dad had sold up and moved to Somerset. I was twelve and went to grammar school in Taunton, taught myself Spanish from a correspondence course, loved French. The desire to discover the world was strong.

# Days Deep Sea:

The 13,000 ton refrigerated cargo liner pitched northwards with a steady, pleasant motion, causing the susurration of the sea foaming past the hull to rise and fall with a rhythmic cadence. It was a dark, but balmy night. All deck lights on the ship were extinguished so that the navigation lights would stand out and be seen with ease by other ships. I leaned on the wing of the bridge and looked off to port where the darker line that was the foothills of New Zealand's Southern Alps could just be seen between the sea and the firmament. Above was a burst of stars - the Milky Way, the Southern Cross, even The Great Bear low on the Northern horizon making a tenuous link with home. The latter also looked down on Rosemary, my girlfriend, back in England. The big diesel engines joined the noise of the bow wave, adding a low, mesmeric background beat. I was at peace, if only for a few idyllic moments.

The year was 1960 and I was a second-year cadet on a fridge ship (refrigerated cargo liner) plying to the Antipodes. Earlier that day we had sailed from Port Chalmers where we had loaded lamb and butter, and now we were cutting a furrow towards the Cook Strait and Wellington. There we would take on the last of the cargo and head west towards Durban, Cape Town, and West Africa, and eventually we would punch through the Bay of Biscay and reach home. The great circle voyage across the Southern Ocean, surprisingly close to the Antarctic Circle, would prove to be cold, grey and unremittingly rough. Don't be fooled by the normal atlas page. The shortest distance between two points on the globe that is our home does not appear as a straight line on its flat representation on a map. Durban would suddenly be oppressively humid, and mosquitos the size of fruit bats would eat us alive in our bunks; but for the moment I could stand lost in reverie. All was for the best in the best of all worlds.

I was on watch with the Third Mate. He was a friendly, mild-mannered man, who got on with his job with quiet competence, never feeling the need to raise his voice to people. For the moment he was in the small chartroom behind the wheelhouse, catching up on some work or other, and had left me to keep an eye on things. Every twenty minutes I went up on the monkey island on top of the wheelhouse and used the compass up there to measure off bearings of lighthouses that I could see. Then I would pass through the wheelhouse and join the Third Mate briefly while I plotted the ship's position on the chart. A satisfyingly regular row of pencil marks progressed upwards towards Timaru and Lyttelton as we made a steady 13 knots.

The twenty minutes were up. I stirred myself from my reverie, climbed the vertical ladder onto the top of the wheelhouse and took the compass bearings. On my way through the small wheelhouse to the chart room I had to pass through a narrow gap between the large wooden wheel and the radar set, and I couldn't help noticing, dark though it was, that there didn't appear to be anyone standing at the wheel. I slipped into the chartroom through the heavy curtain that kept light out of the wheelhouse, muttered a greeting to the Third Mate, and poured briefly over the chart with parallel rulers and a pencil. The position fixed for another twenty minutes, I slipped back out through the drapes and stood at the radar, checking the outline of the coast off to port. Glancing at the helm, I soon realised why the helmsman was not immediately obvious. It was a young AB (Able Bodied Seaman), and he had returned on board straight from the pub just prior to sailing from Port Chalmers. It would not be fair to say that he was drunk, as he wouldn't have been allowed at the helm had that been so. However, perhaps we might say that he was as relaxed as a newt. The aftereffects of the booze made him tired, and he really rather wanted to take the weight off his feet. He had found that he could sit on the wooden grating abaft (to the rear of) the wheel with his back against the bulkhead, place his feet on the base of the wheel, and peer upwards at the gyro compass repeater to see his course. He could then turn the wheel with his feet. This had gone unnoticed in the dark as he had continued to steer in a straight line.

At this very moment, who should come through the curtain but Lecherous Len, the Captain. The origin of his nickname was not known precisely. It was believed to stem from his predilection for choosing the youngest and most attractive women from among the passengers to join him at the Captain's table at mealtimes. (We were a cargo ship, but could take up to twelve passengers without the added regulations that were imposed on passenger vessels.) Apart from his leching, Captain Len had a few other habits that made him a delight for every wag that came across him. For one thing, he habitually walked about with stooped and rounded shoulders, seated on a pigeon chest that had a little potbelly protruding beneath it. However, he was clearly aware that he did not cut the figure that he wished, and periodically he would harrumph loudly, pull in the belly, puff out his chest and throw back his shoulders. Slowly he would forget his appearance once again and would allow his body to subside back into its more usual and less than impressive state. If he was nervous or concentrating hard, the subsiding took place more quickly, necessitating a further harrumph, and others would follow at increasingly short intervals as the puffing up and slumping followed ever more rapidly. As he was a somewhat nervous man, these bouts of throat clearing and shoulder flexing were rather frequent. There was scarcely a person in the crew who failed to imitate this behaviour. Even the Chief Officer had been known to do it behind the Captain's back, invoking immense hilarity in all who witnessed it.

In case you might feel sorry for the man, I should mention that Lecherous Len was not a good man to serve under. He interfered, he showed little respect to his subordinates, and had, to all intents and purposes, a character so unremittingly grey and unattractive that I, who always feel sorry for the underdog, found it hard to feel very much sympathy for him.

When one walks from a lighted room into the dark, it takes a while for the eyes to re-accustom themselves to the lower light levels. It was therefore quite normal for anyone leaving the chartroom to pause for a while by the radar. This served the dual purpose of giving one the opportunity to familiarise oneself with the ship's position, whilst allowing one's vision to become accustomed to the dark. This was precisely what Len did on this occasion. He stepped through the becurtained doorway, harrumphed, threw back his shoulders, and slowly slumped forwards to take a position in front of the radar screen. After a moment or two, he started to glance around him, and, to his surprise, found that he could see no-one at the helm. By now I was standing by the starboard wheelhouse door and noticed the slow movement of his head stop precipitately and he appeared to be transfixed by what he saw by the wheel, or rather by what he didn't see. "Harrumph," he went, and stood to attention, shoulders back, stomach in, chest out, and eyes back on the radar. Then slowly the shoulders sagged, the chest dropped down and became a potbelly, and as his body subsided, he turned surreptitiously to the right and looked once more in the direction of the wheel. Pausing for a second, he harrumphed again, moved slightly away from the radar towards the wheel, and repeated the whole process. This time the next harrumph came quicker, the glance to the right was more deliberate, the stare into the black of the wheelhouse was longer, and the subsequent look at the radar screen was more perfunctory. Harrumphing like a grampus, he eventually ended up standing right next to the wheel and throwing out an arm to see if the body of the helmsman might somehow still be eluding him in the dark. His hand went right past the place where a helmsman should be and made contact with the bulkhead. "Harrumph, harrumph" he went, and was throwing back his shoulders and puffing out his chest as he rocketed back into the chartroom. "By God, sir. Do you realise that there is nobody at the wheel?" he bellowed. "Don't be so bloody silly, sir," replied the Third Mate. The pair of them came back out into the wheelhouse, and the AB was standing at the wheel, steering normally, and whistling through his teeth. With one last "Harrumph", Lecherous Len beat a hasty retreat back to his cabin and wasn't seen again that watch.

I disappeared out onto the wing of the bridge, suppressing my guffaws. For the rest of the watch I chortled repeatedly at the scene that had been enacted before my eyes. Later, I leaned over the rails, looked at the starry sky, saw the dark pencil line of the coast and the white of the bow wave passing down the side of the ship. The noises of the engine and the sea still rumbled and swished their backing music, and I chuckled happily to myself. "May I never work in an office," I thought. "May this communing with nature and following man's eccentricities go on forever." They didn't, but I have tried my best to make them.

There were other ships, older and newer; other trips, shorter and longer. I circumnavigated the world in both directions, first losing a day from my life and then getting it back again thanks to the changing time zones. The start of the trip with Lecherous Len had taken me to Corner Brook in Newfoundland to load newsprint for New Zealand and we had to break ice for several miles to reach the port. As successive tides come in and out, lumps of ice break away and form rims as you approach the ice field. It is known as the floating free. Captain Len was nervous at the prospect of taking his ship through ice and that necessitated several trips from the bridge to his accommodation to visit the loo. During one such visit the Chief Officer, who was no fan of the captain as well as being a bit of a joker, instructed the helmsman to aim at a very large chunk of floating free which resulted in a jarring and scraping. A harrumphing

Len appeared precipitately in the wheelhouse still pulling up his trousers and tucking his shirt in. "Didn't even flush it!" commented the Chief Officer.

In due course we had negotiated a channel through the ice that had frozen over again after an ice breaker had forged a route and a pilot boat came alongside just off the port. A pilot ladder was lowered over the side and the pilot got halfway up it before slipping and falling back into the freezing water. Fortunately he wasn't trapped between the ship and the pilot boat and escaped with a very cold ducking.

From Corner Brook we proceeded up the Saint Laurence and then turned 90 degrees to starboard and continued up the Saguenay River to Port Alfred. (Coincidentally I would later sail on a ship of the same name.) The Saguenay is a deep, but narrow river and the entrance is very fjord-like, with steep cliffs on both sides. This is the heart of French speaking Quebec and, as someone who speaks French, I was given a load of mail to take to the post office in neighbouring Chicoutimi. One of the crew had written to his family in the Rhonda Valley and, not unreasonably, had addressed it to Wales. The postmaster looked at it and said, "C'est oú, ça?". "Where's that?" I told him it was the "Pays de Galles" which is French for Wales. "Never heard of it," he said in French. "Grande Bretagne," (Great Britain) I then tried, but that was no good either and in the end I had to address it to Wales, England. I have often wondered what comments that elicited in Tonypandy!

We carried on loading then in Montreal where a further humorous incident occurred. A rather mild mannered, but strong looking junior engineer was in a bar and had a bit too much to drink. He was involved in some sort of altercation which caused the barman to call the police. Two very bulky Montreal cops turned up, but the engineer refused to go quietly. With one hand he kept both the lawmen at bay while making his way back to his beer. He then continued to hold them off literally single-handedly while using his other hand to pick up and drink the rest of the beer that he had left. As soon as the glass was empty he stopped resisting and went off with the cops, as meek as a lamb.

The ship then went back down the Saint Lawrence and we called at Trois Rivières and Quebec City before going through Panama to New Zealand. Then in due course the earlier scene with the disappearing helmsman occurred.

I had also sailed on the lovely old ship, the Port Dunedin, taking her to La Spezia in Italy to be broken up. Built in 1925, she was the first ever ship to be built with twin diesel engines. Balancing ships' engines to avoid vibration, especially with twin engines and twin propellers, is an issue most will not be familiar with. The Port Dunedin was the first to achieve this balance and thus was the first twin engined motorship. Even so, most twin engined ships had certain revolutions at which these vibrations were noticeable. These were known as critical revs and as the ship accelerated on leaving port it had to pass through these spells of vibration which at times were quite intense. On the Port Dunedin the bands of critical revs were highly extensive, so getting up to full speed on leaving port was an uncomfortable exercise. However, although appearing very old-fashioned, she was immensely strong. Her absolute top speed was 12 knots (22 kph), which made a trip across the Pacific a tedious exercise. Even so, as we sailed down the coast of Portugal towards the Mediterranean we overtook more ships than overtook us.

In 1962 the Cuban missile crisis occurred, and I happened to find myself in the Caribbean on another ship en route from Curaçao to Panama. We were steaming along nowhere near Cuba and heading in the opposite direction. I was on watch when a US destroyer hove into view, rushed alongside us and addressed us through a loudhailer. "Stop your ship, captain. I intend to board you and inspect your vessel." As an allied vessel on the high seas he clearly had no right to do this, so the captain ignored him entirely and we proceeded on our way. Fortunately the destroyer captain thought better than to create an international incident. I will never know how close we came to being the victims of the US navy.

The route across the Pacific could also hold considerable interest. I passed close to the island of Raivavae in the Austral Islands of French Polynesia, and I bet you have never heard of them. In a further episode later in my life the Austral Islands featured in an episode concerning Pitcairn, and the Bounty mutineers settled briefly on another island in the group. On another occasion we passed what seemed to be no more than a stone's throw from one of the Galapagos. Then on a great circle course from the Bluff in the far south of New Zealand en route to Panama we passed close enough to Easter Island to actually see the famous and mysterious stone statues through binoculars. Islanders came out in motorised canoes to try and sell us curios, which was over optimistic.

My last two trips were noticeably different. They were the first two trips of the Port Nicholson, which at the time was the largest refrigerated cargo liner ever built. She quite easily exceeded 20 knots (37 kph) and effectively nearly halved the Pacific crossing time from Panama to New Zealand compared to the Port Dunedin. I first joined her in Belfast at the shipyard where she had been built. Immaculately painted and with the steel decks largely covered with holystoned (scrubbed) wood planking, she was like an enormous yacht or a cruise liner. I have remained in contact with some of my shipmates, though one tragically died by choking on a lump of meat.

In due course the period of my apprenticeship was over and I came ashore and studied briefly at what was then Plymouth Technical College before travelling to London and passing what in those days was called a Second Mate's ticket. Instead of continuing the normal progression of training I would go on to manage, operate and navigate my own ships. This is not what you would call a normal career progression!

Every trip ended in the arms of Rosemary, my childhood sweetheart, and when I had qualified, we married. I had seen the marriages of Merchant Navy officers, and they didn't always work very well. I saw men whose vows were forgotten the moment they set foot ashore in a foreign port, and others who were everlastingly faithful to their wives, only for the wife to use their absence to continue dallying with every man that came along. If both parties were well matched and faithful, they had to put up with constant parting and heartache. Why couldn't Rosemary and I go off and do things together? So we did.

# SOMETHING IN THE CITY – VIA THE ALPS

Try as we did to avoid the rut, the mundane and humdrum were like a magnet and we were drawn inexorably to them against our will. We turned up life's little byways in an effort to reach places and people of interest, only to find that the inviting little track rapidly turned right back into another dual carriageway with traffic hurtling along in both directions. Of all things, by the end of the 1970s I ended up as a company director in charge of a freight company in London. I hated it.

One byway I had tried to turn into led to Aix-les-Bains in Savoie in the French Alps. I worked in the nearby provincial capital of Chambéry in a company called La Société de Transport Pan Européenne. It had a British subsidiary called Pan European Transport. I was tasked with learning the business inside out in the head office before taking over the UK end. We were there for nine months and rented a lovely, but somewhat dilapidated villa that stood above the town and had an amazing view across the Lac du Bourget to the well-known peak of the Dent du Chat, or Cat's Tooth. Our address was Chemin de Bellevue, or Beautiful View Road.

Aix les Bains had a very strong British heritage. In English the name was Aix the Baths and it owed the name to very well-known thermal baths that were renowned for their health-giving properties. It was very fashionable among the Victorians, and indeed

Winston Churchill happened to be visiting there when World War 2 broke out. There were many establishments with British names, and many signs in shop windows saying, 'English Spoken'. That may once have been true, but they were relics of the past. One garage that I used had just such a sign on the door. One day I pointed to it and said, "C'est vrai, ça?" (Is that true?) "J'sais pas. Qu'est-ce que ça veut dire?" he replied. (Don't know! What's it mean?")

The landlady lived in a flat on the second floor with its own external stairway. In her nineties, she was Italian by birth and had first married a Prussian army officer. Because Italy was an ally of Britain in the First World War, she was placed under house arrest and the responsible officer for overseeing this was British, a Colonel Biddulph. When the Prussian failed to return after the war, she married the good colonel. They went to the UK, but in due course in the 1930s had moved to the villa in Aix les Bains. Having been controlled by the British in the First World War, she then had her house commandeered by the Germans in the Second and was under their control. This all gave rise to enormous confusion between languages. She was no linguist and was completely incapable of isolating the different languages. For example, she called our children "les kinder". We also heard how she wanted to buy a blouse when she was in England - 'une chemise' in French. Walking down the high street, she saw a chemist shop and immediately assumed from the name that a chemise would be found in a chemist and couldn't understand why the assistants thought it was funny! The consequence of her linguistic incompetence was a complete failure to be able to make herself understood in France. At times I even had to translate using a melange of languages for her.

This wasn't helped by her name. Madame Biddulph when pronounced in French sounded like Madame Bidule, which translates as Mrs What's-her-name. This made introductions extremely confusing as it sounded as if you were saying, "I'd like to introduce you to Mrs So-and-so!"

Now in her 90s, she had become very eccentric, but remained extremely active, and it would not be unusual to return to the villa and find her washing the garage door from a stepladder, or suchlike.

The company accountant was quite severely handicapped by polio from childhood and he walked with difficulty. He ran the accounts department with an iron fist. Woe betide anyone who whispered to someone at a neighbouring desk. "Monsieur Beltier!" He would roar, or whatever the name of the offender was, and would shake his stick at them. He lived nearby and we often shared a car to and from work. He had the archetypal French car, a 2CV. It was especially adapted for his handicap with a hand accelerator. He drove it with Gallic flair and succeeded in managing the accelerator, the gears, and the steering wheel with his hands and was still able to make copious use of the horn and, when annoyed with another driver, (which was frequent), was also able to wave his stick out through the open roof whilst shouting abuse.

The road just above our house lead up to Alpine peaks and there was a ski slope not too far away. I did have a go at ski du fond. Our two oldest sons, Andy and Duncan, both went to a nearby primary school and had to adapt themselves to learning purely in French. Andy became quite proficient, but when we returned to the UK he went to a school at which a teacher performed the amazing feat of getting him to unlearn it all. What a disgrace!

It was a pleasant and interesting interlude, and it brought my French accent to the point at which the French couldn't tell that I was English. I was variously asked if I was French Canadian, which I certainly don't sound like, but also if I was Belgian, which might have been taken as an insult in the minds of many French people. In those days it was common for the French to tell insulting jokes about Belgians, rather as Americans told Polack jokes. It would be nice to think that we have gone past derogatory racial stereotyping, but I fear that is not the case.

The chairman of the UK company was called Larry de Jong, let's call him. He was an eccentric Dutchman. You may already have surmised that I view calling someone eccentric as a compliment, since life without eccentrics would be a terribly uninteresting existence. His chain sucking of Polo mints and laying a half-sucked mint on the table when a meal arrived was one of his less harmful habits.

However, many of his eccentricities were hard to live with, especially since by then I was a family man. For example, it was his wont to sleep late and start work in the afternoon. By the time the rest of us had done a gruelling day's work, he was just coming to life, and felt that we all needed to be focused on the task of running the most efficient forwarding company in Britain. His means of seeking to achieve this was to insist over and over again that we all completed our day's duties and then retired to a Chinese Restaurant in West London where he would create tensions that he was convinced would be good for everyone. Since that meant that several times a week we weren't finishing our day until well after midnight, what it really achieved was to make everyone tired and ratty. As he did have a certain charisma in an odd sort of way, we didn't all pack it in and seek employment elsewhere. However, my life was really being made a misery by these antics.

It had been yet another evening spent in the Chinese restaurant, interminably chewing over why this person did this, or why that person said that. Ye gods, it was tedious! Periodically Larry would target one person or another for criticism, and I would find it was my role to defend them to try to keep their morale from sinking too far or I would be the one to suffer the consequences on the morrow. This night it had been my turn to be the butt of this destructive management style. I seem to remember that we had a client with whom we had a contra account. In other words, we did work for them and they did work for us, so we owed them money and they owed us money. Generally speaking, we owed them more than they owed us, and they allowed us to subtract what was owed to us and pay them the difference. At this particular moment the balance had swung the other way. Why, Larry wanted to know, had I allowed them to subtract what they owed us when they paid us. The total lack of logic in this criticism was round about par for the course, but there was no-one there who considered it their role to worry about my morale.

I left the restaurant fuming with rage. By this time it was past midnight and I still had a fifty-mile drive home along the M4. My anger buoyed me up for the first thirty miles or so, but exhaustion then took over and I had to pull off at a junction, seek a lay-by and sleep for a while for fear of nodding off at the wheel. Waking a little later, I set off again, but had scarcely travelled further than the next junction before I was being overtaken once more by sleep. I wound down the driver's window and put my head out into the blast of cold night air. I slapped my cheeks. I turned on a tape and sang loudly, but it was all to no avail. Sleep kept creeping up on me, and I had to stop again. All in all, I stopped five times in the fifty miles and it was the middle of the night by the time I reached my own bed.

As my head hit the pillow with relief, my heart was back on that bridge wing and I heard the beat of the engines and the swish of the bow wave. On my face blew the zephyrs of summer winds, and above me were the stars. I yearned once more to chuckle at the funny things in life, practice more honest skills. The time had come to seek a different byway, hopefully one that didn't lead right back onto a major road as the previous one had.

We left our comfortable house in Newbury and ended up in a croft on a peninsula of the Orkney Islands called Deerness. I surmised that there would be a roll for seafarers on an island group, and how right I was. No motorways there. We were up a byway off a byway off a byway. Oh; and by the way, I bought a ship.

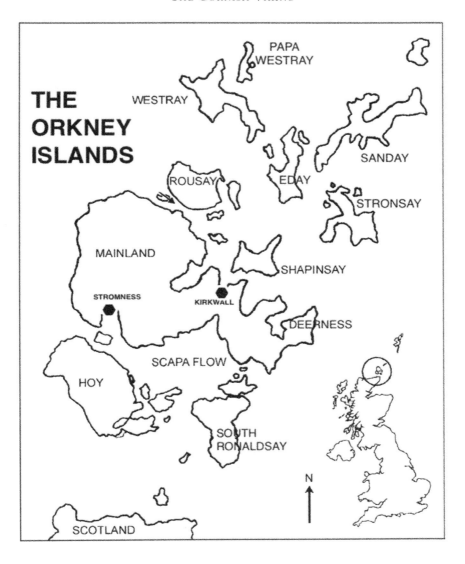

*Map 1: The Orkney Islands*

# ESCAPE TO THE LAND OF
# THE MERRY DANCERS:

L et me first introduce you to the Northern Isles.

The merry dancers is the expression used in the Northern Isles to refer to the northern lights or the aurora borealis. Before living in Orkney I had only ever seen the southern lights, or aurora australis. When berthed in Timaru on the South Island of New Zealand I had once seen an amazing display of the southern lights. Curtains of light filled the sky, flowing and shimmering like a moving silver curtain. Unlike my subsequent sightings of their northern counterparts with which I would become familiar, on that occasion they were only silver, whereas the merry dancers in Orkney would appear in different colours. They could be accompanied by a hard to define background hiss.

The Orkney Islands remain islands of mystery, carrying on their daily affairs for the most part beyond the prying eyes of the rest of the world. Let's face it, most people have heard of Skye, Uist, Harris or even Eigg; but have you heard of Graemsay or Wyre or North Ronaldsay? To find them, go to the far North of Scotland; so far that to go further you would have to swim, fly or take a boat. It is widely supposed that John o'Groats is the most northerly point, but actually that is reserved for Dunnet Head. Standing there and looking out to sea you will espy a big high island. This is Hoy, which is part of Orkney. To get to the islands you will need to catch a ship from Scrabster, which is the port for Thurso. A large and comfortable roll on/roll off ferry will take you and your car from there to the little picturesque port of Stromness, main entry point to the islands. Alternatively you can go from near John o' Groats on a ship which goes on the rather shorter trip to Saint Margaret's Hope on the island of South Ronaldsay. This is an island that is connected to the Orkney Mainland by barriers that you can drive across. Whichever way you go, if you have a delicate stomach, be sure to take your seasick pills. If you go in winter and have a strong stomach - might be an idea to take the pills anyway. The passage won't always be bad, but the stretch of water that you will have to cross is called the Pentland Firth. If anyone reading this makes the sign of the cross at this point, chances are they are a seafarer who knows the waters well! The tide ebbs and flows in and out of the North Sea through this narrow gap, creating numerous tide races, or rousts, as the Norse word has it. Do not be fooled by their names! There are, for example, The Merry Men of Mey and The Swilkie; nice names for dangerous places. The voyage to Stromness will, however, be full of interest. You will reach the West side of Hoy at the point where the famous sea stack named The Old Man of Hoy stands off the Southwest corner of the island. It is the highest sea stack in the land. Next you will steam under the mighty cliffs of St. John's Head. At over 1000ft. they are among the highest perpendicular cliffs in Great Britain. The large and comfortable ferry will be dwarfed by this magnificent sight. In due course the entrance into Scapa Flow will open in front of you and the ship will steam into the quaint fishing port of Stromness. A car or bus journey of some sixteen miles will take you on to Kirkwall, the capital, and starting point of the voyages described in this book. It is a journey through rough and wild island scenery. On the way you will see prehistoric mounds, standing stones, and a lot of water. Of course, you could just bypass all the inconvenience of rough ferry crossings and take the plane to Kirkwall Airport.

Here are some facts about the place:

These islands are called Orkney, or the Orkney Islands. If you call them The Orkneys, expect any Orcadian to flinch. You should not say The Shetlands either. Shetlanders got so fed up with maps of the U. K. that placed them in a box in the Moray Firth that they prepared their own map of the British Isles in which England and Scotland were placed in a box off Sumbergh!

Both Orkney and Shetland are Norse. They are not Celtic or Gaelic and no-one speaks the Gaelic. They did have an old language called Norn, but it died out in the 19ᵗʰ century. The last known speaker died in 1850. It was a Viking tongue, related to Faroese and Icelandic. The names of the islands reflect this linguistic heritage. The -ay suffix means 'island' and the Viking influence can be traced throughout the United Kingdom through this. Thus, Anglesea is 'island of the English' and Lundy in the Bristol Channel means Puffin Island. In Orkney Rousay comes from 'Hrolf's Island' and Sanday clearly means 'Sand Island'.

MacBraynes do not run ships here. Their services are confined to the Western Isles. For many years shipping services to Orkney and Shetland were provided by the old North of Scotland, Orkney and Shetland Shipping Company, and the vessels were known as the North boats. In 1961 the company was absorbed into Coast Lines, which was then a major operator around the coasts of the British Isles. Ten years later they in turn were taken over by P&O. Nowadays the service is operated by Northlink, although the smaller Pentland Ferries run the Gills Bay to Saint Margaret's Hope route. (This might be a good moment to point out that Northern Isles is the collective name for Orkney and Shetland; not to be confused with the North Isles, which are the islands in Orkney to the north of Kirkwall.)

Mainland is the main island of Orkney, unless you are referring to the other Mainland which is the main island of Shetland. What you may think of as the mainland is called Scotland or may just be referred to as "Sooth" (South).

Orcadians in many cases do not think of themselves as Scots. Their ancestors were Norse. In fact, the islands only became part of Scotland as late as the year of 1471 as part of the bride price when Margaret, daughter of Christian I of Denmark, married James III. Orcadians accept that, from many points of view, the islands are

indeed administratively part of Scotland, and they are quite prepared to take money from the Scottish Office and the Highlands
and Islands Development Board. However, since Bergen is closer
to Shetland than Edinburgh and Oslo is closer to Orkney than
London, the inhabitants of the Northern Isles have some reason to
feel that they still have more connections with their Scandinavian
cousins. Indeed, when Scotland was appalled at Maggie Thatcher's
gall of using it as the test bed for the poll tax, an attempt was made
by the Orkney Movement and the Shetland Movement to prove
that, since the terms of the bridal settlement between Margaret
and James III had not been fulfilled in their entirety, neither group
of islands was legally a part of Scotland. They thus argued that they
didn't have to pay the poll tax. The failure of the Danish Royal
Family to support their claim rather counted against them and
their court case failed.

There is, of course, an element of delusion about the fierce pride
in the Norse origins of the islanders. There has been an intermix-
ing of Scottish blood since way before integration with Scotland,
and a new phenomenon is now firmly established. A steady number
of English have taken to moving to the islands, attracted by what
they see as a better, less pressurised way of life. These new arrivals
are known as incomers, or ferry loupers, or even nowadays as 'sooth
moothers' (south mouthers – thoo ken they're frae sooth whin they
open theer mooth).

Although it is recorded that the Norse tongue lasted until 1850
in the form of Norn, there are claims that it may have still been
understood much later than that. As mentioned, it was derived from
Norwegian and bore a resemblance to Faeroese and Icelandic. By
the 20th century Scots English had completely taken over, but many
dialect words survived, especially with respect to the weather, the
sea, and the shore. Hence, a noust is a common word meaning a
place where you can beach and shelter your small boat, a geo (with
a hard 'g') is a landing place among rocks, and a roust is a tide race.
The accent has a sing-song quality that reminds many of a Welsh
accent, but owes more to the Norse ancestry than anything else.

Surprisingly, the Shetland accent is really very different, despite using the same dialect words.

Another part of the culture that has been handed down through the centuries is the musical tradition, which happily marries the twin influences of the Norse and the Scottish. The Northern Isles produce some of the world's finest fiddlers, and music making remains a very important part of everyday life. What is more, it has been a live tradition, with much new music having been written and being mixed with the traditional airs that have been popular for generations. I hope that continues despite the steady disappearance of the traditional ways.

The affairs of the islands are managed by a special type of island local authority called the Orkney Islands Council, (or the OIC), which assumes all the tasks appropriate to the management of some 18,000 people scattered across some 17 inhabited islands. The work of the council and the councillors assumes an importance not afforded to councils elsewhere. Every move made is reported avidly by the two main organs of the islands, Radio Orkney and the Orcadian newspaper. Councillors do not represent parties, but are all independent, and, in the eyes of the populace, should only be barred from standing by the very act of wishing to stand in the first place. They are subjected to an intense scrutiny and scepticism as behoves any holder of public office, but this does not stop the usual number of scandals, both real and perceived.

If you want any further evidence of the difference between Orkney and Scotland, you may wish to consider that, just as Scotland has its own separate legal system from England, so Orkney and Shetland have their own law that is different to the Scots. It is known as udal law, as opposed to feudal law. Udal law differs principally in respect of land tenure. For example, land tenure spreads as far as the low water mark at spring tides, rather than to the high-water mark as practised elsewhere. It also enshrines certain rights to be able to draw up and beach one's boat, and other matters of a highly practical nature in an island community. From time to time the udal principles are tested in the courts of law and are not always upheld. However, if you wish to live in peace with your neighbours, you would be well advised not to challenge those principles of udal law.

Orkney can trace its inhabitants back into the mists of time. There are more Neolithic dwellings per square mile than you would find in any other part of the land. Chambered cairns abound, some of the earliest stone age dwellings in Europe are still visible. Skara Brae, unearthed from the sand of the West Mainland, is a superbly preserved village, and Papa Westray has what may be the earliest houses in Western Europe at the Knapp of Howar. Brochs from the Pictish era are relatively modern and correspondingly quite common, and the Viking influence remains all around, not least in the names of the farms, the towns and the people. Because the land is rich, and the influence of the Gulf Stream keeps the climate moderate, farming has a tradition that covers all the millennia of occupation. However, with rich seas surrounding the islands, the tradition of fishing is also strong.

The islands are famous for their wildlife. Birds bring many a tourist. The razorbill, guillemot, black guillemot and puffin are common as sparrows. You will also see many a Skua, both Arctic and Great. The latter is known locally as a bonxie, and they are something of a pest. Terns abound; Sandwich, Common and Arctic being the commoner species, though you may hope to see a rarer one from time to time. They are a more strident bird than their delicate looks would indicate, but one may pass many hours fascinated at the way they swoop and dive to catch their food. Every bay has its quota of duck, many of which on closer inspection will prove to be Eider. Divers, both Red Throated and Great Northern, are not particularly uncommon and some breed. Geese of all varieties use the islands as a staging post in their migrations. There are waders in profusion, and you may see the occasional eagle or hen harrier. One such visitor from Scandinavia, a fish eagle, was described by a local worthy as being like a barn door with wings. Mammals are also of interest. The secretive sea otter can sometimes be seen making its furtive way along the shoreline. Seals abound, both Atlantic

Greys and Common, and dolphins and whales pass through the islands on their peregrinations. A pod of killer whales might be seen navigating between two islands, or a lone dolphin will pass you by. Then, in the autumn, a great migration takes place and there are hundreds of dolphins purposefully going about their business.

So, what does all that amount to? A small group of islands of great wild beauty, surrounded by strong tides and wild seas, inhabited from megalithic times, rich in agriculture and fishing, and peopled by hard working men and women with a fierce independent streak and a great pride. Why are these islands so little known, then? Remoteness, cost of travel, poor weather, these are the main explanations. If you get the chance, pack your warm clothing and rain wear. Visit empty white strands, surrounded by a panoply of green islands and islets, explore buildings that go back to beyond recorded time, and then retire to a hostelry in the evening and listen to traditional music, while enjoying a single malt straight from one of Orkney's own distilleries. You won't get a tan as if you had been to Marbella or Lloret del Mar, but you may find the experience highly satisfying. I did, and so did my family. Meanwhile, I will try to give you a feel for Orkney, through the eyes of an incomer and a ferryman, a Cornish Viking, and provide an insight into the way of life and the daily round of people, especially in the smaller islands.

This period of my life is now over thirty-five years ago, but, in a rare moment of foresight, I had noted down the tales of events. Now as I write I have just returned to the islands for the first time and visited old friends and retraced some of the routes. The islands have changed and the way of life that had been passed down through generations has been at best diluted and at worst obliterated. I found this very sad, and it places on me an obligation to record events and a lifestyle that have now been consigned to history. In the time covered by this book the island of Westray had some 1,000 inhabitants, and they were all Orcadians. Westray had its own accent, and it was even suggested that Westray folk were somewhat swarthier than people from other islands because one of the Spanish ships from the Armada was wrecked there and some of the survivors settled in Westray. Nowadays the population has fallen below six hundred, of which over half are 'sooth-moothers' - outsiders or incomers. Incomers have helped the economy and kept the schools going, but at the same time they have brought about the loss of some of the old ways. In many ways I found this to be rather sad.

# LET ME INTRODUCE YOU TO:

Having introduced you to the islands, it is also time to introduce you to the family.

The person who had suffered most from the outrageous behaviour of Larry de Jong was my wife, Rosemary. I have mentioned her before as she was already my girlfriend at the time of the incident off the coast of New Zealand. Not only had we been together then, as I write she has now stayed by my side as my wife for 58 years. For me to have met someone who was prepared to put up with me through extraordinary events and in extraordinary places is something that I surely don't fully deserve.

Before leaving for Orkney we already had five children at our Victorian semi in Newbury, and Rosemary needed me at home in the evenings, not fuming in a place where I didn't want to be, doing something that I didn't want to do. Rosemary had the Scots antecedents in the family. With a father from Burntisland and relatives in the West Highlands, she had spent her childhood holidays in Kinlochleven. By the standards of her upbringing in Somerset, that made her much travelled. It seems a long time ago now, but in the pre-M6 days of our youth the journey through the Midlands, over Shap Fell, across the borders and lowlands and into the Highlands was both long and tedious and made by few people. Even today it is amazing how many people from the South have travelled abroad, but never been to Scotland to see some of the most beautiful scenery in the world.

Andy was our eldest son. He had just sat his GCEs and was a quiet, sensitive and intelligent boy. Later, armed with Scottish

Highers, (the nearest Scottish equivalent to an 'A' level), he went away to college back in Somerset, and in due course became a highly professional computer programmer and analyst as well as being skilled in graphic design. It was he who designed the logo for our company, Wide Firth Ferry Ltd. However, he also crewed at times for the family business as well when he was at home.

Number two son Duncan took to boats more than the others. He was also a teenager and was also quite a quiet lad who in Newbury had been lost in a large school which vaunted its excellence but failed dismally to treat its pupils as individuals. He went to Kirkwall Grammar School and got a fair crop of 'O' grades and highers. In his spare time he wasted no opportunity to come out and crew. By his 18th. birthday he had already sat and passed his boatman's licence, and on the very day that he was eligible he took the "Mariana" to sea as skipper. He had studied every nuance of tide, every rock, every combination of route around the North Isles, and was one of the most careful of skippers that I could have wished to employ. When eventually we left Orkney he found that his boating skills were no longer in demand, and he has become a nurse, and now has an encyclopaedic knowledge of this new profession

Dan was a cheeky nine-year-old when we headed north, and his ready smile and sunny disposition soon made him new friends. He was really at an age to take the most advantage of the freedom of life in the islands and could roam almost without let or hindrance. He went at first to the little school at Toab, just across the peninsula that joins Deerness to the East Mainland. He then followed Duncan to the Grammar School in Kirkwall. Later he qualified as a teacher and became a very committed environmentalist and as a Park Ranger now organises and trains volunteers to replant native bush for Auckland City Council in New Zealand. He loved the freedom of the isles and got up to many an escapade.

Next came Tamsyn, or Tammy or just Tam. On our arrival she was just three; small, cute, bright, and, with four brothers, well able to fend for herself. She soon followed Dan to the Toab school where she learned to speak with a broad Orkney lilt and joined in the constant round of staying with friends or having friends over. The Orcadian love of music was soon transmitted to her and she learned to play trumpets and cornets and baritone horns. It is a love and a skill that will stay with her all her life, even though she has grown up to follow Duncan into nursing.

Last but not least was Dave. He was still a foster child when we moved, but he became our fourth son before long. When he was little, he had a head like a bullet, enabling him to dress up in a cloak and spend much of his early time flying horizontally around the house as a superhero saving the world. He got a good start in life from Toab school as well and grew into a deeply thoughtful and serious lad, but tragically developed severe mental illness in his late teenage years and has ceased to live in the real world.

I am proud of them all, but tragically the real Dave is lost to us.

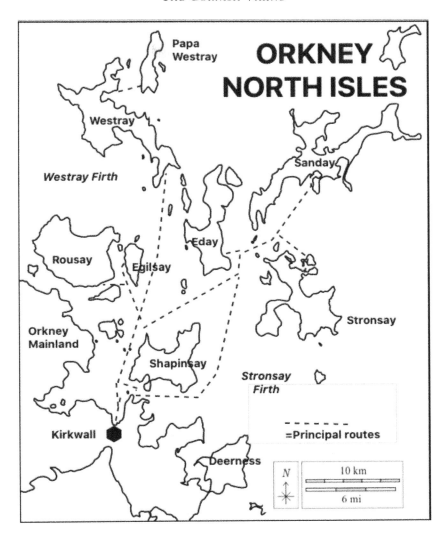

*Map 2: The Orkney North Isles*

# How It All Began

"What on earth am I doing here?" I thought to myself. How often in my life has that question come unbidden into my head? More occasions than I care to remember. I talk myself into doing things and going places, carry them through to fruition, only to find myself face to face with reality and thinking to myself, "What on earth am I doing here?" It was May 3rd. 1982 and I was being tossed up and down unmercifully by a grey North Sea. Rollers swept up behind my craft in a never-ending progression. Steep grey rollers, they were. Steep grey rollers that worried you a little, and created an awkward corkscrewing motion that was guaranteed to seek out any stomach that had been long away from the sea and leave it feeling somewhat delicate.

Off on the port side was a darker grey pencil line that was the shore of the Orkney island of South Ronaldsay, while lying ahead of us was an island that looked like a huge whale basking on the surface of the grey sea. Copinsay sticks out off the Eastern side of the peninsula of Deerness. It starts off at sea level on the Deerness side with a low shoreline, and rises steadily to a height of 70 metres when it suddenly stops and falls precipitately into the sea. The cliffs so formed are an ideal nesting site for sea birds. At the very highest point of the island is a lighthouse, perched precariously on the edge of the sheer drop and peering out into the grey fastness of the North Sea. At the base of the cliffs white spurts of water shot up the rocks. The grey rollers had met their match and were being hurled back into the heaving sea. Why had I picked a day like this for my first sea voyage in the "Golden Mariana"? Why had I not stayed home in my little croft on the far side of Deerness? What madness had overcome me to think that I, a Cornishman, could come to these far flung Orcades and run a ferry service? (Orcades – pronounced Orca-dees - is an ancient name for Orkney).

I had first seen the "Mariana" (to which the name was usually abbreviated) some weeks before. Like me, she was from the Southwest. Built by the long defunct Bideford Shipyard as a stern trawler, she was reputedly named after the hotel in Famagusta where the first owner had spent his honeymoon. Driving across the Churchill barriers from Holm, (which, unlike the word for a small island, is pronounced Ham), I found my way past the Italian Chapel on Lamb Holm and onto the little island of Burray, and then crossed the next barrier, past the ancient wrecks of block ships, and so to South Ronaldsay where she lay at moorings.

These barriers consist of great concrete blocks, piled high one atop the other, with a road constructed across the top. In 1939 a U-boat, the U-47 under Lt. Prien, had slipped into Scapa Flow, past the block ships, and had sunk the battleship "Royal Oak". Eight hundred and thirty-three men had lost their lives. Winston Churchill had determined that such a disaster should not be allowed to happen again, and the orders had gone out to close these eastern entrances to the Flow for good. Italian prisoners of war had been employed in making the blocks. Imprisoned in an alien island world in this alien northern sea, they had done their best to make themselves feel at home, and had used any available materials to construct a beautiful little chapel in a Nissen hut. This triumph of the human spirit over adversity and isolation is preserved as a monument to this day; surely one of the more unusual tourist attractions in the British Isles. Of course, the effect of building the barriers was to take away for ever the individual island status of Burray and South Ronaldsay. Nowadays one just drives across, unless the weather deteriorates. Then great seas can still sweep across the road, leaving it littered with rocks. Risking the drive when the weather is bad is as close as one can get to being in a ship in bad weather, whilst remaining behind the wheel of a car.

On that day some weeks before, I had driven off the Barriers, along the shores of Water Sound, and had turned into the little bay of St. Margaret's Hope with its community nestling at its head. I sought a 52 ft. passenger vessel with a licence for 65 passengers that was for charter or sale. There, moored to buoys in the middle of the bay, were two blue and white vessels. One was an old RAF sea rescue vessel called the "Pentalina", converted to a passenger vessel. The other had the stubby, powerful aspect of a small stern trawler; wide in the beam, but with a passenger cabin built on the after deck where the fishing gear would normally be. I was drawn to her lines. She looked the part - strong, able, reliable. Across her broad stern could be read her name and port of registry; "Golden Mariana" of Kirkwall. She was to become part of my life for the next few years.

In due course I had met Billy Banks, the owner, and was whisked out in a work boat from the quay to have a look over her. Despite the fact that the wheelhouse was damp and cold and the ship was rusty and sad after lying at her moorings all winter, my initial reaction was confirmed. This was a workhorse that would make light of heavy weather, keep its passengers dry and safe, and be ideal for me to open my new North Isles passenger service. After some discussions, I had agreed to charter her for a summer season, with a view to purchasing her later if all went well.

I should provide some background to the new service that I planned. The existing service was provided by an old traditional passenger ship called the Orcadia. She also had a cargo hold serviced by a derrick to lift cargo on and off. In support was a cargo ship called the Islander which was allowed to carry twelve passengers. That is the limit before the added safety requirements for passenger vessels are required. The Orcadia tended to leave Kirkwall in the early morning and would meander laboriously from island to island handling cargo as she went, and often only reaching Westray, the largest of the North Isles, in the late afternoon. Stopping to handle cargo made any timetable largely illusory. Given that you can see Westray from Kirkwall, this was hugely impractical. A Scottish Office study had concluded that North Isles people travelled little by ferry and therefore a better service was not required. Clearly they travelled little by ferry because the service was totally impractical. My plan was to provide two direct services a day to the islands in turn, thereby allowing visitors to spend a day on the islands and islanders to come to Kirkwall for the day to visit family or friends or to go shopping. At the time this was viewed as revolutionary.

Did I go to Orkney to escape the rat race, or was it to take advantage of the opportunity that this poor service provided? I suspect the answer is a bit of both.

So it was that a few weeks after that first sight of the "Mariana", Andy and Duncan had accompanied me over the barriers again. This time on that May morning we had started up the reliable old Gardner engine, turned on the radar set and tuned it in, let slip the moorings and at precisely 23 minutes past 2 we headed out of St. Margaret's Hope and into Scapa Flow. The charts for the area lay across the flat console on the starboard side beneath the wheelhouse windows. We passed around the cliffs of Hoxa Head and down the west side of South Ronaldsay.

The weather was moderate with a Southeast wind of Force 4, but I had no illusions about sea conditions. As long as we stayed in the shelter of the island we would continue to have a calm and pleasant passage; but before we could head northwards for Kirkwall, we had to pass through the dreaded Pentland Firth. The Admiralty Sailing Directions for the area are full of dire warnings: " ... extraordinarily violent and confused seas ... ", " ... even the largest vessel can sustain deck damage ... "," ... extremely dangerous to small vessels, ... ".

Gulp! I had taken advice so that we could round the southern end of South Ronaldsay at the most propitious time, so we had made it out into the North Sea, but the wind had been in the Southeast for some days. Hence, though past the most dangerous part, we were now being followed by the serried grey ranks that I could see ahead beating against the rocky ramparts of Copinsay's cliffs. It was all rather uncomfortable.

Slowly we came up alongside the basking whale of an island and headed for its offspring, a big, unforgiving chunk of rock sticking up to the north of the island and known as the Horse of Copinsay. Great plumes of water leapt high into the air and the sea around the Horse boiled. The tide swirls and eddies around the islands in alarming fashion, forming tide races, or rousts as the local language had them. Duncan surmised that the tide race that churns between Copinsay and its smaller neighbour must be called the Horse race! There's a wag on every vessel.

With the sea now right on our stern we swept past the Skaill Skerries and in past the dark and sombre cliffs of the Deerness Mull, and came at last into the more sheltered waters of Shapinsay Sound. Isn't it strange how quickly we forget? Surrounded by islands, in calm seas, all of a sudden I was at peace. I took the binoculars and scanned the northern shore of Deerness. There, above the big farm of *Halley*, was our little white croft of *Horries*. Rosemary, my wife, would be looking out to see us as we passed. The land closed in around us and we passed through the String between Shapinsay and the Orkney Mainland, and came at last into Kirkwall Bay. At half past seven we tied our craft up in the basin of Kirkwall Harbour and our first trip was over. We had a house; we had a ship. All we now needed was to get some passengers. Would they come?

# At Home in Deerness

Meanwhile, we had settled into "Horries", our little croft near the north shore of Deerness. Deerness is an island in all but name. Joined to the rest of the mainland by a narrow isthmus called Dingieshowe, it combines the attraction of a small island with the ability to drive off it and meet different people. Perhaps as a consequence we found the Deerness folk to be the most friendly and welcoming of any in Orkney. Signs of this appeared that first day when we had rolled up with a self-drive removal truck. Andy and Duncan had come along to lend a hand, as had my father-in-law Dan. Nevertheless, there was a deal of lifting and carrying to be done, and in no time a gruff sounding neighbour appeared, grunted an almost unintelligible greeting, and started to lend a hand. Sandy Cormack was a crofter who farmed some 70 acres. His house, "Bishops", was the only one near to "Horries". As the result of an accident some years before, he moved with a rolling gait. His face had the ruddy hue of someone much out in the elements, until he removed his cap, when a pristine white forehead was displayed. Born and bred in Deerness, he had a wonderful Orkney accent, and for some months we hardly understood a word that he said. It was worth the wait, for he was a warm man, full of a dry humour, and we laughed together over the coming years at many a thing. Belle, his wife, matched him for warmth and friendliness. All in all, we could not have wished for better neighbours.

# A COPINSAY TALE

By that day in 1982 when we passed along the wild east side of Copinsay, the island had already become depopulated. Only the lighthouse keepers remained, and now even they are gone, the light having been made automatic. However, within memory families lived on the island and wrested a bare living from its inauspicious soil. There was even a small school for the children. The families fished. They kept sheep. They grew a few vegetables in the poor soil. They got milk from a cow. Everything else that they needed had to be laboriously carried in aboard a little vessel that put off from the rocks on the Deerness shore opposite. When the winter winds blew, they were cut off. It was a hard life.

In our day, given half a chance, the youngsters of Deerness would purloin a small craft and go across to visit Copinsay. It was only in later years that we heard tales from Dan of escapades with rowing boats in freshening winds and strong tides! At the time the youngsters kept a conspiracy of silence, knowing full well that worried parents would have been aghast.

Deerness had its own village store, complete with a petrol pump, and the lady there had herself been brought up on Copinsay, and it was her that told me the following tale.

The main feature of the little island is the seabird cliffs. In latter years they became the haunt of the bird watcher, and the island's ownership passed into the hands of the Royal Society for the Protection of Birds. In the spring a visitor to the island walks up the hill from the low west side of the island where they had landed, comes to the edge of the cliffs, and peers over. They are met with a cacophony of sound from countless thousand nesting birds, mainly guillemots and razorbills, and the smell of many tons of bird droppings. To get to the island necessitates hiring a small boat, which discourages large numbers of visitors. Thus, the birds are largely left alone.

It was not so in earlier years when the families were still there. In common with many communities on remote islands, - St. Kilda and Tristan da Cunha, for example - the folk would supplement their diet by culling and eating the seabirds' eggs. However, this involved a hazardous operation. Someone had to go down over the side of the cliffs to reach the rocky ledges below. Brought up to it from childhood, the young men were like mountain goats, and could make their way down the side of the cliffs in a way that would bring stark terror to you and me. The only climbing aid they used was to tie some binder twine around their waists, so that the lad who was left on the top of the cliffs could steady them when needed. This practice was known as 'running the lee'. They put the eggs into a bag or 'cubbie' on their backs, and any birds they caught were killed and thrown down to a waiting boat below so that they could be plucked and the feathers sold. (It is not for nothing that it is called an eiderdown - once made from the feathers of the eider duck,)

An English bird watcher came to Copinsay while the families still lived there and was privileged to witness this feat of rock climbing. After a night in the farmhouse two of the sons offered to take him to the cliffs as they were going to run the lee. As you may imagine, he was horrified when, on reaching the cliff top, he saw one of the lads disappear into the abyss, supported by no more than the binder twine. "What happens if the twine breaks?" he asked the young man who had stayed behind at the top. Back came the reply, quick as a flash. "Ach. Hid's nae matterin'. Theer's plenty more back at the hoose!" and the lad turned away lest the Englishman should see the twinkle in his eye.

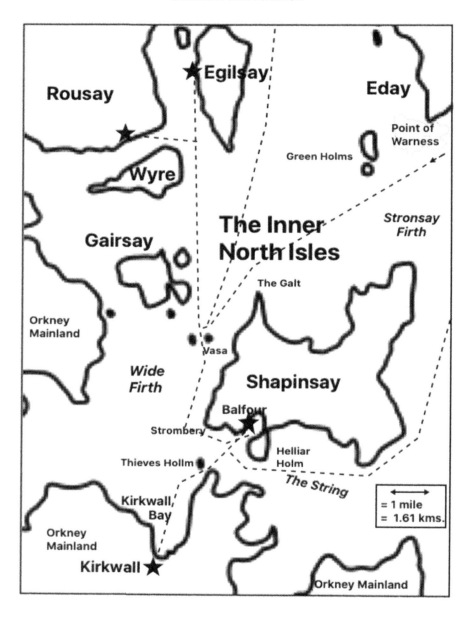

*Map 3: The Inner North Isles*

# LEARNING THE ROPES

Any driver will be familiar with planning a route by road, and planning a route by ship from Lands End to Fremantle is every bit as routine to a navigator. However, planning a route in a small vessel around an island group, where the tides can flow at up to 12 knots (22 kph), and there are myriad rocks, skerries, holms, islets and the like is rather a different proposition. There are three principal unknowns. There is wind direction, sea direction and tide direction. Each one varies from day to day and hour to hour, or even minute to minute, and the combinations are almost limitless. However long you sail your particular patch of sea, there is always the possibility of finding a combination that you haven't seen before. As our first passengers started to entrust themselves to our new service, I had to learn, and learn quickly, and that meant picking the brains of the local folk who knew the waters well.

However, it wasn't long before I learned lesson number one of small vessel operations, this one being relative to local pilotage. I have had it confirmed over and over again during many subsequent years of operating vessels in Africa. It is thus:

*Not everyone who says they know, does know!*

After suffering from listening to advice from people who didn't know what they were talking about, I soon learned to be very choosy about who I believed and who I didn't!

You will benefit greatly from following our perambulations on a map in the following section

It was a Thursday in our first season. That meant that we went to Shapinsay, Rousay and Egilsay. It was a fine enough day with big spring tides running. We left on the flood tide, taking a sprinkling of passengers, and made our way out of the Basin in Kirkwall and headed out into the Bay. All voyages out of Kirkwall began over the same route and after a week or two of operations we were already getting rather blasé about the trip to Shapinsay. Truth to tell, however, this part of the trip had as much of historical interest as the rather more remote corners in which we might find ourselves further out in the Isles. Astern of us lay the old town. It nestled around the head of the Bay with hills on either side, but the town itself was in a flat cleft that led straight through to a second port that lay on Scapa Flow. Commanding all else as it stood up clear in the cleft was the impressive spire of St. Magnus' Cathedral. Most impressive view of all of this fine old 12th. Century building is from further out beyond Kirkwall Bay in the Wide Firth. This is a place of shoals and rocks and churning tides; not easy to find one's way safely; but if one lines the spire of the Cathedral up with the point of Strombery on the western corner of Shapinsay, the navigator can follow that line past every obstruction and come safely into Kirkwall Bay. I often mused on whether the Vikings, mighty seafarers that they were, placed the spire with this very fact in mind. If it were so, this is the grandest navigation mark to be found in the land. You may find it interesting to look at the story behind the cathedral and how it came to be built, in which case you should look at the end section of the book; **Orkneyjar and Hjaltland – Some History of the Islands.**

As we travelled towards Egilsay on that day, I told the passengers the stories outlined in that historical chapter, with many more tales of yore. There were new accounts from the more recent past as well as from the distant Viking history. We passed between Thieves Holm and Carness. Musings as to how this unremarkable little islet came to be named also appear in the history section, but it has another tale to tell from the more recent past. The indentation halfway along it on the eastern side was the spot where the 244 ft. "St. Rognvald" (pr: Ronald) ran onto the Holm one stormy night. She had been loaded with cattle for Aberdeen and the master had sailed rather tentatively. Would the weather be too bad for the animals when he rounded the Mull of Deerness? It transpired that it was, so he turned and headed back towards Kirkwall. As you come up The String, there are a number of headlands that you pass on the port side. First there is Rerwick. Then follow the Head of Work and Carness, and lastly you need to round Thieves Holm. On the radar the aspect of these different points of land looks similar. On this occasion, Johnny Walker, that well known, but very inferior seaman who prances across the labels of a well-known whisky brand, was in command of the ship. He is known for his poor capacity for concentration, and he mistook the radar echo of Carness for that of Thieves Holm. Consequently, he turned into Kirkwall Bay much too early and the ship ran so high onto the Holm that one would think that, with a couple of knots more, she could have bounced over onto the far side and continued on her way. It has been said that the helmsman knew full well what was happening but was so fed up with having to disobey Johnny's orders when he wasn't paid to captain the ship that for once he just did what he was told!

One poor farmer was in terror for the whole of the following day. Every beast that he owned had been shipped on board, and you could not get insurance cover for that particular voyage by sea. All was well, however, and every animal was saved. Later, a salvage company blasted the rocks from under the bows and pulled her off on a high tide. It is the effects of the blasting that have left the dent in the rocks that I pointed out to the tourists on our trip.

I also told the passengers stories from the second world war. Not only was Scapa Flow a key harbour for the Navy, but there were many other military activities on the islands. On the point of Carness there used to be gun batteries, but Kirkwall did not rate as highly as London, so they were removed and transported south for the defence of the capital. Rather than let it be seen that the local defences had been weakened, dummy wooden ones were put in their place and, to make it appear that these false guns were in regular use, they were made to turn in the wind so their position could be seen to change regularly.

There was more subterfuge further out in the bay. Dummy warships floated there at anchor, including a phoney aircraft carrier, hoping to confuse German bomber pilots. Local seafarers pointed out that they wouldn't fool anybody, as there were no birds flocking around to snatch the scraps being thrown overboard. Accordingly, a little boat put off each day and tipped offal around the bows of each dummy ship. Now there's attention to detail.

So our trip to Egilsay continued. We called at Shapinsay, let off some folk, and carried on out, around Strombery and into the Wide Firth. Once more there was a story attached to every rock and every bay. If the stones could but talk, what tales we would hear.

At this spot we were at a hub. To the south of us we looked back over Thieves Holm towards Kirkwall and the cathedral. The western side of the bay was boarded by the hills of the West Mainland, with the Hill of Wideford highest of them all, its summit covered with radio aerials. Then we looked westwards into the Bay of Firth, with more hills on the Rendall shore beyond. To the northwest was a passage out into the Western Ocean through Eynhallow Sound, and moving clockwise around the horizon were all the holms and islands that were our destination; Rousay, or Rolf's Island, the highest of them; Gairsay, or Garek's Island lay between us; Wyre and Egilsay were low lying and harder to spot. To the north was another exit out into the Westray Firth, route to all the outer isles. Then, looking east we could see down The String, past the lighthouse on Helliar Holm, past the Stronsay Firth to the Mull of Deerness and the North Sea. Whichever way we looked we saw a panoply of land and sea and sky, the colours a delicate mix of blues and greens. There was much to see on Shapinsay as well, but I will return to that later.

As we proceeded up the west side of Shapinsay, we headed towards a narrow channel between the shore and a skerry. It is known as Vasa (Pr. Vassee). The water is quite deep through the channel, but the passage is very narrow. It is one of those places where lining the cathedral up with Strombery shows you where it is safe to go. The tide whistles through here at a great rate of knots. The Shapinsay side was a pebble bank, whereas Vasa Skerry was just a rock that could be covered at high water, all except a beacon. On the grey rock a seal or two might often bask, though it was never one of their most popular locations. Sometimes scarfies, which is the local name for cormorants, would stand and dry their wings. (Unlike most sea birds, their feathers are not waterproof so that air bubbles cannot collect and hamper them when they swim under water.) Nearby was a navigation buoy which was a favourite haunt of tysties (black guillemots), a bird that is gregarious with others of its own species, but doesn't mix with the ordinary guillemot, nor with the razorbill or puffin. This time I had a strong spring tide behind me, and we shot through between the skerry and the bank of pebbles feeling for all the world like a speed boat.

On either side of the Point of Vasa were two bays. To the north was the Bay of Furrowend, which is deep. When the tide flowed against us, we would inch our way through the narrow channel, and, at the first possible opportunity, turn into the bay, where the tide formed a back eddy and flowed in the other direction. As we left the main flow of water it felt as if a giant restraining hand was suddenly released and the boat would surge ahead with renewed speed and a feeling of relief. Before Vasa was another less well-formed bay with shallow water, and this was known as Hebdon's Vasa. Hebdon was a Westray man who owned his own small boat. Visiting Shapinsay one day, he imbibed freely, and set off for home again in poor visibility. In his drink-befuddled mind, he mistook the two bays and ran into the first one instead of the second, and promptly ran aground.

Leaving Vasa behind we headed across to the Hen of Gairsay and Sweyn Holm, passing another old wartime gun emplacement on Salt Ness to starboard and Taing Skerry to port. The passengers noted the different colour of the rock on this islet. It appeared to be almost white, owing to the tons of guano that had been deposited there over the years as a result of the cormorant colony that inhabited the spot. We followed around the end of Wyre and berthed on the rather inefficient jetty of Rousay. Dropping a sprinkling of tourists, exchanging banter with Tommy Gibson, the pier master, we were soon on our way again to Egilsay. What history still surrounded us. We had been passing through the territory of that arch-Viking, Svein Asleifarson, who had lived on Gairsay. At the same time Kolbein Hruga had lived on Wyre and had built a stone keep that was the ultimate in des. res. in its day. Way back beyond the Viking days, the early inhabitants had also left their marks on this corner of the islands, with chambered cairns from the Neolithic era. Moving ahead to the 19th. century, Lt. General Traill-Burroughs had lived at Trumland House on Rousay and had held a running battle with his crofters and the Free Kirk Minister which had made him notorious as the worst type of landlord. Then, in latter years the poet Edwin Muir had passed his formative childhood years on Wyre. A historian could fill a book with tales from the history of those places that were within our immediate view as we passed through Rousay Sound and Wyre Sound.

But more striking still than the historical connections of this out-of-the-way spot must be the beauty that surrounded us. In fine weather, if Kirkwall Bay and the Wide Firth represented a nautical idyll, Rousay Sound was breath taking. On every side green islands crowded in on us, seals raised their inquisitive heads and peered at our passage, terns wheeled and cried above before plummeting into the water, only to reappear moments later with a small fish in their beaks. The high land of Rousay made a perfect backdrop to the steely green waters. This was the sort of place to which people came to be at peace. Yet there on the Rousay bank, where Wyre Sound becomes Rousay Sound, there stood two kirks, one next to the other. The second was built next door to the first for the express purpose of annoying the other minister and worshippers. What a strange thing human nature is.

At the north end of Egilsay there came into sight quite a long stone pier. It was a nice, looking pier; a sturdy looking pier, a pier that a ship might expect to lie alongside with relative equanimity. There was just one minor inconvenience - not much water! This rather obvious disadvantage was blamed, like the placing of St. Magnus' plaque, on an earlier laird, who had quite arbitrarily chosen this poor site, when a much better one, with deeper water, lay no more than half a nautical mile away.

Perhaps it is time to state my second law of boat operations. It is an observation based on numerous experiences of trying to get vessels alongside piers that lacked some, or even all, of the prime requirements for a good pier. The law reads as follows:

*Anyone who designs piers should themselves be made to put ships alongside them.*

It was said that the designer of the rather poor pier at Rousay had fled to Australia.

Egilsay is a peaceful place. The name comes either from Egil's Island, or else the Norsemen adapted the Celtic word *eiglais* for a church. And there just above the pier is a fine circular tower to a little kirk, named, naturally, after St. Magnus. There is no longer a roof, and the tower was lowered by 15 feet in the 19th. Century. On every occasion that I walked ashore there, I felt myself to be wrapped around with peaceful feelings. Could this be ascribed to the saintly Magnus? My thoughts go back as I write to balmy summer days, with the smell of new mown silage, the cry of curlews, the shriek of terns and that most soothing of bird cries, the twittering of skylarks. Strangely, the peace that I felt as a visitor to the island was not felt by the inhabitants, who somehow managed to be permanently at odds with each other. After generations of Norse descendants had inhabited the island, nearly every croft and farm was now inhabited by incomers or 'sooth-moothers' like myself. There was a former seed salesman from Wales, a Rhodesian farmer deprived of his vast acres in Africa, and a goodly number of self-sufficiency dreamers, determined to seek a simpler life than the one they had come to know in the cities of lowland Scotland and England. In total there were somewhere around twenty five of them. One might divide the people into two quite distinct camps. There were those who kept goats and never did any housework, and there were those who tried to farm, but found it a great struggle in such a remote spot. Still, learning to live with your neighbours when you have so little choice is not an easy matter, and all small communities seem to be bedevilled with feuds and arguments which sometimes spread down through the decades and are passed from generation to generation. The Egilsay rows were a source of great amusement to the Orcadians, though one has to admire the efforts they made to adapt to a lifestyle that was completely alien to anything they had experienced before. Still, they did rather ask for trouble, such as on the occasion when one third of the island ended up behind bars in Kirkwall over an argument about a lawn mower!

Just opposite on a part of Rousay called Scockness there occurred an argument between an Orcadian and an incomer that was a classic of its type. The neighbours had feuded over a land boundary for a long while, until eventually the Orcadian felt himself to have been goaded beyond endurance. Words no longer sufficed, and so he punched the Englishman on the nose. Thinking of the money he would gain in damages, the Englishman spluttered, "I've just been waiting for you to do that."

"That's guid," responded the Orcadian, "Thoo'll no be mindin' if I do hid again," and promptly punched him a second time.

We steamed in to the pier on Egilsay, and there, waiting to take the boat to the town for some shopping, was the last Orcadian and his family. One by one, the Orcadians had gone until this man was the only one left. Even his wife and family were English. It was to men like him that I turned to learn my way around the difficult waters that ran between the islands, and as we steamed back through the Wide Firth to Kirkwall, I quizzed him as to the best route to take if I needed to pass northwards out of the Sound of Rousay and into the Westray Firth.

If you look at the chart you will see that the passage concerned is blocked by a small island called the Holm of Scockness. Between the Holm and Rousay the route is easy to see. You must keep two thirds out from the Rousay side, and one third out from the side of the Holm. The Rousay side of the channel has a ledge of rock sticking out, and the fast flowing tide is squeezed into a narrow gap next to the Holm. This restriction of the water flow is so pronounced that at spring tides the water is held up on one side or the other and escapes by bursting past the gap and can actually be seen by the naked eye to be running downhill. This is known as Longataing. On the Egilsay side was Howie Sound, and this was an altogether more complicated proposition. The channel was shoal almost everywhere, and there were rocks just where you didn't want rocks. I had been loath to try it and had always used the somewhat longer route through Longataing.

As we returned to Kirkwall that day, the last Egilsay Oradian tried to explain the rather circuitous route that needed to be followed to navigate Howie safely, but I resolved not to try it until I had far greater confidence in my knowledge of the route, and that meant going through the Sound with someone who had local knowledge. I didn't want to be like another local boatman who carried diving parties, and one day decided to show off his intimate knowledge of the waters by taking his vessel through Howie. He had worked out a part of the route that involved lining up what seemed to be an old black shed with a hillock of land by the pier. Taking care to tell everyone how complicated the passage was, he got well into the sound, only to find that the shed had gone, and he had to turn round and go the other way. His 'shed' had been an ancient hay rick that had lain there so long that it had turned black. Eventually, someone had fed his leading mark to the cattle!

Our trip to the town passed without incident. We swung into the Basin, came alongside the steps, and the family set off for a day around Kirkwall.

At 6 o'clock in the evening we were back alongside the steps ready to sail again, and we looked in vain for our return passenger. It was by now a very low tide and all the boats in the Basin had sunk to a level that was well beneath the level of the piers. Sailing time came round at 6:30 and there was still no sign of them, even though they had purchased return tickets. Where could they be? Could they have taken another route home? If we sailed without them, would we condemn them to an unexpected night in a hotel? I fretted and fussed, climbing the steps frequently to see if there was any sign of them walking down Bridge Street towards the pier. Eventually, I decided to make a quick foray into Kirkwall to see if I could spot them. First and most obvious place to look was in the bar of the Kirkwall Hotel, standing as it did right by the pier entrance. I hit the jackpot first time. There they all were supping ale in the corner of the bar.

"Are you not coming back to Egilsay tonight then?" I asked.

"We are that," answered the husband, "but thee boat isn'a theer yet in the Basin."

"Of course it is, " I replied. "We've been tied up at the steps since six o'clock."

"That canna be, fer we looked," he said. By this time they had gathered their messages (shopping) together and picked up that ubiquitous little brown bag that is known throughout Scotland as the carry-oot, and carries the exact amount of alcohol that is needed to see a passenger through their journey, (be it a journey by transport or their journey through life)! Leaving the Kirkwall Hotel, the family was aghast to look down into the Basin and see that the "Mariana" was indeed lying there. The tide was so low that he had failed to see her and had sat happily boozing in the pub waiting for the arrival of a vessel that was already there. He was as contrite as could be. He was contrite as only someone who has just had a good long session in the pub can be.

"Ah canna tell thee how grateful we are that thoo cummed tae luik fer us," he said over and over as we retraced our passage out through Kirkwall Bay and across the Wide Firth. "If theer's anything we can do tae thank thee, jist say the word." Suddenly he recalled our conversation of the morning about how to make a passage through Howie Sound. "Ah tell thee what, boy. Whin we gets tae Egilsay, ah'll tek thee through Howie and show thee the route. "Frankly, when I had wished for someone with local knowledge to show me through Howie, I hadn't had in mind someone who had been boozing for some hours, and had now got well and truly stuck into the carry-oot. By now our friend was slurring his speech and had become distinctly unsteady on his feet. The Wide Firth was calm, but everywhere that he walked it seemed almighty rough. "Come on, boy. T'is nae bother. We'll be oot and back afore thoo kens it, and once through, thoo'll ne'er need tae be showed again."

In due course we arrived back at Egilsay pier, and this family were the last passengers. We put them all ashore, and then the husband and I set sail again. However, this time I turned the wheel to starboard and we headed north into Howie, with a mosaic of rocks and shoal patches ahead of us. We proceeded parallel to the pier, but inside the first rocks, turned slightly to port and still kept parallel to the coast. In due course this route meant that we were headed straight at a small cliff face. "Dinna worry aboot yon peedie cliff. Theer's deep watter right up tae hid," he said, as he swayed from side to side and peered out of half-closed, bloodshot eyes. I confess that I was reluctant to go in too close to the shore, and he grabbed the wheel with a sudden lurch, saying, "Theer's plenty o' watter, boy. Any amount. Thoo can'st pretty near gae right in and touch yon cliff," and he swayed alarmingly while turning the helm until we were worryingly close to the rock face. I gulped, and my fists were clenched, my knuckles white as I stood by, ready to leap into action at the first sign of him getting anything wrong. "But dinna gae too far, fer theer's rocks ahead, and theer's more over theer tae port," and he swung the wheel and we headed mercifully away from the cliff at forty five degrees, cutting between two parallel ridges of rock, one sticking out from the Holm and the other from the Egilsay side. We were through and clear. There was nothing now between us and Westray except the Firth itself, though that alone was a formidable obstacle on a poor day.

It remained to reverse our passage. I took the helm again and followed the route I had just been shown. In due course we came again to Egilsay pier, and our drunken friend, swaying alarmingly, timed a sway to perfection and launched himself onto the pier. With a cheery wave and another lurch, he got into his car and drove unsteadily away, his debt for keeping us waiting paid in full.

Ever after on my way back from Westray, if the tide was ebbing and conditions were right, I would let the tide push me away to the west as I came across the Firth, and I could slip inside of the Kili Holm, and thread my way through Howie. The passengers were rewarded by the beautiful views of Rousay, and the St. Magnus Kirk on Egilsay. On the Holm of Scockness itself numerous Atlantic grey seals basked on a beach, giving a fine view to the visitors. Some navigation is learned in a classroom, with books of tables and logarithms, but some, it seems, is learned by entrusting the wheel of your boat to a local worthy in his cups and letting him pass on to you the benefits of generations of accumulated knowledge.

# A VIKING INTERLUDE

In the last chapter we sailed quickly past the island of Gairsay and said little about it. Gairsay consists in essence of just one big hill, with a little bit tacked onto its Eastern side. There appears to be little to recommend it, though the rough grassland clearly lends itself to the keeping of sheep. If one studies it as one sails past in the Wide Firth, a single dwelling can be seen over on the West side. It appears to be a substantial place, and is actually the one farm on the island. However, that this farm is more than meets the eye may be guessed at from its name. Laingskaill, which, when translated from the Old Norse, *Langa Skali*, means Long Hall. The Norse long halls were military and drinking halls, and the name is a clear indication of a Viking pedigree. Not that the farm today is an old Norse building, but it is on the site of one such, that was built here by one of the most notable Vikings of all. We mentioned him in passing - Svein Asleifarson. I had better point out straight away that his name is spelt in two different ways. I often opt for the shorter one - Svein Asleifsson. I have provided a brief history of this extraordinary character in the final section of the book - **Orkneyjar and Hjaltland – Some History of the Islands**

# Of Westray, Bad Weather
# & School Bairns

In an earlier chapter we were travelling through the Wide Firth to Rousay, Egilsay and Wyre and I went on to tell you more about the earlier inhabitants of islands in the Wide Firth. One day, with a load of primary school children aboard, we had a closer encounter with Sweyn Holm and Gairsay than we had intended.

A party from a Kirkwall school had been out to spend a couple of days on Papa Westray, (usually abbreviated to Papay). We agreed to do an extra run on the Sunday afternoon to bring them all back. Our operator's licence did not permit us to travel as far from Kirkwall as Papay, so we devised a very popular way of getting people there and back. We landed as usual at the jetty at Rapness on Westray where we were met by Davey Hulme's mini-buses. The passengers were then driven the length of Westray to the main harbour at Pierowall and carried across to Papay in the little school boat run by Tommy Rendall. This cut out a stretch of sea which could be rough, and was also a great deal quicker. Papay had its own primary school, but, as the children got older, they had to journey each day to their larger neighbour to attend the secondary school there. If they then wished to pursue any form of academic studies, ultimately they were obliged to go to Kirkwall and attend the Grammar School, while staying in a hostel. Once at the pier on Papay, Bob Henderson, the manager of the Co-op on the island, would meet the visitors in a Land Rover and set them on their way to a great day's activities; bird watching, exploring archaeological sites, looking for the rare *primula scotica*, (which is often known as the Scottish primrose), and the like. The meals were great, people were friendly, and it was voted a great success by the visitors. Even the hole in the floor in the Land Rover that let in the rain, and the fact that the tourists might get called on to push start it just added to the fun.

Getting the school children to Papay posed no problems, but on the Saturday, day before they were due to return, the weather forecast was ominously poor. I was sufficiently worried that I made contact with the teacher in charge and expressed my concern. The conversation did not help assuage my fears. The party leaders were obviously very determined to travel and would brook no contemplation of missing school on the Monday. On the Sunday morning I telephoned the Met. Office at Kirkwall airport and had a long chat with them to try and determine exactly what the weather was supposed to do. The wind was to go into the Northeast and blow. Briefly in the early afternoon, however, around about the time of slack water in the Westray Firth, there was what the yachties love to call a window, a spell when the conditions would permit us to travel without let or hindrance.

I ought to explain that there were certain restrictions placed on us as passenger carriers with respect to the weather conditions that we were allowed to operate in. There were two licences that were displayed for all to see on board. One was for partially sheltered waters which enabled us to go anywhere between Kirkwall, Shapinsay, Rousay, Egilsay and Wyre in any conditions at any time of the year. To venture further, however, we had to restrict ourselves to between the beginning of April and the end of October, between one hour before sunrise and one hour after sunset, provided "the weather is settled and the sea is calm". In the far northern summer, the sunrise and sunset restriction concerned us not one jot. It just never got dark. However, the problem that beset me was the interpretation of settled weather and calm seas. Orkney prides itself on having up to four kinds of weather in any one day -fog, sun, wind, rain, for example. Viewed from one point of view, the weather was never settled! Furthermore, what represented a calm sea to a fisher-man might appear like a boiling cauldron to someone else. To make matters worse, a calm sea at one state of the tide had mountains of water that bore a passing likeness to the Cairngorms when the tide changed. The boat operator was in a no-win situation. Faced with running a service that was rather more important than just a trip round the bay, every move had to bear scrutiny from both the knowledgeable and those whose knowledge was self-proclaimed. If the skipper failed to sail, the experts on the quay would mutter, "Whit's up wi' yon fellow. Hid's no that bad. The man's feared o' a peedie lump o' tide!" (A lump of tide is the local expression used to describe rough seas caused by the effects of a combination of wind and tide. When seas meet a fast tide from the opposite direction, the ensuing waves are very steep and dangerous.) On the other hand, if one sailed and had a bad trip, someone on the quay who might look remarkably like the same person, would be heard to say, "Yon skipper's no safe. The fellow's a madman takkin' passengers tae sea on a day the like o' this!" This phenomenon led me to evolve my third law of small vessel operations. It reads thus:

*The best skipper is always on the quay!*

I suppose under the circumstances, it is inevitable that once in a while any skipper will get it wrong. This tale is about one such occur-rence. The strange thing is that the problems actually occurred once we were within the limits where there were no restrictions, in conditions that I had never seen before and never saw again, despite plying that particular stretch of water at least five hundred times a year.

The trip home for the youngsters started well enough. They all got onto the "Amerance", Tommy Rendall's school boat, and made their way to Pierowall. With the wind in the unusual quarter of Northeast, they made the trip in the lee of Papay, and with any seas safely following from astern. No-one was worried, and none were seasick. They alighted at the new harbour which housed some of the Westray fishing fleet tied up for a weekend ashore; big, able fish-ing vessels that were clean and modern more in the Scandinavian style. It had been a grey day, with a blustery wind and threatening rain, and the town looked desolate. Pierowall, set around its bay of the same name, always seemed to me to be more a collection of houses than a proper centre. True it was here there were shops, a bakery, the pub and the kirks, even a castle, but each building was sufficiently separated from its neighbour that the overall impression was more that of a random collection of buildings than of a town as one envisages a town. Nonetheless, it was normally a vibrant place and the centre of a very active community life. This was especially true at the various places of worship, of which the Pierowall Hotel was prominent on the weekend evenings, and the kirks on a Sunday morning. However, there was nothing at all vibrant on this particular Sunday. The first rain had started, and was being blown horizontally across the piers, over the bay and through Pierowall. It found its way under the hoods of the youngsters' anoraks and started to soak their bags and possessions. Davey Hulme's minibuses were waiting for them and they climbed gratefully into the dry and set off around the bay, past the Hotel, and on down the spine of the island. In due course they arrived at the peninsula of Rapness at the southern end, and the buses turned and twisted in and out of little coves until they reached the end of the road, went over a cattle grid and came at last to a field above the jetty. As they drove the last mile following the Rapness shore, their destination could be seen at times. Then the bus would twist into a bay and the jetty would be lost to view for a while, only to reappear, a little nearer each time. The waters of Rapness Sound were grey, white flecked and uninviting, and there, alongside the little jetty, the "Golden Mariana" lay waiting for them. Even at the jetty she seemed to be bucking and heaving.

I had set out for Westray, to collect them with Duncan crewing for me, together with a lad who was an auxiliary coastguard and had been studying to take his boatman's licence to allow him to skipper small passenger vessels. He suffered from two rather major obstacles to the furthering of his nautical career. Firstly, he had an appalling sense of direction, and frequently wanted us to take the vessel to the east of Shapinsay when we wanted to go to Westray. If you look at the map you will see that this is like being in London and travelling via Dover to reach Southampton. His other difficulty was a complete inability to manoeuvre the vessel. The "Mariana" had two levers to control the engines. The lefthand one had three positions: astern, neutral and ahead. The other was a straightforward throttle. Roger failed completely to get the hang of this, and twiddled them backwards and forwards at random, leading to the engine racing in neutral, or else the ship going the opposite way to that which was intended. However, he sailed with us as purser and in the ensuing trip his strong qualities made themselves clear.

As we had left the Basin, Kirkwall Bay was no longer the blue and pleasant waterway it was in calmer times. The sea was grey, the sky was grey, even the green of the islands was dulled and muted. It was a poor day. White horses lined the route ahead of us. We pushed out past Strombery where we came into the shelter provided by Shapinsay from the North-easterly. In due course we came to the Galt, a headland and rocks that stand out from the Northwest corner of the island, and I turned up to starboard and headed across towards Eday to get into the shelter of the land again. This was where we entered the Firth. Orkney has three Firths; Westray, Stronsay and the Pentland. They are passages of water that are open to the Atlantic on one side and the North Sea on the other. Just as the Pentland Firth is notoriously rough and difficult, so are the combined Firths of Westray and Stronsay. Fortunately, however, they were at their worst when the wind or sea was either in the northwest or the southeast. northeast would not be so bad, I fondly imagined.

Deprived of the shelter of the land, the boat started to pitch and toss, climbing over one peak of water to crash headlong into the following trough. To cap it all, it started to rain. "If it comes on much harder," I said, "the rain will start to flatten the sea." It is true that this can happen, but not, I suspect, where the tides are churning around as they do in these difficult waters. Truth to tell, I was whistling in the wind to keep my spirits up. In the back of my mind was the worry of what the seas would be like as we returned with our young charges. We made our way up to the Eday land where at last the seas eased off, and we headed northwards between the islet of Rusk Holm and the small uninhabited island of Faray. Midway between the two is a shoal and Jim o' The Ness had showed me the inner route through here. It was an impressive one. Coming close to the rocks on the Northeast corner of the Holm, we would turn and run parallel to the shore, so close that we could easily look at the rare breed of sheep that lived there. At the North end of the Holm stand two cairns, one above the other, and sticking out from the shore is a reef on which enormous Atlantic rollers break, travelling for league upon league across the Ocean, before being squeezed into the entrance to the Firth and breaking on this inauspicious little lump of rock. Coming from the Faray side, the ship appears to be heading right into these seas, and an impressive sight it can be. However, when the two cairns come into line, the helmsman turns hard to starboard and follows the line of the cairns all along the inner side of the reef, with breaking waves just yards away to port. Eventually, the reef past, the boat can head in reasonable waters straight across to the jetty at Rapness.

This was no time to be taking short cuts. We went the longer way around, and eventually crossed the Sound to the little strip of rough concrete that is grandly called Rapness Jetty. As we approached there were already folks there to meet us and take a line. It was as well. With a North-easterly blowing, seas came through the Sound of Weatherness, and broke straight onto the North side of the jetty, which was the usable side. Of all the wind directions at Rapness, while none were good, this was the worst. With old tyres festooned down our port side, I gingerly allowed the "Mariana" to drift down on the wind until we rested uneasily alongside. Whenever we did an extra run it soon became common knowledge, so there were other passengers already there and waiting to board. They seated themselves in the passenger cabin, and we sat and waited for Davey Hulme's buses to hove into view along the road that could be seen snaking along the shore of Rapness Bay.

Of all the places we went to in the North Isles, Rapness must have been my favourite. There was just something about the place that seemed to epitomise the whole of the story behind our ferry service. It was beautiful, it was isolated, it was bleak. Somehow the wind always seemed to blow, and even when it felt quite warm elsewhere in the Isles, at Rapness it always felt chilly. The jetty always had water enough for any state of the tide, but it was awkward to use, and there was always some motion setting in from somewhere. If the sea was in the west or northwest, a surge reached into the Bay, and we also surged - up and down the jetty. If the wind was in the south or southeast, seas might break over the jetty making it hard to lie alongside, and we have already seen that the northeast was worst of all. In fact, I used to say that Rapness Jetty was a grand place to lie at as long as the wind wasn't in the northeast, east, southeast, south, southwest, west or northwest. That left north. It was great when the wind was in the north!

Jetty was a somewhat grand name for it. There had always been a landing place there on some rocks. Westray folk wanted to have a proper pier built there because it was so much nearer to Kirkwall than was Pierowall. Not only did it save some eight nautical miles compared to Pierowall, but those eight miles could be the worst of the lot in a northerly. However, the powers that were opted to build a harbour at Pierowall for the fishing fleet, so Westray were told they could have no more. Fed up with seeing the lifeboat having to battle its way to Pierowall whenever someone was ill and needed evacuating, the Westray folk clubbed together and built Rapness Jetty themselves. It was done on a strictly limited budget, so the jetty was just rough concrete piled onto the rocks that were already there. They followed the line of the rocks as well, so the jetty had a kink in the middle of it. At high water the part beyond the kink was covered, so a boat lying alongside the end of the jetty had to move up to beyond the kink as the tide rose. And if the tide rose still further on a high water springs, there was scarcely any visible jetty left, and we had to creep up to the approach to the jetty with our bows almost up against the face of the little cliff at its head. The trouble was, having had the jetty built for the evacuation by lifeboat of the sick, the air ambulance service started, so for many years Rapness lay deserted, except for the occasional fishing boat, or someone running a hire service to Kirkwall. It wasn't until the "Mariana" came along that suddenly this end of the island saw a great influx of people passing through. Cath Burger at the nearby farm said she looked forward to the first service of the summer as it was a mark of the changing of the seasons. In latter years everything has changed and there is now a ro-ro terminal further up the bay, which is a compliment to our own endeavours because we had proved beyond doubt that the service should run from there and not Pierowall.

The jetty led up a concrete rise and disappeared onto one of Jim Burgher's fields. Across the top of the approach was some barbed wire, and when Jim had cattle in the field, he would ask us to pull the wire across when we left. We often said to the last passenger to board, "Would the last person to leave Westray please close the gate and switch out the light!" Into the field would drive the mini-buses and the cars that came down to meet or deliver the Westray folk. When it was wet they often had a great deal of difficulty leaving again, and there might be much pushing and slithering on the wet grass of the field. If it got dark, the ranks of vehicles could be relied on to turn on their lights and illuminate the scene for us, and a quick call on the CB would always find somebody who would blow their horn for us on a foggy day.

On the top of the small rise beyond the jetty was The Ness farm, with Cath and Jim Burgher, their son Ian and daughter Frances. What fine people to have for our pier masters. Whenever we approached, one of them would always come down to take a line for us. Sometimes, when the tide was high and the wind in the southeast, Ian would don his fisherman's waders and would stand in breaking seas on the jetty, ready to snatch at a line and put it on a bollard for us before the wind blew us too far away. Furthermore, their help started way before we arrived. After leaving Kirkwall we would call them on the CB for what we called a Firthcast. Whatever the weather, there could still be a heavy sea running in the Westray Firth, product of some disturbance way out in the Atlantic. Sure sign of this were waves breaking on the Rusk Holm. "Three three for the Referee or the Velvet Lady," we would call, using their CB handles. (Jim was a football referee, and I think Cath must have had a favourite velvet coat.) We always used channel 33 on the CB. A lot of isles folk had embraced what was then a modern means of communication, providing as it did a cheap way of widening their circle of acquaintances or of keeping in touch with friends and family across the waters. It also meant that they could call us direct on their CBs and check on our movements.

"On channel," Jim or Cath would soon reply when we called.

"What's it like in the Firth, Jim?"

"Hid doesn'a luik a' that nice. Theer's been a lot o' westerly motion on and theer's a lot o' white brakkin' on the Holm. If ah was thee, ah'd be makkin' fer the back o' Rusk Holm today and keep out o' hid."

This was the spot that we found ourselves in on that grey Sunday afternoon, as we lay uncomfortably waiting for Davey Hulme to arrive with his cargo of school children. I hoped they wouldn't be long as I desperately needed to get across the Firth before the flood tide set in. In fact, I worried as to whether they would come at all. Davey had a reputation for being forgetful, and it was not unknown for him to just fail to turn up. On our regular run when we called there twice in the day, we would see him off in the morning by saying, "See you tonight, Davey." "Aye," he would reply. "Ah'll try to mind on.[1]" Perhaps twice a summer he would indeed forget, and we would have to call someone on the CB and get them to phone him up and remind him. He would arrive at the rush some quarter of an hour later, and alight flustered from his bus saying, "Ah fergot tae mind on!" (tr. I forgot to remember!).

On this occasion all was well. In due course, two buses wound into sight further up the bay. They ducked out of sight several times and reappeared, each time getting nearer, until they pulled into the field and came to a halt just above us. Shepherded by the teachers, they came down the jetty while Duncan, the purser and I helped steady them on the slippery surface of the concrete, grabbed them if they seemed in danger of being blown over by a gust of wind, and then helped them over the entrance point of the boat, which continued to dance up and down from the seas that were sweeping down on us. In an effort to steady the vessel, we kept the engine running and in gear so that the forward motion of the boat acted against a spring, which is a line led from the fore part of the vessel to a bollard on the jetty that was level with the stern. This kept the vessel tight against the jetty, but under the conditions it was no more than slightly successful. With one eye on the time, I encouraged the school party to hurry, and we soon had them on board with all their packs and bags. Helpers on the jetty threw off the lines, and I put the engine astern. The square shape of the stern was not designed to head into waves, so as we pulled away, the seas buffeted us and great clouds of spray flew over us from the stern to the bow. Wallowing in the waves as we turned hard round, we started to make our way across towards the lee of the Faray shore.

As we were now heading into the wind, we pitched easily enough into short seas and I was happy enough with progress. We seemed to be just in time to cross the Firth before the flood tide set in against the direction of the wind. Suddenly a voice came across the ether, "Three three for the "Golden Mariana". "Golden Mariana" are thoo on channel?"

"On channel," I replied.

"Ah'm in a car headed fer Rapness, and we're jist headin' doon alang the Rapness shore. Ah ken we're late and ah can see thee've already sailed, but ah have tae get tae the toon fer ah've urgent business the morn's morning. Cuild thoo no jist cum back alaing by the jetty and pick me up?"

I always tried to be helpful, but on this occasion I vacillated, torn between catching the tide and helping a customer. We weren't far off the jetty still. It wouldn't take long to go back, let the latecomer leap on board, and we would be on our way again. I weighed it all up, turned the wheel, and made the wrong decision. I squeezed the mike button on the CB. "Just get ready to jump on board the second we're back at the jetty. I'm rushing to catch the tide in the Firth."

Back we went. I had seen the car at once, dipping in and out of sight as the buses had done not many minutes before. Others had heard the conversation on the CB and stood by to take a line from us. If anything, the seas were worse. We spent some while as I tried to ease the vessel against the rough jetty without the waves battering us too hard against it and causing damage. At last it was done, our passenger scrambled on board carrying his suitcase with him, I shouted to cast off the lines again, and once more I came astern into a buffeting from the waves.

Full ahead, I made every revolution that the engine would allow. There was not a second to be lost. All around us was a grey heaving sea, with white foam being blown from the tops of the waves. We headed down to the south end of Rusk Holm and on towards the Muckle Green Holm. Slack water was still with us in some spots; in others it seemed to me that the flood tide had started. In other places it was clear that the tide was still on the ebb. As tide swirls around all the different channels it plays strange tricks. For example, the tide turned at a completely different time in the Sound of Rapness than it did in the Firth no more than a mile away. There seemed to be a formlessness about the sea. The waves no longer flowed in serried ranks. Instead waves suddenly appeared from nowhere, rose to a peak and then we would fall into a great hole that had suddenly materialised on the far side of them. By now it was raining in sheets, and our world had been reduced to a few square metres of heaving water. Remembering my optimistic hope that if the rain got heavier it would flatten the sea, Duncan, who was jammed into one corner of the wheelhouse, was heard to mutter. "I don't know about the rain flattening the sea. It looks to me more as if its knocking great dents in it!"

The youngsters were far from happy. If they had been Isles children they would have been used to these conditions. As it was, many Kirkwall ones were far from used to being in boats, and even less used to being in boats that showed such a great reluctance to stay on an even keel. The first ones started to be sick. They also showed a great predilection for open air and wanted to go outside, where they were in danger of being swept away by several tons of ocean. This was where our purser came into his own. While Duncan and I looked after the boat, he looked after the kids. He shepherded them, calmed them, got them out of danger when they tried to escape on deck. Still, we made progress. We see-sawed our way to the south end of the Little Green Holm, from whence we could set a course towards the Galt at the northwest corner of Shapinsay. I felt that the worst was over. The "Mariana" was a fine boat with the sea on the stern. Some vessels are dangerous in such conditions. The sea picks up the stern of the vessel, forces it forward so that the bow digs into a wave, and then continues to push the stern of the vessel so that you are twisted around and broach beam on to the waves. This can be very dangerous, especially when the waves are exceedingly sharp. It can invoke a rolling that is so extreme that one must worry for the stability of the boat. As long as I could keep the sea on the stern, the motion was tolerable. It meant hard work for the helmsman because the following sea still tried to exert this twisting motion, so the man at the wheel had his work cut out, twirling the helm backwards and forwards. However, once we reached the Galt Buoy, I would be able to turn in behind the Shapinsay land and we would be sheltered again.

It was not to be. With calm waters in sight, a combination of conditions occurred that were as rare as they were unexpected. Just when I thought that I could reasonably hope to be near salvation, the seas just got worse and worse. How could it be? By now we were inside the officially designated partially sheltered waters, plying a route that we used hundreds of times a year. It had never been like this before. Instead of turning in behind Shapinsay, I had no choice but to continue running before the sea. To turn beam on was unthinkable under the conditions. I stood at the wheel, holding a little rotating knob in my right hand that enabled me to twirl the wheel quickly. Glancing over my shoulder, I watched the seas pile up astern of us, and then twirled first one way and then the other to keep the stern lined up with the direction of the waves. The sweat was pouring from my brow. The trouble was, we were headed down wind straight at the little island of Sweyn Holm, and there was nothing I could do to avoid it. I had to work the ship back towards the lee that would be provided by Shapinsay. That meant that I had to turn into the seas and punch my way straight into them. Well, so be it. I waited and waited, watching over my shoulder for a series of seas that were slightly less fierce. Eventually I took the plunge. Over went the wheel, around we came, and with a couple of heavy rolls were heading back into the seas, instead of following them. Instantly the motion of the little ship changed dramatically. Instead of a relatively smooth wallowing movement, we now started to career up the side of very steep waves, reared into the air as we reached their summit, and then plunged with great thuds and crashes into the troughs, followed by a shock as we hit the following wave. Tons of sea water swept our fore deck, spray lashed against the wheelhouse, and all was noise and pandemonium. It was more than the youngsters could stand. Screams started to come from the passenger cabin and the fear was beyond our purser's ability to stem. I couldn't put them through more of that, so I waited my chance and then turned again.

A relative calm redescended as we swooped along, being driven by these abnormal seas - and we were still headed directly at Sweyn Holm. I had two choices. Either I headed inch by inch away to the south and passed through a narrow channel between the Holm and a piece of Gairsay that stood out from the rest and was known as the Hen o' Gairsay, or else I worked my way inch by inch to the northwards and carried on through the Sound of Gairsay. It wasn't where I wanted to go, but needs must when the devil drives. There is a small channel between the Holm and Gairsay, but I didn't know it. Now was not the time to experiment. Besides which, conditions didn't favour getting a chart out and studying it. Instead, I inched my way ever to the north. I dripped sweat. Children wanted to lean over the side to be sick, and I was too busy to do more than thank our purser and encourage him in the good work he was doing. From time to time there would be a call on the CB from a worried parent, waiting in their car at Kirkwall Pier. "Whit like is it oot theer? Are the bairns all safe?" Yes, they are safe, and no, it's not very nice out here. At last I was clear of the Holm and looked straight down the Sound of Gairsay ahead of us. We raced onwards, the seas pushing us still, and then suddenly we passed a line between Gairsay and Wyre that represented the end of the obstruction that the Sound posed to the tide, and within the length of the ship, all was calm. What a relief! The change to calm waters had been instantaneous and dramatic.

To understand this phenomenon, consider a placid lake with a river flowing out of it. The surface of the lake may be mirror-like, but where the river leaves it, placid water continues right up to the spot where the water starts to flow downstream. Then you will see little ripples and overfalls. The same thing happens to the tide. It remains calm up to the spot where it starts to flow out of an obstruction. The wind gets under the ripples and turns them into small waves, then bigger waves, and lastly into the nasty, steep monsters that we had been through.

It was only later that I managed to work out why we experienced these conditions in that place at that time. As the tide turns, there comes a moment in the cycle when the tide floods through the Sound of Gairsay sweeping first east and then northwards in the Firth where it continues for a little while to ebb between Rousay and Westray. It doesn't last long. After a short while, the flood sets in everywhere, and a weaker tide comes through the Sound of Gairsay and heads down the Wide Firth and out through The String. We had just caught it at the wrong moment when there happened to be a rare gale of northeast wind blowing directly against it, and creating a tide race into which we had sailed all unsuspecting. In well over two thousand passages through that piece of water, I never saw it again.

We continued around the back of Gairsay, sailed along the Rendall shore out of any strong flow of tide, and punched our way back into Kirkwall Bay from a totally unexpected direction.

"Three, three for the "Golden Mariana". How's it goin' boy? Where are thee noo?"

"We're just coming up the Rendall shore, at the back of Gairsay, and we'll be in in another half hour."

There was a pause. "Whit the hell is thee doin' all oot theer?"

We tied up and handed the children over to their relieved parents. The next day we had a letter of thanks from the school for having looked after the children so well under the circumstances. There was also a letter from a parent which also thanked us for our solicitude and fine seamanship in trying conditions, but it concluded, "though little Sophie never wants to travel in a boat again!"

Doubtless, the little man was there on the pier, muttering, "Yon skipper's no safe. The man's a madman takkin' passengers tae sea on a day the like o' this!" For once I would have had to agree with him; but then, anyone can be wise after the event.

# About Westray and Weddings

Westray is a place that merits more description. It is a place that few in Britain have even heard of, and yet it is a place of great interest. It stands to the Northwest of Orkney, cut off from easy access to the Orkney Mainland by the wild waters of the Westray Firth. From the southern tip one can see past Rousay, Eday and Shapinsay as far as Kirkwall and the hills of the West Mainland; but to the North is nothing but ocean, wild and open. On a fine day, however, from a high piece of land, a bluish grey lump might be seen on the far horizon - the island of Foula, perhaps the most remote inhabited outcrop of the British Isles of all. So remote is it that its inhabitants never acknowledged the change when the Gregorian calendar was adopted in 1582, and to this day the Foula Islanders celebrate Christmas in January. Easily the most populous of all the islands aside from the Mainland, Westray nonetheless maintained a uniquely Orcadian way of life. In those days there was scarcely an incomer who had infiltrated their society. Indeed, it was widely believed that Westray folk would not sell to incomers. Personally, I don't really believe that, because Westray folk are warm folk, and the welcome they gave to me and the boat service was as warm as it could be. Rather, the demand for the farms and crofts was so high among the islanders themselves, that few were the buildings that ever reached the outside market. The land is rich and the farmers are hard-working. The seas are rich and the fishermen had generations of experience passed down to them on how to wrest a living from the waters.

Sadly, how things have changed. Now some forty years later the population has dwindled to under six hundred, of which more than half are "sooth-moothers", or incomers.

Each island has developed in a unique way, and I don't doubt that a skilled philologist could tell apart the accents of each. Certainly Westray had its own accent, and, as mentioned earlier, the people themselves are reputed to be rather swarthier than other Orcadians as a result of the stranding of one of the Spanish warships that was blown around Britain by the gales that defeated the Armada. Generations of marriage within small communities has meant that certain surnames predominate on the islands. Westray has more than its share of Drever and Pottinger, Harcus and Costie, for example, just as half the Fair Isle seems to be called Stout. This can often lead to confusion as it is not uncommon for two people in a small community to end up with the same Christian name as well. To overcome this, often people aren't designated by their surname and Christian name. One of them is dropped in favour of the name of their property. Thus, Tom Pottinger who lived at Tuquoy became Tam o' Tuquoy, and Jim Burgher who overlooked Rapness jetty from his farm called The Ness was known as Jim o' The Ness. At times all vestiges of a person's name might be dropped in favour of the name of the property, such that one might hear someone say, "Ah'll be talkin' tae Stenaquoy the morn's morn," meaning, "I'll be talking to the man from Stenaquoy tomorrow morning."

Such was the richness of the land and the industriousness of those who worked it that a couple of the farmers had banded together to operate their own light aircraft. At sea some fishermen continued to run small creel boats, but the more ambitious had gone out and searched for grants from the Orkney Islands Council, the Highlands and Island Development Board and the banks, as a result of which Westray had in those days a fine fleet of new or nearly new ships. Such was the employment that they created that they had to turn to the Mainland and to other islands to find sufficient crew. A wise observer once commented to me that behind every successful fishing community there lay either the Kirk or the bottle. So hard is the life of the deep-sea fisherman that he can only ply his trade if either his senses are dulled or if he can place himself in the hands of a higher authority. In the case of Westray, they had kept their options open and pursued both alternatives. Some followed the route which led to the Pierowall Hotel, others were staunch worshippers at one or other of Westray's churches. Not only was there the Church of Scotland, but many people were Brethren. Papay was especially strong in this denomination and was consequently perceived as being much more straightlaced. Needless to say, some people hedged their bets and followed both Bible and bottle.

This incongruous marriage of influences was especially evident, appropriately enough, at weddings. Isles weddings were famous on the Mainland, or perhaps infamous would be a better adjective. They were known for their gay abandon, for the amounts of alcohol consumed and for their sheer stamina. Of Isles weddings, Westray weddings stood out. We came to do many a special matrimonial run, and it was my great privilege to be invited to many of them. Once the service was over and the guests had retired to the hall, a fiddle and accordion band would strike up and the dancing would be fast and furious, matched only by the consumption of liquor. Around the hall, amid the dancers, stewards would circulate carrying two completely different types of beverage. First was the Bride's Cog. This consisted of a two horned wooden vessel, filled with what I have heard described as a sort of alcoholic curry. I have no idea what went into the Cog, but whatever it was, it was powerful stuff and great for keeping out the chill. Much more mundane and prosaic was the other drink that was passed around in common or garden plastic buckets - home brew. Can you imagine what a plastic bucket full of home brew actually looks like? Making this devil's concoction was an island speciality. Depending on the batch, it might be consigned to friends and welcome visitors, or it might be kept for people that you would rather see the back of. Copious amounts would be prepared when a wedding was in the offing. The effects of the mixture of these two drinks, not to mention a free flow of drams, either from the bar or a half bottle in the pocket, was dramatic.

The ethos of an Isles wedding was best summed up for me by the following account of a VHF radio conversation that was overheard by Alec Costie, skipper of one of the Westray fleet. It refers not to Westray, but to Westray's Shetland equivalent, the island of Whalsay. The difference between Orcadians and Shetlanders is described by referring to an Orcadian as a farmer with a boat, whereas the Shetlander is a fisherman with a bit of land. This balance still applies when Westray and Whalsay are compared. Westray had a grand modern fleet of vessels, but Whalsay had bigger and better. Indeed, Whalsay, which is also largely unheard of throughout the rest of the land, probably has a higher percentage of people who have a share in a ship than any other community in Britain and the vessels themselves are so immaculate as to be almost yachtlike. Alec was tuned in to Channel 14 on the VHF, the channel that is used by fishermen to converse with each other, and he overheard the skipper of a big Whalsay boat. He had been fishing out to the west of Shetland and was talking to the radar repair man called Magnus who was employed by the fisherman's co-operative in the port of Scalloway, ancient capital of Shetland. The conversation went like this:

"Theer's a peedie fault on the Decca, Magny. Woulds't thoo come doon and hae a peedie look at it. Theer's nae rush. Over." (There's a small fault on the Decca radar, Magny. Would you come down and have a little look at it. There's no rush.)

"Aye, Geordie. That'll be nae bother. When will thoo be in? Over." (OK, Geordie. That will be no bother. When will you be in?)

"We're awa' in noo, Magny, but thoo canst come doon and tak thee time, fer we'll jist be tyin' her up and awa off tae the lass's weddin'. Over" (We're coming in now, Magny, but you can come down and take your time for we'll just be tying her up and away to the lass's wedding.)

"Ah didn'a ken thee lass wis gettin' married, Geordie. Tell me, boy, whit day is the ceremony? Over" (I didn't know your lass was getting married, Geordie. Tell me, boy, what day is the ceremony?)

"Hid's Thursday the 20th, Friday the 21st and Saturday the 22nd!"

That's island weddings for you!

# RUSK HOLM AND FARAY

In a previous chapter we were heading around the back of Rusk Holm, between that little lump of rock and the uninhabited island of Faray, and I took you through the impressive short cut that Jim o' The Ness had shown me one time. What a strange place Rusk Holm is. You may wish to hear more about it.

As for Faray, it was not always uninhabited, and the houses and school could still be clearly seen. Descendants, or even some of its last inhabitants, would sometimes wish to make a pilgrimage there. There was a lady from Shetland who had been brought up in the schoolhouse, and an American who had come back seeking his roots. When we carried the school children in from Papay the weather was foul. It was not always thus, and whenever someone wanted to go to Faray strangely it was always fine. On those occasions that people asked if they could get to Faray, I always warned them that it would be subject to weather conditions. Not once were they ever disappointed, and they enjoyed glorious days of hot sunshine, scudding white cumulus, the lazy drone of insects and the cry of the seabirds, the curlews and the skylarks. We couldn't land them there ourselves. Instead, Ian Burgher, who kept a little creel boat moored on a buoy in the little bay by Rapness Jetty, would take them off our hands, run over with them and land on rocks or a beach on the Faray shore opposite. The jetty, such as it was, was on the other side of Faray in the Sound of Faray. It was a poor landing place, and in the old days the island steamer could only lie off and land goods in little boats called flit boats. When it came to transferring cattle and larger items, there were real difficulties. In any case, when the winter winds blow from the north, heavy seas sweep down the Sound of Faray, and often the island could be cut off for weeks. There was a time when privations of this nature were acceptable, but in our consumer age, none but the determined hermit would put up with such an existence.

Back in the 1930s the Faray islanders were offered some improvements to their lot. There was money available to spend on their infrastructure. They could either have a decent pier, or else they could have a better road along the island. After much discussion, they opted for the road, so Faray now has as good a road as one might wish to find where humans rarely tread! Mind you, there is no guarantee that they would have fared better if they had opted for the pier. On the island of Stroma in the Pentland Firth the islanders were provided with a brand-new pier. "This is jist the job," they thought, as they ordered in boats to their new pier to carry away their belongings and set up life elsewhere.

The old crofts and buildings on Faray are still clear to see, and the island is green and fertile, so it is easy to see why people once lived there. But why anyone should ever want to live on Rusk Holm escapes me entirely. Nonetheless, signs of habitation there are. Rusk Holm is little more than a breakwater for Faray. It is divided into two sections. The main part to the north is a chunk of rock onto which rocks and pebbles have been flung by the great westerly seas of winter. As depressions in the Atlantic cause gales of great ferocity, rollers speed in towards the Westray Firth, and are squeezed between Rousay and Westray. Enormous seas are created, and they hammer onto Rusk Holm like a blacksmith at an anvil so that it is almost hard to understand how it has lasted there all these years. In the centre, protected by these stones, there remains a small area where grass can grow and where a rude stone hut was built for kelpers and shepherds. (A kelper is someone who gathers tangles, which is seaweed that can give up iodine and other valuable minerals.) It is here that earlier folk seem to have tended the little land that there is. Was this a hermit, some religious order committed to a life of hardship, some criminal in exile? I would love to know the history of this unpropitious rock.

The south end of the Holm is just a strata of rock that covers and uncovers with the tide, separated from the main part of the Holm by a little neck that is slightly lower lying than the rest. Nothing would live there, one might think, other than marine molluscs. Nothing, though, could be more wrong. The south end of the Holm is home to the Sooth Enders, one flock of the rare breed of Rusk Holm sheep. Hang on, do I hear you cry? How can they live there if the rocks get covered by the tide? These sheep, whose forefathers have inhabited the Holm back into the mists of time, have an in-built tidal clock. As soon as the tide starts to rise dangerously, and before the neck of rock onto the main Holm gets covered, they manage to make their way back onto the comparatively safe ground of the North end, where they stay until their clock informs them that the tide has now started to go out again. Why do they do this? In a word, food. No, there is, of course, no grass growing on the rocks. If there were the sheep would not be interested. It is not grass that they eat, but seaweed. Some sheep never become Sooth Enders. When they are born, some automatically join one flock, and some the other. There is no apparent rhyme nor reason to it.

On the island of North Ronaldsay there is a better known and more numerous breed of rare sheep that also eat seaweed. Like the Rusk Holm sheep they are small and lean. Being a much larger island, the inhabitants have plenty of agriculture, and the last thing that they want is to have sheep spoiling everything. Generations of islanders have therefore maintained a dyke or wall that surrounds the whole of North Ronaldsay and keeps the sheep on the shore where they have come to thrive on the seaweed.

The Rusk Holm sheep are not infallible. Sometimes they find they have lingered too long over a juicy clump and return to the neck to find it covered. To help them, a small cairn has been set up by the neck with a spiral path around it. The forgetful sheep can walk up the spiral and stay at the top above the level of high tide.

Nonetheless, there is still a constant attrition, and when the gales of winter blow, many is the carcass that is washed up on the Faray shore beyond.

The meat from these animals if very lean and has a strong taste to it, which make it a welcome change from the mild, fatty, frozen stuff we normally purchase. Once a year on a fine day the families that have the traditional rights to the sheep go over from Rapness, taking home brew with them, and they spend a day tending and culling the flock. It is a great day out for all and is awaited with eager anticipation. For a while afterwards, Holmie, as their meat is called, finds its way onto the menus of a few select folk. It is delicious. Kathleen Burgher, Jim and Cath's daughter, had left the nest at The Ness and lived in Kirkwall. Phoning of a Sunday at that time of the year, she said, "Dinna tell me that thoo're eatin' Holmie, fer I cuildn'a bear to think o' hid. It jist maks me mooth watter!"

Mansy Flaws was the operator of the Rousay boat. He lived on Wyre and ran across twice daily to the jetty at Tingwall, on the Rendall shore. Mansy was a great character. He could suddenly entertain his passengers with a tune on the Jews harp, and I have seen him get out his fiddle for a play. He was hired once by a party to take them round the little Holms and islets in the search for rare breeds. They went to many a little island; the Holm of Scockness - none there; the Killi Holm - none there. Then, by a stroke of good fortune they found the sheep on the Rusk Holm and were delighted. Mansy must have chortled to himself. He knew full well where the rare breeds were. Why did no-one think to ask him? Perhaps they equated geographical remoteness with a lack of awareness and knowledge. Nothing could have been further from the truth.

I am left with the mystery of Rusk Holm, and I doubt if it has enough importance for anyone to assuage my curiosity. Who were they, these strange former inhabitants of Rusk Holm? How could they live with the violence of the seas breaking on the western side? What persuaded anybody to live in such a wild and uncompromising place?

# TROUBLE WITH SCRAP

Disposal of rubbish is something that we all take for granted in our sanitised and organised lives. We put out our bags of rubbish at regular intervals, and lo and behold they disappear. There is rarely any need to wonder what to do with some possession that we have cast off. The worst that might happen is that we will have to pile an old fridge into the back of a vehicle and take it to the local Council tip, where there will be an area designated *Electrical Items*. And if our car fails catastrophically and is no longer worth the repair, there is always a friendly neighbourhood scrap dealer who will take it off our hands.

In the UK cars over three years old must pass a safety test to ensure that the brakes and steering are in good order, the tyres have sufficient tread, the lights all work and can be dipped and the vehicle is roadworthy. This is under the Ministry of Transport and the test is called an MOT and is undertaken by garages which are licensed to undertake the task and issue a certificate. On the Orkney Mainland, if your car failed its MOT and was clearly on its last legs, there was an alternative way of getting rid of it. You "sold it to the Isles". MOTs posed something of a problem if you lived on an island where there was no garage licensed for MOTs, or even where there was no garage at all. It would scarcely have been reasonable to expect someone living on Westray, say, to ship their car on the steamer into Kirkwall once a year, get it MOTed and then ship it back again. Hence people living on the Isles were exempted from the provisions of the MOT regulations, as long as the car remained on the island. Once that car arrived in Kirkwall, however, MOTed it had to be. Thus there was a thriving market for people on the Mainland to sell their MOT failures out to an island where they didn't need an MOT. Not that Isles folk were relieved of the obligation to keep their cars up to the legal requirements. There was nothing to say that they didn't have to have all their lights working, or any loophole in the law which allowed them to drive about with no exhaust and hardly any brakes. On the other hand, who was going to stop them?

Fair play. The police did try. They surreptitiously got on the Loganair Islander flight out to an island, but the moment they alighted at their destination the word of their arrival spread at a speed which vastly exceeded the police's ability to get about. Thus, all the rotten old heaps that could usually be seen on the island's road or roads would be safely ensconced in a barn or at the back of a croft long before the poor policeman had any chance of apprehending them. In the case of Rousay, there was no air strip, and the police had to travel on the local ferry. This meant that the warning was even better. The skipper would get on the radio. "Tell them at the shop that ah've got theer bread aboard." Bread was the key word. It meant that they were carrying an unwelcome visitor. So good was Rousay's system that their vehicles were in an even worse state than those of other islands. Apart from those suffering from general decrepitude, there was one with a tractor exhaust welded straight up through the bonnet like a funnel, and another that had no bodywork at all, just a chassis with an engine and some random seats bolted on for the occupants, including an old armchair. By the time the policeman arrived, all he saw driving around would be the postman or the nurse, since they would be the only ones with halfway legal vehicles. The upholders of the law must have thought that activity on the Isles was at a far lower ebb than it really was, since every time they travelled there, there was hardly anything moving!

As a ferry operator, I was inevitably incorporated into this carry on. Apart from anything else, one of my own cars was "sold to the Isles". Moreover, from time to time I would get dragged into the perennial battle of wits, as the following little tale will illustrate.

One day, when en route to Westray, the Velvet Lady came on the CB. "Theer's a wifey frae Pierowall thit's on the phone and wants me tae ask thee something. Ah dinna ken hoo tae put this. Let's jist say, does thoo hae a body aboord that shuildn'a be aboord?" I laughed. "No Cath," I replied. "All our passengers are members of the general public!"

Every now and then some poor person on one of the islands would be right out in a remote corner and would fail to hear that the roads were temporarily a no-go area. All unsuspecting, they would drive happily back towards a more populous part of the island, only to find themselves confronted with an official personage in a dark uniform. It would be a fair cop, fines would be demanded and paid, the police had that little bit of success to encourage them in further endeavours, and life would return to its normal merry-go-round.

So far, so good; but what happened when an Isles car, already an MOT reject, finally came to the end of its life? Salty air and rough roads made their lives 'solitary, poor, nasty, brutish and short', to borrow Thomas Hobbes' description of the lives of the poor. When I was in the Isles, I never lacked for a lift or the use of a vehicle. Someone would always proffer transport if ever I wanted to leave the landing place. On Westray our good friend Billy Stout would offer to run me up to Pierowall if I needed to go, or else would lend me his car. Billy drove one of the mini-buses, and was also a great helper, voluntarily taking it on himself to help organise numbers for buses, numbers to travel on to Papay, and so on. One day I alighted at Rapness and he proffered me a lift to Pierowall in his Austin Ambassador. It was a prime example of an Isles car; rusty, dirty, decrepit. I opened the passenger door to a creaking sound and against a certain resistance created by rust and lack of lubrication. Climbing into the seat, there was a further creaking sound, and I found that I was lowered gently but inexorably back to ground level, leaving my feet in the usual position under the dashboard. The chassis was so weak that it had given way altogether and dropped me back down onto the ground, seat and all. Billy didn't bat an eyelid. "Sorry aboot that, "he said. "Thee'll jist have tae sit in the back." With some difficulty I extricated myself from my unusual sitting position and did as he bid. Billy reached over, caught hold of the seat, levered the whole lot back up off the ground, selected first gear and set off without any further thought!

Yes, scrap is a problem on a small island. Some of them are festooned with old rotting hulks, many of them models that, were one to clear away the grass and nettles, might excite one's historical interest. Other islands have a mutually agreed dumping area, which had the advantage of keeping the wrecks out of view, unless, like Wyre, the dumping area happened to be on the corner of the island that we first came to when sailing from the Wide Firth! Shapinsay had another system, all its own.

Shapinsay is the nearest island to Kirkwall, and as a result is not so isolated as the outer isles. Its name is widely purported to mean 'sheep island', but this is not so. The Norse for sheep is a quite different word. It appears to stem from 'Hjalpandi's island' though nobody seems to know who Hjalpandi was. Anyway, it had its own regular ferry service using a strange little craft called the "Clytus". (Nowadays it has all been modernised. The island has its own small ro-ro.) Shapinsay folk were used to travelling into Kirkwall to get their weekly shopping. Then, if they wanted to go to the cinema, or attend some other evening event, Alfie Nicholson would run a hire for them in the little "Sheena" for a very reasonable charge. Our reason for going there was not to compete, but to allow a direct connection between Shapinsay and the other islands, and at times we carried a fair number of passengers, off out to see family, or tourists who were island hopping. Because of the timing of our evening runs, we even enabled some people to travel home after work. One resident of Shapinsay ran his own shipping company, which enjoyed some success for a number of years. He lived on the island and worked in Kirkwall. Often he commuted in his own little motorless yacht, and we would pass him crossing The String, sails drawing in a brisk wind, pipe stuck firmly in his mouth, quite imperturbable as his small craft bucked and tossed in the tide lumps that bedevil that stretch of water. (A tide lump is the term used in the Northern Isles for a wave created by the wind or sea being in opposition to the flowing tide.) If he was tired after work, or when the weather deteriorated, he would slip quietly on board before our evening departure and travel home with us, thereby being one of the first commuters from the island.

The other thing that Shapinsay had is a castle; a genuine turreted, inhabited castle. It wasn't unduly old and had never been conceived for defensive purposes, but, in the style of a French chateau, it was a notable and noteworthy edifice. What is more, it stood in a prominent position, looking right across The String towards the Mainland, which made it quite a sight for passengers as we made our way out of Kirkwall and approached the island. Constructed by David Balfour and designed by David Bryce in 1847 from money made in London from trade with India, the building had been filled with fine things. The owners at that time went by the somewhat non-Orcadian name of Zawadski, which would explain the presence at Shapinsay pier from time to time in the summers of yachts bearing the ensign of Poland. Mrs Zawadski worked hard to preserve Balfour Castle, while Chris, her son, worked equally as hard at running the farm that went with the property. For example, Mrs Z was a leading light behind the all-inclusive trips that we used to make to Shapinsay twice a week. Loading up in Kirkwall, on a fine Sunday afternoon we could hope to fill up our 65 seats and return for a second batch. I turned on the public address system and gave a running commentary.

After crossing the rough patch in The String, we ran into Elwick Bay, with the castle to port and the little island of Helliar Holm with its prominent lighthouse to starboard. There was much to see. On the port side of the bay was the pier, and in front of it was a round tower called the Douche. That was part of the landscaping designed by David Bryce, and was supposed to be a saltwater shower; hence its name, (douche is French for shower). Beyond the pier was a castellated gatehouse, which had become a pub, and another round tower was a sham which had actually been designed to camouflage the gas holder, all by Bryce. Running along the shore from the pier was a picturesque row of estate cottages, because Balfour had, at the same time, swept away the old run-rig hotch potch of land tenure and laid out a modern system of fields on the island. Doubtless, this was not well received at the time, but it did lay down the basis for the island's agricultural prosperity in the modern day. Then, at the head of the bay, was a very prominent white house called Elwick Bank that was also the work of Bryce, and had been the estate factor's house, and latterly belonged to the Doctor. On the shore below it at the head of the bay was an old wreck on the foreshore. This was the last resting place of a fine old vessel called the "Iona", which had been the Shapinsay mail boat for 70 years since she was built in 1893 and until she caught fire at the pier in 1964. Her remains had been beached there in an imposing spot.

I pointed all this out to the trippers, but it was across to the other side of the bay that we headed, because there, on rocks that joined the Helliar Holm to Shapinsay at all but high tides, was a favourite haunt of the common seal. Its name belies its status, as it is rare and not even the commoner of the seals in Orkney waters. That falls to the Atlantic grey. The grey is much bigger and has a Roman nose, while the common seal has a head that is more dog-like. They basked on the rocks in some profusion. The pups are born in the spring and added to the excitement of the passengers. I would drift slowly in towards the rocks, leave the engine to idle, and just drift along the shore. Cameras clicked, children shouted with excitement, there was many an ooh and an aah. We tried not to alarm them, but some would get curious, and they would flop across the rocks and into the water, only for their heads to pop up closer to the vessel, where they would stare at us. Who was watching who? I longed for a seal to produce a camera, aim it at the tourists and photograph them in return.

From there I headed straight across to the other side of the bay and landed them all at the pier. Mrs Z would be there with helpers, and off they would all go for a guided tour of the castle, followed by tea in a little café run by Sue Elliott. There they had a sumptuous repast, while also visiting the workshop of Sue's husband Marvin, who was a wood carver of considerable repute. In due course, they all repaired on board and we took them back to Kirkwall. It was such a popular trip that Shapinsay won a Highlands and Islands Development Board tourism award on the strength of it. (It was not the only one that we helped an island to gain, since another year Eday was a recipient as well.)

"What has all this got to do with scrap," I hear you say. Just be patient. I'm coming to that now.

It was a fine Sunday afternoon, and we were crowded out by people on the castle trip. I had told them all about the dummy guns on Carness, the holmgangers on Thieves Holm, and I had pointed out Gairsay further up the Firth and told them about Svein Asleifsson. It was clear and sunny, not a bit like the other trip day with a southeast wind when everywhere was shrouded in thick fog, and I had heard myself say on the intercom, "And now, ladies and gentlemen, on the port side further up the Firth you could see Gairsay, if it wasn't thick fog!" The String was blue and pleasant, just enough of a bump to be interesting. Off down The String we could see Rerwick Head and the Deerness Mull in the distance, and closer was the fine lighthouse with its imposing dwelling on Helliar Holm on our starboard bow. Oh to live in a place like that. The Commissioners for Northern Lights had automated the lighthouse and sold off the keepers' houses. Someone from England had bought them and then never turned up to live there. They deteriorated a little every year. What a shame.

Suddenly, I spied something ahead in the water. It was large enough. It seemed to be a white box-like object floating in the water. I eased back the engine, and we pottered up to take a look. It was a freezer! What on earth was a freezer doing floating up and down in

The String? It had a great potential for doing damage to some poor unsuspecting vessel that might run into it, but, with a boat full of passengers I was in no position to do much about it myself. As if that wasn't enough, what did I now espy heading straight towards it at a good rate of knots but a small Kirkwall boat called the "Arun Mist". The "Arun Mist" will appear again before the reader struggles to the end of this book, so let me tell you a little about her. She was a wooden vessel with two quite powerful large Cummins engines in her. About 35 feet long, she had what is known as a semi-planing hull. That means that she couldn't rise right up in the water and skim along at very high speeds, but she was able to rise a little and achieve the reasonable speed of 14 knots. It was 14 knots that she was now making - straight at the freezer!

"'Arun Mist', 'Arun Mist'. This is 'Golden Mariana', 'Golden Mariana'. Please go to Channel 12," I called them on the VHF radio. We moved to a working channel and made contact.

"'Arun Mist'. This is 'Golden Mariana'. I thought you might like to know that you are steaming straight at a sizeable freezer that seems to be drifting up and down The String not under command," I told them.

"Crikey," came the reply. "Yes, I see it ahead of me now." (You will note that the skipper was not Orcadian!). "Thanks for letting me know. I shudder to think what would have happened if we had hit that. I'll tell you what, I'll take it in tow and get it out of the way into Shapinsay before somebody smashes into it."

We carried on our way and thought no more of it. Basking under the northern sun, we went close under the lighthouse, on into the bay, and stopped near the seals. Everyone thronged around the portholes or squeezed themselves onto our limited deck space. It was a happy gathering of folk. Then, in due course, I turned the bow across the bay and steamed at full speed for the pier, manoeuvred past the Shapinsay ferry "Clytus" and a couple of visiting yachts, and made my way alongside the steps. Mrs Z welcomed the visitors, and the crew and I helped them ashore one by one. Chattering excitedly, the crowd disappeared off the pier, past the gatehouse and on towards Balfour Castle. We were left in peace. It was the one time during the week when we really had almost nothing to do but wait. I helped myself to a coffee from the coffee machine, plonked myself down in the pilot's chair and crunched my way through a packet of Monster Munch, which was always a very popular sale item.

It was at just such a moment on another trip that we heard an urgent sounding call on the VHF to Pentland Coastguard, which is the regional Coastguard centre based in Kirkwall. Idly wondering what this stranger wanted the Coastguard for, we flicked across to their channel, 67, and listened in. From his accent, the caller was clearly a Wicker. Wick people have a very distinctive burr to the way they speak.

"Pentland Coastguard. This is the *"Day Dawn²"*. *We're trawlin' aff Copinsay, mindin' oor ain business, and this big ship has steamed reet up tae us and dropped his pick on oor nets! Boy, boy! Whit a mess! Boy, boy. Boy, boy!"* We glanced at each other in surprise. The idea of a large vessel dropping its anchor right onto the nets of a fishing vessel was novel, to say the least.

Clearly the coastguard was surprised as well. There was a brief pause while they considered their response to the problem. *""Day Dawn", this is Pentland Coastguard. Can you read the name of the other vessel?"* they replied.

At this moment, instead of the dulcet tones of the Wicker, a very English voice cut in. *"Pentland Coastguard. This is the "Grampian Surveyor". I believe the fellow is referring to us. However, we are not, repeat not, at anchor. We are undertaking survey work for BT and are attached to the Fair Isle telephone cable."*

All over Orkney, from our wheelhouse to the Coastguard station, and in every other vessel listening in came a great guffaw of laughter. It was clear what had happened. The Wick trawler had set his nets and then left his wheelhouse to go for some lunch, with no-one keeping a look out. Relying on his fishing signals to keep any other vessel out of his way, he had had the bad fortune to come up against a vessel that was even more hampered than he was. Steaming blithely and blindly on, they had wrapped their trawl around the telephone cable which was no longer lying out of the way on the seabed, but which was now hoisted up to the survey vessel for some inspection work to take place. There was little more that the Wicker could say, and he was last heard still muttering over the radio, *"Mighty. Whit a mess. Boy, boy. Whit a mess!"*

Stuart Ryrie was crewing for me that day, and I will introduce him to you later. He summed it all up very well. "Yon Wicker shuild luik on the bright side. At least he can mak a cheap link call while he has the chance." (A link call is a telephone call made from a ship by radio and connected to the phone line by a coast radio station.)

There was no such entertainment this day. After a brief rest, I decided to go for a stroll up the pier. It was a grand day to be out and about. From the end of the pier I walked up towards the Gatehouse pub, but was loathe to go too far. First house in the row belonged to a local fishing boat owner and skipper of the fishing vessel "Our Catherine". The ship was nowhere to be seen, but if nonetheless he was at home, passing his house was hazardous. You were not allowed to go by without calling in, and not allowed to cross his threshold without taking delivery of the largest dram you could imagine, and not allowed to have less than half a glass without having it topped up. Instead I mooched over to the Peedie Pier, a little stone slipway that ran parallel to the main pier, and where small boats could be pulled up and creels could be discharged. A couple of local lads were standing there, so I went over to pass the time of day.

"Grand day," I said.

"Hid is that," they replied. "Theer's plenty cummed fer the castle trip today, then."

"Yes, we had the best part of sixty today." We were running out of things to talk about, when there around the end of the pier chugged the "Arun Mist", towing the recalcitrant hunk of kitchen equipment.

"The "Arun Mist" has a freezer in tow," I said. "We spotted it floating up and down The String, so they're towing it in before someone runs into it."

Consternation immediately registered itself on the lads' faces. "Bloody hell," said the one. "Ah dinna bloody well believe it." "Sod it," said the other. "We're ne'er goin' tae get rid o' the bloody thing!"

"Why whatever's the matter," I asked in my innocence.

"Hid's jist that we've bin tryin' tae get rid o' that bloody freezer since first thing this mornin'. 'Tis like a soddin' boomerang." They went on to tell me the tale.

Shapinsay had devised its own particular way of getting rid of scrapped cars. It involved the "Our Catherine". Not for Shapinsay the rusting heap of old wrecks in one corner of the island, nor even a peppering of such individual ruined vehicles around and about. When they wished to get rid of a car, they just towed it down to the pier, and next time the "Our Catherine" went to sea, they would attach a line to it and tow it off the pier and out to sea. Once they had left shallow waters and arrived in The String, the skipper would let the tow slip and the body of the no longer loved nor wanted vehicle was consigned to the deep. That morning there was a mini pick-up that was to take its final voyage. Meanwhile, someone else had another thing to dispose of. Yes, you've guessed it in one. It was a freezer. "Ah ken whit we'll do. We'll lash it tae the back o' yon pick-up and they can get rid o' hid at the same time."

The skipper was a friendly man, a large man and a powerful man, built like a brick convenience! He had been an army box-ing champ. When you met him he was mild mannered and polite, but there was clearly another side to him, for he had the most ferocious reputation. No-one dared to cross him, for if he should once get angry with you, he was wont to use you as a sparring partner. Thus, his crew were inclined to obey him without ques-tion. For all that, he was not the world's most successful fishing skipper. His original vessel, the "Boy Graham" had sunk, the crew fortuitously saved by a friend whose boat was nearby at the time. He was left without a ship for a good while. Meanwhile, the "Our Catherine" slowly deteriorated in the basin in Kirkwall, result of a bankruptcy. Eventually our man decided that the time had come to go back to sea, and he bought her for a song, painted her up and got her in reasonable working order. She was a beamy wooden vessel of some 70 ft. in length and was too big for the creeling in local waters, and not big enough to compete with the big newer Westray boats out in the Atlantic or the North Sea. Consequently, Johnno would often end up after sand eels off the Fair Isle. It isn't the easiest of catches to handle as they slide around in the hold almost like a liquid, and I have seen the "Our Catherine" returning home with her decks almost awash. The life of his new ship was also to be 'solitary, poor, nasty, brutish and short', rather like an Isles car. It wasn't long before she went the way of her predecessor and disappeared beneath the waves somewhere off the Noup Head on Westray, her crew fortuitously taking to a liferaft from whence they were collected by the Stromness lifeboat! I saw the skipper the next day. "What happened," I asked. "Hid was a freak wave," he replied. Later I recounted this explanation to someone else, who muttered, "Aye, hid's a freak wave that's jist followin' him aboot."

Early that Sunday morning, the skipper had repaired on board. The crew made the mini pick-up fast, cast off the lines, and eased the boat away from the pier. The towing warp came taught, took the strain, and the mini left the pier with a splash and forged through the sea behind them as they left Shapinsay bound for the Fair Isle. Once beyond Helliar Holm, it remained to cut the mini free and they could be on their way. There were no last rites, no ceremony, just a sharp fisherman's knife, and the mini was separated from its final human contact, but as the crew started to turn their backs on the vehicle and busy themselves with the coming trip, they couldn't help noticing one rather important fact. The mini had failed to sink! There wasn't a glug. It didn't even look like sinking. Instead, it floated along The String on the tide.

"We canna leave the thing theer," said the skipper. "Hid's far too big to gang floatin' up and doon The String. Whitever's the matter wi' hid?"

"Ah dinna ken," answered one of the crew. "They've always sunk before."

They manoeuvred back alongside the vehicle and one of them reached across and wound down the cab windows, making sure that the cab was full of water. It didn't sink. Then they stretched over the bulwark of the boat and, with considerable difficulty, reached underwater until they found the tyre valves and deflated the tyres. It didn't sink. With a certain amount of colourful and descriptive language about minis that wanted to be boats, they paused to reflect. There was little more they could do. Suddenly one of them had an idea.

"Thoo kens whit hid is. Hid's that bloody freezer whit's keepin' hid afloat."

"By heck, boy. Ah think thoo're right. Cut the bugger loose."

In a moment with a deft flick of a knife, the lashing that held the freezer in the back of the pick-up was severed, and there was an instant response. Without a word of farewell, other than a few glugs as the cab filled and the air was expelled, the mini slid gently beneath the waters of The String, never to be seen again. It had hung tenaciously to life, but in the end the final battle had been lost.

"Hid's all very well," said the skipper, "but that bloody freezer is still floatin' 'up and doon. We canna wait any longer. Hid'll jist have tae stay theer."

"Thoo canna do that. Whit happens if some peedie boat like Alfie Nicholson's "Sheena" shuild hit hid?" one of them replied. "Open yon door. That shuild surely let the watter in." Already soaked from their efforts to sink the mini, once more they reached into the sea and opened the freezer door. It didn't sink.

"Ah ken. Hid's double skinned. Theer must be air trapped between yon ooter layer and the inner. Let's knock holes in hid and let the watter in." So they set to with a hammer and chisel and knocked holes in the outer skin of the freezer. It didn't sink.

That was the last straw. They had been messing about in The String by then for a couple of hours, and the crew had been half in and half out of the water for much of that time. "That's hid!" commanded the skipper. "We canna mess aboot any more. Hid'll

jist have tae stay theer and sink by hidself. Ah'm fer the Fair Isle,"
and they sailed off down The String, up the east side of Shapinsay,
out past Kettletoft, rounded Start Point and made for the sand eels.

And there we were, some hours later, watching the freezer making its way back into Shapinsay, bloodied, but not bowed. It was
hauled out of the water, carried away and they set fire to it. That
finished it off. It had, of course, been the insulation that had kept
it afloat.

# FULL ASTERN

I promised to introduce the reader to Stuart Ryrie. Stuart was my right-hand man and stand-by skipper. Product of a culture in which men between the ages of 15 and 25 feel themselves obliged to be guided exclusively by testosterone and booze, Stuart stood out as a shining example of probity. He had no family advantage, no example to follow, and yet he was sober, industrious and polite. Furthermore, he was an excellent young seaman and a credit to young people as a whole. After a season as my second in command, he took over as relief skipper, and a very competent one at that. The trouble for Stuart was that I could only employ him in the summer season, so during the winter he filled in with other jobs. He was also an auxiliary coastguard, and at various times served on other vessels, including Alec Costie's Westray fishing boat. One winter he took over the job as relief skipper on the "Hoy Head" for the Orkney Islands Shipping Company when she was standing in on the Shapinsay run for the "Clytus". In due course he became a top captain in the North Sea and the decorated coxswain of the Kirkwall lifeboat.

The "Hoy Head" was something of a mixture of a boat. She had been built as an Admiralty supply boat, taking stores out to Naval ships. Heavily constructed of wood, she was 74 feet long and could carry up to 38 tons of cargo in her hold. However, somewhere along the way she had been granted a Class IV passenger certificate to allow her to carry passengers in partially sheltered waters, even though she lacked certain of the attributes such as a steel subdivided hull. This meant that, when the Shipping Company sent the "Clytus" away for her annual refit, or if she was out of service for any other reason, they could substitute her on the Shapinsay run. The two crew for the "Clytus" both lived on Shapinsay and the boat lay there overnight, but of the "Hoy Head's" crew, Stuart and the deckie both lived in Kirkwall, while the engineer lived in Shapinsay. (Being larger, "Hoy Head" needed an extra crew member.) This meant that Stuart and the deckie would bring the vessel back to Kirkwall after dropping the engineer at the end of the last trip of the day. The following morning they would start her up and make their way back to Shapinsay where the engineer would be waiting to take a line from them at the pier prior to taking their first passengers. It all worked well enough, until one day when disaster nearly struck as a result of a combination of the lack of the engineer and an unusual characteristic about the old boat's design.

On a small vessel the skipper might reasonably expect to be able to step out of the wheelhouse and lend a hand on deck when coming alongside. However, the "Hoy Head's" wheelhouse stood above the deck housing, with only a vertical ladder to gain access. The skipper stood up there in lofty isolation, lord of all he surveyed, but unable to influence it except by shouting instructions. What was more, there were no engine room controls up there. In other words, he could not control the engine from the wheelhouse. To explain what this means I would draw your attention to your car. There are wires and levers from your foot pedals which pass through the bulkhead into the engine compartment, so that when you press, say, the accelerator, the engine's speed increases. Imagine what it would be like if you had no such controls, but instead had to signal to a very small Scotsman who sat under the bonnet and controlled the engine for you. This is exactly how things worked on the "Hoy Head". There was an engine room telegraph with which the skipper rang down to the engine room the instructions, 'STOP, SLOW AHEAD, HALF ASTERN, FULL AHEAD,' and so on. A similar telegraph in the engine room was read by the engineer who then complied with the signal that had been rung down from on high. They are beautiful old brass objects, these telegraphs, but even large ships have done away with them now. Not so our Shapinsay relief boat.

All of this posed something of a problem when there were just two crew on board. One of them had to be down below to control the engine, and the skipper, as we have already seen, was stuck up top out of the way. Neither of them could be in two places at once, so who would throw a line ashore when they came alongside? Stuart and the deckie devised a system. As they approached the pier on Shapinsay, the deckie would repair below to the engine and Stuart would ring first 'FULL ASTERN' to slow her down. Then, timing it to perfection so the vessel just had enough way on her to drift as far as the pier and no further, he would ring 'STOP ENGINES'. On receipt of this signal, the deckie would put the engine into neutral and race up on deck, grab a line that he had prepared earlier, and throw it into the hands of the waiting engineer on the pier. These arrangements all worked well enough and after a few days of practice, the two of them had perfected the system surprisingly well.

There came a day, ostensibly like any other, when the system failed! The deckie and Stuart scrambled on board in Kirkwall, started up the engine, and Stuart manoeuvred the ship away from the pier. As soon as 'FULL AHEAD' was rung on the telegraph, the deckie came up on deck, went into the galley, and put the kettle on for the first brew of the day. They made their steady 9 knots out by Thieves Holm and across The String. The pier was getting near. Stuart lined the ship up for their approach, waited, waited, and then rang 'FULL ASTERN'. Nothing happened. The ship ploughed straight on at full speed towards the pier, and then, to his horror, Stuart spotted the deckie standing all unconcerned in the bow of the vessel, the line already in his hand, waiting to throw it ashore. He had completely forgotten that there was no engineer on board! With a great bellow out of the wheelhouse window, Stuart grabbed the big, heavy old wheel, and frantically tugged and heaved it around. Slowly, agonisingly, the bow moved. The pier was getting nearer with alarming speed - well, at 9 knots, to be precise. Almost at the last moment the swing gathered some momentum, and instead of a thundering crash, they hit the pier a glancing blow. The "Hoy Head" shuddered and bounced away into clear waters again. It is said that seagoing consists of 99% boredom and 1% stark terror. Stuart put this incident firmly into the 1% category!

# Football Hooligans

At the sound of the words *football hooligans*, most transport operators' faces blanche, and they break out into a cold sweat. Even in our remote corner of the land, we were not immune from this scourge, though the Orkney football hooligan had a number of redeeming features, as a result of which my attitude towards them was much more ambivalent. Whatever else one might say about them, they certainly livened up our routine! Besides which, there was something about the Orcadian nautical variety of the species that may make them of interest to the armchair traveller who has never met their like.

We soon got into a routine of twice daily trips out to the Isles. Come rain or shine, we set out from Kirkwall on a regular run each morning; tourists out, shoppers and locals back; and then at night we reversed the process. However, almost from the outset, local people would come up to us and ask, "Will thoo be doin' hires?" It was clear that we should. The need for special runs was the result of a great lack in the social life of the islands. There was a time when islanders would cram onto any little fishing vessel and head off to a neighbouring island for a dance or a wedding, but in our day we have tried to legislate away every risk from our lives, without any appreciation that some sort of risk is part of the human condition. One episode a few years before had brought down the wrath of officialdom on much inter-island travel, and effectively brought to an end a great amount of social intercourse. A football team from Sanday, with all its supporters, packed onto a local fishing boat and headed over to the neighbouring island of Stronsay for a match.

On the way back they were distinctly merry and the boat was badly overloaded. One reveller, no longer sure which way was up, fell into the sea. Manoeuvring a small, overloaded fishing boat alongside someone floating in the water was no easy matter, and by the time the man was fished out, he was already far gone. He had gone in beerlogged and come out waterlogged. By great good fortune, one of the supporters was also the Sanday doctor, and he was able to bring back the man from the jaws of death. Unfortunately, the Department of Transport made it quite clear that large numbers of inebriated travellers piling into small boats would not be tolerated, unless the boats were licensed to carry passengers and had all the appropriate life-saving equipment and other facilities. At a stroke, much summer fun on the Isles was curtailed, and from then on fishing vessels could only carry twelve people at the most. Just the manager as the one supporter following the team scarcely represented an uproarious day out. Hence the great interest in whether we would do hires.

Over the coming seasons we did hires for a great diversity of events. There were dances, weddings, funerals, choir outings, concerts, school kids at the Kirkwall hostel going home for half term or for the weekend, fishing boat crews paying off their ships, patients discharged from hospital, and, most of all, there were football matches. In Orkney football is a summer sport. Since the summer temperature rarely exceeds 15° Centigrade, there is little about the summer to prevent one from playing. On the other hand, in winter there might be snow, ice, frost, waterlogged pitches and, most particularly, there would almost always be wind. It is one thing to play in England in blustery conditions, but 45 knots of wind coming straight off the sea does rather tend to spoil the match, since most of the teams' time would be spent chasing the ball to stop it from blowing away. Besides which, teams could travel in the summer, where winter weather made it too hazardous. The only adverse climactic feature in summer might be fog. We did carry the Kirkwall team of Hotspurs out to Westray once, and, by an oversight, they were running out of beer ON THE WAY TO THE MATCH! They inveigled me into calling at Shapinsay so they could buy more on the way. It was a day of thick fog, and we drifted slowly into Rapness, found the jetty, and watched the players, already far from sober, stagger up to the field and disappear into the mist. As the captain left, I consoled him. "At least if you can't see the ball, you'll never know whether to blame the fog or the ale!"

Isles teams were unable to take part in any league because of their special travel problems, but they did compete in the Parish Cup and the North Isles Cup. Both of these competitions involved home and away legs, so we had two hires for each fixture. Usually this would mean taking one of the Mainland teams out to visit their competitors, and then a week later bringing the Isles team in to Kirkwall for the return leg. Fortunately, there were really only two islands that could participate at this level -Westray and Sanday. Other communities were too small to support a full eleven. Otherwise we would have had great difficulty in coping with the demand. Sanday were the ones that really took it seriously and hence they tended to stay in the competition longer before they were knocked out. The only year that Westray got worked up about it and really trained hard and did well was after they had been beaten by tiny neighbour Papay in the North Isles sports. They were shamed into reaching the quarterfinals of the Parish Cup that year.

We became something of experts in the behaviour of football teams and their supporters. Strangely, each team had its own particular manner of whiling away a trip. For example, South Ronaldsay had many players who were used to travelling by boat each day to the island of Flotta where they worked at the oil terminal. They had their own way of passing the time; they gambled. A couple of card schools would form and they would pass the trip quietly, with nothing worse than an occasional head poking around the wheelhouse door and saying, "Wuolds't thoo hae the change o' a poond?" Another team sang a lot. Yet another swapped our ensign for a pair of underpants. (It was returned later. Pranks were usually good natured, and there was an innate honesty about most people.) Some brought just the team, while others brought Mum, Dad, Uncle and Auntie and all the nephews and nieces and made a family day of it, but when it came time to go home - mostly they drank.

Just as they all had different ways of passing the voyage, so they all had a different favourite snack and beverage. This applied to all runs, not just the football trips. For example, Eday folk had a passion for Monster Munch. Westray folk liked tomato soup; but woe betide us if we were carrying a Sanday football party and had no chicken soup. They purchased prodigious quantities of the stuff from our vending machine. What is more, unlike the beer, they didn't seem to spill any. Eventually I asked them, "What is it with the chicken soup?" but was met with embarrassed laughs. Eventually, I told them I had worked it out. "I know now why you always buy so much of the soup. You're putting drams in it!"

The story would not be complete if I failed to mention one further passenger who invariably accompanied the teams from the Mainland. He was not made welcome, but sat quietly by himself, a man apart. Was this some football loving pariah, you may ask? Well, sort of. It was the referee. You will have seen by now that Sanday were the team to watch. They always progressed through to the latter stages of the competition. They carried the largest crowd of supporters with them. They made the most mess. They drank the most booze. They bought the most chicken soup. They caused the most problems. They caused the most fun. One year they reached the semi-final of the Parish Cup. The first leg was away to South Ronaldsay and they won 4-2. Already convinced in their minds that they only had to turn up at the Sanday leg to win, they started to plan their victory lap around Bignold Park in Kirkwall on the day of the final. Unfortunately, South Ronaldsay had other ideas. Furthermore, their first team was often depleted because key members might be on shift on the island of Flotta at the Occidental refinery. The following week with a stronger team they travelled out to Sanday and thrashed them. With the Sanday supporters venting their spleen on the ref, he had to be whisked away from the field and kept at a secret location on the island until the "Mariana" returned late that evening. Unfortunately, it was clear where he would be at boarding time, and he crept on board to a barrage of boos and catcalls. As we pulled away from the Kettletoft Pier, a shower of stones and rubbish were hurled after the boat! One might have thought that at least he would be popular with the winners, but he still passed the trip sitting quietly by himself, unwanted and ignored.

To give you a flavour of these football runs, I am going to describe two trips in greater detail. Hang onto your lifebelts. It's going to be a rough ride!

There was something rather different about Sanday folk, something indefinable. One sensed it rather than understood it. For a start, they seemed to act in a group, rather than as individuals. When we went to Sanday, either no-one would turn up, or a great crowd would be there. Even the relationship between the Orcadians and the Incomers was different. There seemed little animosity, but they got on with different lives, different pursuits. Incomers had a judo club, Orcadians played football. It was Sanday which had had the reputation for having bands of hippies living there in the 60s, escaping from the 20th. Century, and there were constant rumours of drugs and muffled oars on quiet beaches delivering the next illicit batch.

When we first started operating, the people who were the keenest to get football runs going again were, of course, Sanday. Their Captain was a Glaswegian who had nonetheless integrated into the Sanday life very well. He was usually known by his CB handle, The Clydesider. For some weeks we would get calls on the CB as fixtures were firmed up. There was a growing sense of excitement and anticipation. Football runs were starting again.

As we went to Sanday on Saturdays anyway, there was no need to lay on an extra run to bring them to Kirkwall in the morning, but on the other hand, they were quite determined that they would not be ready to return at our usual sailing time of 6 p.m. That meant that we would have to do our regular evening run and then set out a third time to take them all home again, leaving Kirkwall at gone 11 p.m. When the day dawned it was a fairly typical Orkney day, like a curate's egg. We set out from Kirkwall with the usual set of tourists, called at Shapinsay and then continued on our way along past Vasa and out to The Galt, from whence I set a course for the Green Holms. Passing close along the southern side of them, we saw Atlantic Grey seals on the Little Holm, and then went close in under the cliffs of the Muckle Holm, where there are the caves which might include the one that Svein Asleifsson hid in. (See the chapter at the end entitled '**Orkneyjar and Hjaltland – Some History of the Islands**'.)

The Green Holms are the cross-roads of sea routes in the North Isles. In certain conditions of wind and tide, almost any route around the islands may pass close to the Green Holms. They stood right in the way of the rush of water that flooded in through the Westray Firth and continued on its way into the North Sea by the Stronsay Firth. The narrow channel between the Holms and the Eday shore was the spot where the flow of water was compressed the most on its route, and hence the water flowed faster there than anywhere. Indeed, it is now the site of a tidal flow generator. At this spot in calm conditions our passengers were able to witness a very striking phenomenon. Behind the Muckle Green Holm we were out of the tide and the water was almost slack, but the moment that we poked our nose out of its shelter, the tide on the flood could be seen flowing past in front of us like a river in spate. The boundary between the slack water and the flowing water was sharp and clear cut. Sometimes we played a mean trick on people. There were always numerous candidates who wanted to steer the ship. By chance this was the very spot where we thought to ask them. They took the wheel in the slack water, but when they crossed the dividing line, the bow was suddenly being moved sideways at some 8 knots while the stern remained in the still water. This exerted a considerable twisting moment and the "Mariana" would heel hard over and start to spin to starboard. The look of horror on the face of the unsuspecting passenger caused much childish merriment to the crew, and invariably the passenger would thrust the wheel back at us as though it had suddenly become too hot to touch.

Our voyage continued across the Bay of Greentoft, around the Point of Veness on the southeast corner of Eday, and along to the pier at Backaland. We will revisit Eday later. Backaland was our second operating centre for the DTI, as it was then known; (Department of Trade & Industry). In those days most of their inspectors were old salts, perhaps ships' engineers with a lifetime of experience at sea. These were practical and reasonable men rather than the born bureaucrat who feels that it is his job to stop anyone from doing anything that might be worth doing. Sanday and Stronsay were too far away from Kirkwall to allow us to offer a service there. The limit placed on small passenger vessels was 15 nautical miles from departure and no more than three miles from land. We were safe on the latter count, but by no stretch of the imagination could Sanday or Stronsay be said to be less than 15 miles by sea from Kirkwall. However, our friendly regional examiner came up with a solution. If we ran a service to Eday from our operating centre in Kirkwall, and then immediately succeeded it with a service from Eday to Sanday, everyone would be happy. Let us give thanks for reasonable, practical officials. They sometimes appear to be an endangered species.

All of this leads me on to my fourth law of small boat operations. You may feel that its application spreads beyond the marine field, and I have certainly experienced it repeatedly in subsequent years in the field of development in poor nations. It is thus:

*For every person who is trying to do something, there are nine who are trying to think of reasons why they should not!*

We called at Backaland, dropped off the day trippers for Eday, and carried on our way towards Sanday. This involved crossing the Sound of Eday and passing through the gap between Spur Ness on Sanday and the north end of Stronsay. This gap was narrowed by islands, the largest of which is on the Stronsay side and is called Little Linga, also known locally as the Peedie Holm of Huip. On the Sanday side is a small group of islets called the Holms of Spurness. The main channel through is an easy one and goes right through the middle between the Holms of Spurness and Little Linga. However, there is also a safe channel for smaller vessels on the northern side of the gap between the Spurness Holms and Spur Ness itself. This other channel is called The Keld. Although there was little advantage in using it under normal circumstances, there was a set of conditions when it could be a great help - a south-easterly. Once we were past Spur Ness we entered Sanday Sound, and if the wind went into the southeast we needed every bit of help we could get.

Sanday is one of the largest of the North Isles. It is also the flattest. Spur Ness, where we find ourselves in this tale, is the one place on the island where the land is any more than just above sea level. It rises to a massive 50 metres. If you look at a map of Sanday you will see that it is shaped something like an irregular straggling star, with various arms radiating off in different directions. The arm that ends in Spur Ness is the only one that has hills. The rest of the island is unremittingly flat and, as its name implies, sandy. The wilder, hillier islands of Rousay and Hoy are very beautiful, and there is grandeur about some of the cliffs and high moorland, but Sanday has a softer, quieter quality about it. Make no mistake, the winds blow as fiercely here as anywhere, and there is nothing to stop them. The seas break with every bit as much ferocity as they do on the Atlantic side of the islands, if not more so. Indeed, Sanday was feared by the old-time seamen, because it was too low lying to be easily seen in any sort of adverse conditions. As a result, Sanday is a ship's graveyard, with a considerable number of wrecks around its shores. There is little that is soft about Sanday on a poor winter's day. However, on a summer's day, with a blue sky and scudding clouds, the soft drone of insects, the cry of the sea birds, the smell of the small wildflowers in the short rough grass, there is a feeling of laziness and peace about the place; a balminess that might seem more like that of more southern climes.

The main part of Sanday is around the pier at Kettletoft, which is close to the centre of the spokes, facing out towards the south. Nowadays the ro-ro ferry terminal is at the Southwest corner of Sanday, which is far more practical, but in those days the pier was the only landing site for all but the smallest of vessels. The pier at Kettletoft stands in Kettletoft Bay, where it is protected from southeast seas by the peninsula of Els Ness and the little Holm of Elsness that lies off its shore. It is not an ideal place for the pier of one of the larger islands for the simple reason that it has little enough water alongside it. The other defect of its location was that it meant that ships coming to the island had to brave the waters of Sanday Sound, and when the wind goes into the southeast and comes on to blow, there would be few to contradict me when I say that Sanday Sound is not a nice place to be.

The problem of Kettletoft Pier was not Sanday's alone. It affected every one of the outer North Isles. Before we came along with the "Mariana", the only way of travelling to these islands was either by an expensive air service, or by the North Isles steamer. (The term steamer was no longer technically correct, since steam had disappeared with the withdrawal of the old "Earl Sigurd" in 1969. Latterly all vessels in service around the islands have been motorships. The term, however, persevered.) For a number of years this boat service had been operated by the passenger/cargo vessel "Orcadia", supplemented by a cargo service from a coaster called the "Islander". The "Orcadia" was not really the best of ships. Built in 1962 in Aberdeen, she was 164 ft. long and made a round trip to all the outer North Isles three or four times a week. To her credit, she ran the service successfully for some thirty years, but I could not resist the impression that she had been designed by a committee. Someone wanted cargo space - put a good size hold in her; someone wanted room for day passengers - put ample passenger lounges on her; someone pointed out that sailings would be exceedingly early in the morning - put a number of passenger cabins in; someone wanted very shallow draught, (and thus flat bottomed and top heavy). The result was a vessel which rolled like a pig, yet was still too deep draughted to get alongside Kettletoft Pier at low water. To be fair, they were trying to reconcile the irreconcilable, and it would have been hard to have done better. However, the net outcome was that all sailing times around all the outer North Isles were dictated by the time that the vessels could get alongside in Sanday. The "Orcadia" used to leave Kirkwall at a time dictated by its expected arrival at Kettletoft, and she ploughed slowly from Stronsay to Sanday to Eday to Westray to Papay, before trundling back to Kirkwall again. On other days the order would be the other way around. At each place various items of cargo, varying from groceries to a prize bull in a pen were winched ashore on a derrick, and any product from the island was in turn loaded aboard. If you were unfortunate enough to be travelling to Westray and had to visit every other island, the trip would take you all day. It made a nice round trip sea cruise for a tourist, but they had no chance to alight and see the sights of interest. So clumsy was this service that local folk only used it if they had to.

Just as travelling to Pierowall inflicted an unpleasant trip on passengers when a northerly was blowing into the North Sound, so a South-easterly had the same effect in Sanday Sound. Because of the shape of the Sound, the seas tended to funnel in, and met shallow waters. Anything unpleasant happening in the North Sea was made that much worse when it reached the approaches to Kettletoft. For many years the Scottish Office showed a great deal of reluctance to improve the type of service, and it seemed likely that the best that could be expected was for them to fund a replacement for the "Orcadia" in due course. Using passenger statistics, they attempted to show that there was no demand for a better service, and even claimed that the outer isles had little potential for tourism. (Philistines!) They seemed to fail to understand the point that, with such a clumsy and time-consuming service, few travelled because the service was so poor. Given an improved service, passenger numbers could reasonably be expected to increase considerably. I like to think that it was the "Mariana" that finally gave the lie to the Scottish Office's curmudgeonly ideas, and eventually in later years they had to agree to provide small roll on/roll off vessels and invested in the appropriate jetties. The Westray one was to be near our jetty at Rapness, just a little further into the Bay, and the Sanday one was to be at Loth on Eday Sound a little way north of Spur Ness. As a result, many of the trials and tribulations of travel among the islands are now a thing of the past. Gone are the tidal delays, gone is the heavy rolling through Sanday Sound in a Southeaster, gone are the monster waves straight from the Arctic that troubled the ships that fought their way northwards to Pierowall. In fact, gone are the days of the football trip on a small boat, the isolated life of an island with poor contact with the outside world, the gatherings around the piers and jetties to see who or what had arrived from outside, the riotous goings on with a dance trip, the lads climbing down the cliffs for the birds' eggs. Instead, the Isles are connected to the Internet, they have social media, and phone, electricity and TV. I am left with the feeling that our service was witnessing the end of an era and the end of a way of life. It hasn't yet changed completely, but many of the tales I am now recounting could no longer happen thirty-five years later. It is as good an excuse as any to recount them.

The day of the first Sanday football trip had so far passed off without incident. We left Backaland on Eday, made our way into Sanday Sound, sailed towards the Holm of Elsness, and then headed into Kettletoft Bay, where we soon approached the Pier. It is a substantial pier of stone, with the odd house nearby, and, most importantly, the Kettletoft Hotel. It suffered from the usual operational difficulties. The steps were hard to get to. For a start, the approach was very shallow, so at low tide we drifted in very, very slowly, all the while listening for the knock of a stone on the bottom beneath us, or the scrape as we touched mud or sand. Furthermore, we couldn't lie right alongside the steps because the stern was held out at an angle by a widening of the pier. Instead, we put the nose up to them and produced a little set of wooden steps so that people could climb up onto the wide rail around the bow, and thence ashore.

I have already mentioned that Sanday folk tended to do things in groups. They travelled in groups or stayed away in groups. It was normal for one or two folks to come down to the pier when we came in and engage in the usual banter, whether they were travelling or not. Stuart Ryrie was a master at this.

"Whit fer do thee come doon tae the pier jist tae see a boat cummin' in. Have thoo nae got hames tae gang tae?"

"We have that, but tis better than the telly tae come doon and watch thee Kirkwall eens."

Or else: "Whit? Sober already? The state o' thee the other night when we put thee ashore, I thought thoo'd still be dronk!"

"Ach. Ah cuildn'a brink mesel' tae sail with thee if ah hadna had me fill o' drink!"

Then again, there was the memorable Rapness encounter the week after Stuart had, unusually for him, succumbed to the home brew at a Westray wedding.

Jim o' The Ness: "Whit? Here again? Ah'm jist surprised thoo've the nerve tae show thee face after last week. You Kirkwall eens canna tak a drink."

Stuart: "How wis ah tae ken thoo wis makkin' the home brew oot o' creosote!"

This time we expected a knot of people to be waiting for us. After all, there would be at least eleven footballers. What we weren't expecting was the great throng that milled about on the pier, clearly headed for Kirkwall. Sanday and his wife were going 'tae the toon' for the match. They piled on board, chattering away, and settled themselves on the rows of benches in the passenger cabin. Every seat was filled. They spilled out onto the small after deck and leaned over the railings, they joined us in the wheelhouse for a yarn. There was a festive mood abroad. We pulled away from the pier, traversed Sanday Sound, called again at Eday, made our way past the Green Holms, cut across to The Galt, down through the Wide Firth and into Kirkwall Bay. The happy gathering spewed forth like an invading army onto the pier in Kirkwall. We sensed the air of excitement and expectancy. Football trips were starting again!

In the evening we did our normal run and returned late to Kirkwall. We hoped there would be time to relax briefly before our third trip of the day to Sanday. Perhaps we could put our feet up for a moment, send someone to the chippy at the head of the pier for sustenance. Some hope! There by the steps in the basin was the same throng starting to foregather. This time, however, they were clearly showing the signs of why they didn't want to return earlier in the evening. The extra part of the day out was clearly to enable them to make a bold effort at drinking Kirkwall dry. The volume of noise had expanded. It was no longer the excited chatter of the morning, but a loud hubbub of noise, interspersed with regular shouts and guffaws, like a pub at closing time on a busy Saturday night. The crowd had been swollen by the friends and erstwhile opponents who had come down to see them off. Many of them showed signs of being the worse for wear after their evening of steady boozing. And every passenger carried that brown paper package, the carry-oot. (A bag containing a half bottle of Scotch!)

Well, we might as well get on with it. "Would all you Sanday ones get on board now and we'll be on our way," I yelled. Everybody came, friends and all. In no time the passenger cabin was a heaving mass of tipsy humanity. To overcome the din, I turned on the PA system at full volume. "Would all those who are not travelling, kindly go ashore as we intend to sail." Everybody left, or at least, a goodly number of both passengers and visitors left, leaving a mix of about half and half on board and the same on the quay. I stepped ashore and started to round up all those that I recognised as being Sanday folk, but as fast as I shepherded one group on board, someone else would be squeezing past them in the other direction going ashore again. It was worse than a sheepdog trying to sort sheep. I yelled, I cajoled, I herded, I pushed. Slowly, but surely I got the Sanday folk onto the boat and the Kirkwall folk onto the pier. Posting Stuart and Andy on the steps to prevent any further mingling, I set about trying to count the number of passengers we had on board, but they kept moving about. It was like counting maggots in a bait box. After several attempts I had counted between 60 and 67, but slowly the correct figure of 65 predominated. "Is anyone missing," I yelled. The cry was taken up by others. At last I felt able to sail. I had done everything in my power to check that no-one was missing and there were no stow-aways. We had gone about five minutes and were rapidly approaching Iceland Skerry, when a head popped around the wheelhouse door. "Theer's een fellow thit's nae here."

"Are you sure," I replied.

"Well, he's nae that sober, so it cuild be he's passed oot some place, but ah dinna think so. We last seed un gaein' up tae the chippy fer a fish supper."

"Oh, hell," I groaned, turned the wheel, and headed back to the pier again. We pulled back alongside. Nobody ashore batted an eyelid, seemingly taking our return for granted. Taking care not to allow a further interchange of passengers and visitors, we sent the missing man's friends off to find him. They were soon back, leading him with them. "He hadna even noticed we wis gone," they reported. Off we went for the second time.

(A fortnight later we did another Sanday football run. This time we were just leaving the Basin, when a drunken face that clearly belonged to a Deerness man appeared at the entrance to the passenger cabin and, with a big smile, said, "Ah dinna want tae gae tae Sanday!" but that's another story.)

After a pleasant run in the morning, the wind had got up and we had a hashy sort of a trip back out again. It was choppy on the sea and very rough in the passenger cabin. The beer was flowing freely, the half bottles of whiskey were circulating freely, the conversation flowed freely, and the chicken soup was served, but not freely as we charged 25p a cup. Between the booze and the soup, there must have been prodigious quantities of liquids consumed that night. The conversation among those passengers that gathered in the wheelhouse started off following well defined norms, but deteriorated into the babble of drunks as the voyage progressed. One man commandeered the CB and spoke endlessly to others on Sunday, repeating himself over and over again, telling of the match, their evening in the toon, the match, their evening in the match, the toon. When he finally finished, another drunk took his place and it started all over again. We bucked and heaved our way past the Green Holms again and made our way for the compulsory stop at Eday pier. It was quite a dark night by Northern Isles summer standards, and I spent a good bit of time navigating on the radar. Back in the cabin, some people were beginning to succumb. Now when we went to serve yet more chicken soup from the vending machine, we found we were having to step over prostrate bodies. They slept where they fell, and everyone else ignored them.

Meanwhile, back in the wheelhouse, we could look through the sound of Spurness and as we pitched and tossed in the choppy waters, we could see ahead the lights of Kettletoft. The man on the CB got it into his head that, for reasons that were only clear to his drink-befuddled brain, we were in reality heading for Whitehall on Stronsay. I foolishly argued with him when I should have known better. "No, it's Kettletoft," I said.

"Hid's nae Kettletoft. Hid's Stronsay. Whit fer are thee takkin' us tae Whiteha' ?"

"Look," I said. "Whose navigating? You or me? It's Kettletoft. There's no doubt it's Kettletoft."

"Whit fer are thee takkin' us tae Whiteha' ?"

"Look. I'm not going to argue. When we get there, if it's Kettletoft, I'm right. If it's Whitehall, you're right. All right?" and I refused to discuss the matter further.

At long last, the pitching eased away and we were off Els Ness and headed in towards the pier. Alongside again, we cajoled and encouraged those who could to go ashore, and to help those who were no longer walking so well. We were left with a couple who refused to awaken properly, and we half pulled them and hoisted them over the side and onto the steps, from whence they were dragged away. As folks jumped into their cars and weaved unsteadily away, they waved cheerily to us. "Grand trip, boy." "Whit a grand day oot," "We're surely glad thoo's started the footba' trips again," and then, ominously, "See thee again hin twa weeks." Whatever had we let ourselves in for?

The departure of the passengers had revealed a terrible scene. The cabin was like a war zone. Empty beer cans littered the floor. Many more cans weren't even empty, but rolled around depositing their contents on the deck. Empty cardboard cups lay squashed into every conceivable corner. Cigarette ends, usually well dunked in stale beer were everywhere. One worthy had passed out and had been laying in his own sick. Our work was far from over. With one man on the wheel, the other two knuckled under. Every can had to be gathered up, and any remaining contents poured over the side. Even many half bottles were still half full of their amber fluid. Over the stern that went as well. There must have been some very drunk fish in Sanday Sound that night. Then out came the dustpan and broom, followed by the mop and the disinfectant. It took us most of the trip back to Spurness before we were straight again.

Back on Sanday the night's doings were far from over. There were six car accidents as the revellers endeavoured to find their homes. Our navigational expert must still have been thinking that we had arrived on Stronsay. His accident was the worst. He drove into a dyke, smashed up his car, and broke his arm. (In Scotland a dyke is a low wall.) As we headed home, the ambulance flight was called and a Loganair Islander flew to Sanday, collected him, and took him back to Kirkwall where he was ensconced in the Balfour Hospital before the "Mariana" was back and safely tied up and the crew away off home to their beds. Think how much easier it would have been on everyone if he could have just got someone in the town to break his arm for him so he could have walked to the hospital by himself!

For us on board there followed a welcome interlude. The three of us gathered in the wheelhouse and supped coffee. To the north, the sun had disappeared over the horizon near midnight, and now it was rising again at around three in the morning. The wind and the sea had dropped. The engine gave off a steady thrum, and we ploughed a calm and pleasant furrow towards home again. It was a moment of quiet and relaxation. A night owl somewhere in the islands called us up on the CB for a yarn and wanted to know "whit like the Sanday eens was on theer wa hame." I told him. He laughed. We didn't.

The football runs continued each season. That first one was perhaps the worst. After Sanday's next trip there was only one accident when a returning supporter got into his car on the pier, selected reverse by mistake and nearly backed off the edge of the pier. The car teetered there, but he succeeded in getting out and all was well. I told the Sanday folk that the Royal Society for the Prevention of Accidents was thinking of banning football trips. It wasn't until a couple of seasons later that the next trip occurred that I want to tell you about. Sanday continued to perform well, though never quite making it to the final of the Parish Cup. However, on this occasion they did win the North Isles cup. Exactly as before, we collected them at around 11 p.m. at the steps in Kirkwall. They were, if anything, even more happy than usual as they had a victory to celebrate. We had developed better tactics at dealing with them, and they were less excited as football runs had become more commonplace. It seemed as if we were headed for a fairly normal run. Far from it!

It all started normally enough. We went between Thieves Holm and Carness and headed Eastwards down The String so as to round the Fitt of Shapinsay. By experimenting we found that this way was slightly quicker at certain states of the tide than the more usual route around The Galt. There was little in it, but it made a change. In the passenger cabin the usual frantic boozing was going on. Sales of chicken soup were at their usual astronomical levels. The first intimation of disaster sounded innocent enough. The VHF crackled into life:

"Pentland Coastguard, Pentland Coastguard. This is "Arun Mist", "Arun Mist".

""Arun Mist". This is Pentland Coastguard. Channel 67."

"Six seven. Going up."

Such messages were a constant background to our work. Fishing boats called for weather forecasts, a tanker called for a pilot in Scapa Flow, a Peterhead fishing vessel called up his mate for a chat. However, this particular exchange intrigued me somewhat. Whatever was the "Arun Mist" doing out at this time of the night? I flicked the radio across to Channel 67 to see what the call was all about, only to be more intrigued than ever.

"Pentland Coastguard. This is "Arun Mist". Would you be kind enough to pass a message through to Kirkwall Police Station. Please tell them Code Blue, Code Blue."

Whatever was all that about? No-one in the wheelhouse knew. I had a sudden thought. Roger, the auxiliary Coastguard, was at the vending machine selling another fix of chicken soup to some-one. When he returned I asked him if he knew what Code Blue meant.

"I dinna ken exactly," he said, "but ah think it might be the code fer Sanday."

That all made horrible sense. If there was anywhere in Scotland where you would be guaranteed to find drunk drivers that night, it would be leaving Sanday pier after we had dropped them all off. I figured that an ounce of prevention was worth a great deal of cure, so I called The Clydesider from the cabin.

"I've got a horrible feeling that you'll find the police are waiting for you on Sanday," I told him, and stated my reasons.

"By heck," he responded. "I hope no'." He reached for the CB mike and started to call through the channels, trying to find someone on Sanday who could tell him what was going on. Eventually he located someone who was sober enough to hold a rational conversation.

"Is tha' reet the po-liss is theer waitin' fer us," he asked in his broad Glasgow accent.

"Ah dinna ken, boy," answered his respondent. "Ah've nae seen them at a'. Theer's been nae talk o'hid aroond these parts. Ah'll tell thee whit. Ah'll check up, and if ah finds oot anything, ah'll gi' thee a ca' back." Somewhat relieved, The Clydesider went back to his drink.

We hadn't gone much further when there was a call for us on the CB. "Three, three for the "Golden Mariana".

"On channel," I replied.

"Cuild ah hae a peedie word wi' The Clydesider, boy?" I called him and he made his way back to the wheelhouse and answered the CB.

"By heck, boy. Thoo wis right. The bluebottles is jist pullin' in tae the pier noo. Whit like is everyone?"

"They're a' dronk, every one" was the reply.

When The Clydesider shouted in the passenger cabin, "Theer's po-liss at the Pier," a hush fell on the festivities. Panic ensued.

Every man sought his own path to salvation. The benches in the cabin were full of people flaked out trying to sleep it off. The monstrous consumption of chicken soup ceased and was replaced by black coffees. Many sought the fresh air of the open deck to clear their heads. One man paced up and down, hoping exercise would do the trick. Yet another stood forlornly at the door to the wheelhouse, looking down at the tatty tennis shoes he wore on his feet. "Me hoose is near eight mile frae the pier. Ah'll ne'er mak it. If ah'd only kenned ah'd have weared me guid shoes!" In the wheelhouse one man took it on himself to try to organise transport for them from more sober folk who had stayed at home. For a long time he called and called on the CB, searching for Sanday night owls who were still at their sets. He called long and hard, going through a long list of CB handles of friends of his. At two o'clock in the morning he was still trying. Eventually he gave up in disgust. "A' they that's sober's abed, and they that's still up's a' dronk," he said in disgust, and retired to the cabin again.

It was a subdued party that arrived at Kettletoft that night. There was no laughter, no drunken chatter, as they all trooped ashore. The most we got from them was a quiet, "See thee then, boy," as they left. Quietly they slunk off, worrying to a person about how they were going to fare. It was not until later that we heard. The reason for the police presence had nothing to do with them. A visitor at the hotel had gone berserk with an axe. While the police apprehended him, our passengers sidled away to their homes quietly with sighs of relief.

# COMINGS AND GOINGS

I should correct any impression that every trip was a riotous gathering of inebriated islanders, up to all sorts of pranks and carryings on. Nothing could be further from the truth. Mostly the days rolled by with a succession of visitors drinking in the beauty, bird watchers enthralled at the puffins, razorbills, guillemots and terns, islanders heading south for their holidays and returning a couple of weeks later, others heading to the town to visit family, or just for the messages· (which is the Scots term for the shopping). These comings and goings covered the whole gambit of human emotions. We might witness the joy of brother or sister, returned with their families from the Antipodes or North America to see the family again. For a while these colonial cousins would often come aboard for trips to town or to the other islands. Then, a couple of weeks later there would be a tearful gathering at the pier or jetty as the families parted again, perhaps not to see each other for many years. Sometimes we would take elderly folk away from their island for the last time as they headed for a retirement home in Kirkwall, and they might pass a new family of incomers, headed out to see a croft that had been advertised.

There was the American bird watcher who had come to the Islands just to see puffins. "No problem," we assured him. "We always see loads of puffins."

"That's what they all say," he replied. "Ah've travelled the world to see puffins and ah'm always told, 'No problems', and ah've never seen one yet." We went out across the Westray Firth and back. Guess what - no puffins! I told him he should go on a bus tour with David

Lea, who was a former RSPB official. "Ah went yesterday, and there were no puffins," he replied. Later I mentioned this conversation to David, and he confirmed the story. "I'm thinking of making some wooden cut out puffins and placing them in strategic positions on the cliffs," he told me, and on board we reflected on having some balloons with puffins painted on them, so that someone could blow them up and release them from the after deck. One time a very rare Scops Owl was sighted on Papa Westray, and within hours twitchers started to arrive from the four corners of the kingdom. We did think that a stuffed Scops Owl on a wire would do wonders for Papay tourism. It wouldn't have taken that many bird watchers for Papay to record a 100% increase in tourist numbers.

It is true that much that happened was tinged with humour, often unconscious, and often tinged with pathos. There was the Eday alcoholic. He would regularly head for Kirkwall with a return ticket and a list of messages from his wife, but we knew full well he would not be back that night. The money for the messages was spent at the hostelries, and he would be too far gone by the time we returned in the evening. It was a couple of years before I ever saw him sober, when he proved to be a quiet, shy man. Normally he was a shambling, slim figure with the disconcerting habit of putting his face very close to yours. Unfortunately this brought home to you another characteristic. He had home brewed breath. His eyes were glazed and his speech slurred. Also he loved the "Mariana", and would repeat over and over, "Golden Mariana, Golden Mariana" for reasons that were not entirely clear. He also repeatedly tried to take the helm. If he ever succeeded he was very hard to extricate. Trying to keep him from this trick was rather like warding off the advances of an evil-smelling octopus as he placed one arm around my neck for support, distracted me with a gust of fetid breath, and made a surprise grab for the wheel. One trip after just leaving Eday we were surprised to be overtaken by Geordie Swann, the doctor's husband, in his speed boat. He came alongside and our drunken friend, in his usual parlous condition, was bundled over the side. Thanks, Geordie! I think it was a case that a drunkard was better off the island than on. Eventually he came to realise that the only way to achieve his heart's desire and get an interest in the "Mariana" was to marry into the family, so he started to propose marriage to me. Being happily married already I felt there was really very little he could offer me, so I turned him down!

However, there was sadness as well. One of our best customers was an Eday man. He had moved to Kirkwall, but still kept his boat on Eday and travelled backwards and forwards to go to the creels. What a nice man he was, and I would call him a friend. He was quiet and helpful, and would step calmly aboard in the morning, dressed in a blue fisherman's smock, ready for a day's work. Often he would take the wheel for the crew to give them a spell, or give a hand with the lines. For part of the trip he would chat to us in the wheelhouse, and then would go and sit quietly in the cabin. But there was more about him than met the eye. He had been married and had a son but was divorced from his wife. His trouble stemmed from deep, dark depressions that would come over him, when he was convinced that he was useless and that his life was worth nothing. Then, though normally sober, he would drink himself into a stupor. I was told that there had been some problem with drugs when he had been away at sea on the big ships, and it had affected his mental stability. How true this was, I know not. Still, he loved his little lad, and would often take him with him to the creels during the school holidays, and it was clear that he would do anything for the little chap. We never saw the other morose and depressed side; only the quiet, pleasant, rather shy man who would always help you if he could. One day he fell into dark despair again and set to drinking. Every failure in his life, his worthlessness, bubbled up in his drink fuddled brain, and he made his way down to the pier - and just kept walking right over the end. The cold waters of Kirkwall Bay brought an end to his sadness. When I heard the news, tears sprang to my eyes. What a loss of a nice man. What a waste. He was worth so much more than he himself had realised.

There was another very sad event that took place on Rousay while we were there. It was a tradition for the groom-to-be at his stag night to be on the receiving end of a 'blackening'. It was a sort of modern equivalent of a tar and feathering, but involved plastering the recipient with black goo, probably grease. On this occasion the groom got wind of what was planned and managed to escape. He made his way down to the pier on Rousay. However, suspecting that he was being followed, he borrowed a canoe that was lying nearby. He set off in the dark, probably headed for Wyre just across the water. There was no news of his whereabouts for some days, but then his body was found. How very sad for the bride-to-be!

# Deerness Folk

When I first determined to write down all the unusual happenings that we experienced when we were running our ferry service, I was left with an impression, which may also be that of the reader, that the overriding feature of life in the Isles is that of humour. Yet I had lived that life and the impression had not been confirmed by the reality. We did not go around in a permanent mood of laughter and hilarity. Life pursued its normal round, interspersed with moments of sadness, pathos, happiness, joy and laughter, just as happens in the lives of all but a few. So why do so many of the tales of those years leave an impression of being funny? The answer, I suspect, stems from the character of the people. Island life has bred in them a rugged individuality which causes people to make their own personalised responses to situations and to seek personalised remedies to problems. Out on the land in all weathers, or braving wind and rain from a small boat are lonely and solitary tasks and this has encouraged people to maintain this individuality that has been lost in the modern technological society of our towns and cities. By the nature of an individual response to a circumstance, it is quite likely to be different to what is expected, and surprise is the essence of humour. Whereas we have been homogenised and pasteurised, the milk straight from the cow is full of impurities, but maintains a fuller richer taste. I want to tell you about our life in the parish of Deerness, but most of it could be "Got up, went to work, came home, went to bed", so instead I am going to describe some of the people who were our friends and neighbours. There is humour attached to this tactic, but do not make the mistake of thinking that there was no more to them than this. They are people of rich character, warm and welcoming, whose lives were enhanced by the fact that at times they did and said the unexpected.

We had gone to live in a little croft called "Horries". It was painted white, and was tucked low into the side of a hill. The stone walls were thick and it was roofed not with tiles, but with roofing stanes, large flat square stones, that could not just blow away in the first gale. It had a fair-sized double bedroom and two very small singles. What had been another double bedroom we turned into an open-plan dining room with the kitchen, and gave ourselves bed space by the simple devise of having a large residential caravan at the back of the house. The living room was pleasant with an old Rayburn stove to keep it warm. The house did suffer from the minor defect that when the wind outside blew at Force 8, the wind inside was only marginally less at around a Force 5! Fortunately, judicious stuffing of foam into cracks reduced the problem to no more than a healthy draught. The views from the house were stunning. To the north we looked out over the Stronsay Firth and could see Stronsay, Sanday and Eday, with a glimpse of the hills of Westray on the horizon. Moving anti-clockwise, to the northwest we looked across the neighbouring parish of Tankerness on the far side of Deer Sound, and beyond stood Shapinsay and the high land of Rousay and Gairsay. Then, to the West was the inner part of the Deer Sound, with the hills of the West mainland beyond. Just below the house at the bottom of the hill was Halley beach, a long sandy strand that lacked only one attribute of the best holiday beaches in the world - there were hardly any people on it. On the south side we had our contact with the outside world from a little road that led to our house and then continued a short way up the hill before turning into a track that proceeded onwards to the highest point of land in Deerness. Up the hill to the East we were surrounded by barns, of which a couple belonged to "Horries", and the better ones were still being used by the farm of "Halley". There were other barns to the north, including an old ugly one which was a Nissen hut plastered all over with reinforced concrete. With no little effort I managed to knock it down as it spoiled the view.

To seek out an example of the kindest of people who welcomed us to Deerness, I have to go no further than just across the road to our neighbours, Sandy and Belle Cormack of "Bishops". They were already in their last years of farming this small 70 acre property, and Sandy epitomised the crofter who had a lifetime of hard toil behind him. Slightly lame from a tractor accident, blinded in one eye at the same time, he was just as one would imagine an elderly farmer to be. Never rushed, he could be seen from the crack of dawn till last light, limping from job to job or mounted behind the wheel of an elderly tractor, dressed in plain, hard-wearing, practical farm clothes. His features were a ruddy brown, stained by wind and weather. On his head was implanted a flat cap, which was almost permanently in place. On the rare occasions that it was removed, it became obvious that the face was indeed weather beaten, because the balding head that normally remained concealed was a startling pallid white. Belle was also the archetypal farmer's wife, small, slightly rotund, garbed in flowery dresses, often with an apron on, she cooked and baked and tended the chickens, and when she was needed, she donned her boots and coat and would go out into the fields and biers and lend a hand. In common with most Orkney farmers, their main concern was with the rearing of beef cattle. Much of the other work was associated with this. For example, the growing and cutting of silage to feed the herd during the winter months was a major task, for in the autumn and winter the beasts could not stay in the fields, but were brought into the barns where they spent the hard months cooped up and waiting for the return of spring.

We first met Sandy within minutes of our arrival with the removal truck. He was there, not to be nosy and get in the way, but to help shift the furniture. With the briefest of introductions, he was hefting beds and sofas and boxes of books with the rest of us. It was a kind act, but one which we found hard to place into context, for the simple reason that we couldn't understand a word he said! Furthermore, it was to be another six months at least before bit by bit I had come to grips with his broadest of Orkney accents. There is a fundamental error of the English. We mistake a lack of clarity of English speech with not having anything worthwhile to say. In fact, getting to understand Sandy merited the wait, for he had much of worth to say, and often it could be very funny. Sandy was the possessor of a wicked sense of humour, and it was one that was often lost on his friends and neighbours. I believe he greatly appreciated having an audience of someone who could chuckle, or even roar with laughter, at some wry or cutting barb that he had just delivered. Often some guttural, unintelligible sounding grunt would have me in paroxysms of mirth. At times it was the turn of phrase which was so amusing. I do like a good turn of phrase.

One day Sandy had been going to the Deerness Stores and gave me a lift in his car, and the following conversation took place:

Sandy confessed to me that he wasn't as slim as he used to be, and blamed it on his liking for eggs.

"Whit an eggs ah eat," he said. What an eggs I eat, meaning, 'I eat far too many eggs.' "Salt too," he continued.

"With me, it's pepper," I told him. "I take an enormous amount of pepper."

"Aye. Ah work wi' the pepper too!" was his rejoinder. I work with the pepper, meaning 'I always take a lot of pepper.' This seemed to me to be a highly descriptive way of describing his addiction to pepper. It was a great turn of phrase, and one which he used to good effect on another occasion. This time we were at Johnny's. In Deerness there were two centres for the dissemination of information. One was the shop, used by both men and women, and the other was all-male - Johnny's. Our corner of Deerness was reached by a side road, called the Kirbister Road that turned left off the main road and headed as far as the North Shore where it came to an end at the farm of "Halley". Before its end, another little road turned up the hill known as the Laing Gate to the right and swept round in a loop before coming back to the main road again at the shop. A further small road turned left at the top of the Laing Gate and went as far as "Horries" and "Bishops". At the junction between the main road and the Kirbister Road was a corrugated iron shack. At this inauspicious place, Johnny Aitken carried on his business. It was a business vital to the well-being of the community. He fixed things. It mattered little what needed fixing; he seemed able to fix it, whatever it was. If your car broke down, Johnny mended it. If the frame of your bike snapped, Johnny welded it. If your tractor wouldn't start, Johnny started it. If you wanted some special tool for the farm, Johnny designed and built it. At the end of the job some small exchange of coin would take place, and one would go happily on one's way, wondering how he could make a living. He must have been the last person in the land who would still charge 50p for doing some small job on a car. Naturally, in an agricultural community, his services were much in demand, and when Johnny was in attendance, you could often find quite a group of the men of the parish, all waiting for him to help with some task or other. And while they waited, what was more natural than that they should discuss local matters of importance - gossip, in other words.

On this occasion, Sandy and I joined a number of other local worthies while we waited for Johnny to finish building a moon rocket for someone, or whatever task he had agreed to undertake that day. Talk had turned to AIDS. In those days AIDS was still a mystery killer, and little enough was known about it by the general public. The tabloids had irresponsibly cottoned on to the spread of the virus through the gay community and had dubbed it the gay plague, thereby setting back for a number of years a true under-standing of the disease by the person in the street. For some rea-son, the gathering was comparing the spread of AIDS to the spread of anthrax through cattle. Sandy saw a weakness in this logic and debunked the conversation in one sentence. "Aye," he said. "But beasts dinna work at the poofin'." Nobody saw anything the least bit humorous in this statement, but Sandy glanced at me and I saw his eyes twinkling, and I suppressed a desire to burst out laughing. On the way home in the car he did give vent to a satisfied chuckle of merriment. It was indeed a well-turned phrase.

I am sure that sometimes it was the phraseology which lent itself to a situation, and Sandy might say something that was not of itself funny, but which came across in that way because a word or phrase was so apt. One day we were discussing wife beating, heaven knows why. Sandy managed, as usual, to see an appropriate circumstance from everyday life with which to punctuate our conversation. He referred to someone he knew who was a cowed individual with a wife whose large body was nonetheless still disproportionately small compared to her mouth, which was always open and always had the volume turned up. "Well, theer's wan thing," he observed. "Jimmy'll nae be batterin' that gurt wife o' his'n! Mighty; whit a breuch comes oot o' that wife's mooth!" One does not have to be familiar with the word breuch to understand exactly what it means.

This sense of humour would have served others well. It is an unfortunate truth that some families in the islands fall out with others, and what starts as a disagreement becomes a feud that can last down through the generations. With only a limited population to mix with, it is hard to escape the consequences of such rows. The makings of one had occurred between Sandy and Belle and the previous occupants of "Horries", who by chance had also been called Cormack, though were not related. Behind it all were chickens. Belle, in common with many others in those days, kept chickens. In the days before battery farming many a housewife in the isles supplemented the family income by selling eggs. The trouble was, the Cormacks of "Horries" had an aversion to Belle's hens crossing the road onto their property. Well, you know free range chickens, they have this annoying habit of ranging freely. I don't doubt Belle gave them a good talking to. "Listen, thoo hens. The Cormacks dinna want thee on theer side o' the road." It certainly didn't work. One might imagine her training the chickens. "Sit! Stay!" but no effort dissuaded the hens from crossing onto the neighbour's land. The matter was creating a very definite friction between the neighbouring crofts, and Sandy and Belle were at their wits end to know what to do. At length an event occurred of wonderful surrealism. One unruly hen not only crossed the road, but couldn't help noticing that "Horries'" door was open. Always on the lookout for one more tasty snippet, the chicken walked daintily inside, clucking quietly to itself, proceeded down the little passage-way and into the kitchen. There was nobody at home. She clucked about and cleared up every crumb that she could find, leaving the usual little calling cards on the stone floor, as hens are wont to do, and then turned her attention to another door that also stood ajar. Onwards, onwards she went, into the dark recesses of Bert's room, the son's bedroom. There was no food here, but by crikey, that bed looked mighty comfortable and that was the very moment when she got caught short. She was on strange territory, far from home, and an egg was coming. Improvise, she told herself, and hopped onto Bert's bed - and laid the egg! Now, given the state of relations between the two families Cormack, one might have supposed that this would have brought things to the boil. Seemingly, however, the monstrous gall of the bird completely took the wind out of the "Horries" family's sails. Without a word of criticism or complaint, they told Sandy and Belle what had happened - and GAVE THEM THE EGG BACK! Ten years later Sandy was still chuckling about it.

Sandy must have been a bit of a lad in his day. Many a hint he dropped to that affect. He told me the tale of a friend of his from school days, for example. His friend Fred was brilliant at maths. "Ah ne'er did a sum frae the start o' the term tae the end," he told me. "Fred did ma eens and his eens in nae time at a'. Hand whin hid cam tae a test ah cuildna do a one!" Does that sound familiar? It did poor Fred no good, it seems. He went 'sooth' to work, had a nervous breakdown and became an alcoholic. He was fortunate, though, and "met this wife whit pulled en through." Unfortunately, the effort proved such a strain on her that she became an alcoholic in her turn and ended up "wi'oot the breath tae light her ain fag." What years of unhappiness lay hidden in that short anecdote, and I could tell that Sandy too was sad at the way life had treated his friend, and taken him from Deerness away from people who cared about him.

Although we lived very close to Bishop's, weeks might go by with no more than a cheery wave, but we always knew we could rely on our neighbours if we needed a hand. It was this friendly, but relaxed relationship which Sandy and Belle liked. They didn't like the idea of having people opposite who were watching their every move. Although we were incomers, we got their vote of gratitude for that. Then, of a sudden, Sandy and I would find ourselves walking along together, or perhaps he would give me a lift in his car, and often there would be some little tale that was worth remembering. He told me one day of an old chap, well past his prime, who had done some work for the people at the Hall of Tankerness in the parish across Deer Sound. It had been agreed that he would take his pay in potatoes - a sack full, and the workers at the Ha' thought to play a trick on the old chap. They filled the largest sack that they could possibly find until it was bulging with tatties and was far too heavy for one man to lift, they thought. They then hid themselves and settled back to have a good laugh at the old fellow's expense. In due course he came up the road with his horse and cart, but the laugh was on the men of the Ha' for he lifted the sack in one easy motion and flung it on the cart without even bothering to lower the tail gate!

There was a young chap who lived nearby. He was a good Orkney lad who played football, worked where he could on the land and was not averse to "a few peedie drinks." One night it was he who came to disturb the peace of our corner of Deerness. We were sat quietly in the living room, watching TV. Outside it was already dark. Suddenly, to our amazement, a car passed the house at high speed. Since the road ended no more than a few yards above "Horries" where it became a rough track, you might imagine our surprise. We went to the small window that looked out on the road out of curiosity and were just in time to see another car rush past at great speed as well. This second one had a distinguishing feature. On the top of it was a blue flashing light. My goodness, what excitement, a police chase! Discussing this event that had come to disturb our equilibrium, we suddenly saw the two cars returning down the hill at a much more sedate speed. Both were being driven by policemen, and the young man was seated forlornly in the back of the Panda car. He had been in Kirkwall and had decided to stop for some refreshment at the pub that was halfway from Kirkwall and was known as the Quoyburray. Inevitably there were others in there that he knew, and one drink led to another, so that it was not until later in the evening that he continued his by now unsteady way home. Unfortunately, one of his rear lights was not working, so, modest though his driving was, the police car had every excuse to pull out behind him from the little car park on Dingieshowe, the isthmus that joined Deerness to the rest of the Mainland. Our young friend was worried. He was even more worried when he reached the top of the brae into Deerness, turned onto the Kirbister road at Johnny's, and the police car followed him. To check if it was coincidence or not, he increased his speed a bit. So did the police car. He increased his speed a bit further. So did the police car. By the time that they had reached the turning off to the right and headed up the Laing Gate, he was going as fast as his old car would let him. So was the police car. By now the young man could think of only one escape. If he could reach the end of our road and leap from the car, he would surely be able to run for it and outstrip any flat-footed PC Plod. He knew he would get done for dangerous driving and speeding, but at least he would avoid blowing into the little bag. Just after the breakneck chase past our house he screeched to a halt, leapt from the car, and took to the fields. All he needed to do was to leave the law sufficiently far behind that they would lose sight of him in the gloom. He had failed to allow for one small thing. Although it was true that one of the police was a rather tubby, unfit individual, the other one proved to be a cross country runner of some ability and he overhauled our Deerness lad and apprehended him with some ease! He had a lot of time walking during the coming twelve months during which he could ponder the results of his miscalculation.

Nearby was a house with a nice old lady who was housebound. It was a rude croft, with a barn or two at the back. Unfortunately she was now aged and infirm. A large lady, she couldn't get about very easily anymore and rarely left the house. However, she did love to have a visitor and a chat. She had a fund of stories about life in Deerness in earlier years, apart from keeping up to date with every last item of gossip. Sharing the house with her was her nephew, a man so rotund that he had the shape of a ba', that ball stuffed with cork that forms the centrepiece of the historic Christmas and New Year game in Kirkwall. Indeed, so fat was the nephew that Sandy Cormack once said to me, ""Yon fellow hasnae tied his left boot since 1953."

Over the years when we lived in Deerness we would go visiting our neighbours from time to time in the traditional fashion. Entry to this lady's croft was at the back. A knock on the door would elicit the sound of shuffling steps, the door would open, and a booming voice would welcome you, with instructions to "cum awa in and sit doon." The old croft assaulted your nose with a smell of years of peat fires, cooking bere bannocks on the Rayburn stove and a hint of the cowshed from the nephew's trousers. (A bere bannock is a traditional Orkney bread made from bere meal, which is an ancient type of barley.) In no time a mug of tea would be proffered with a piece, which is the Scots word for a snack. The old lady would talk with relish about anything that might be going on, or which was of interest from the past, interspersed from time to time with a booming laugh of pure joy and merriment. Her feet were housebound, but she certainly never allowed her brain to be the same.

"Ah dinna ken whit fer thoo wants tae visit a poor body like me," she said on one visit.

"You've always got such interesting tales to tell," was my response.

"Aye," she said. "Me mooth were aye me best part!" I mentioned this to Sandy one day and he replied that "She was sum lass in her day,"

I remember as if it was yesterday sitting in their living room and the nephew was watching the Miss World competition on the 26" TV that stood in the corner. He was rooting for an unexpected participant. "We're fer Miss Iceland, fer we must show solidarity wi' us eens frae the north". There was something wonderfully incongruous about the scene, a mixing of eras. The croft was much as any croft had been for centuries, but that box in the corner spelt the coming of the electronic age. Did it also mean the passing of the era that had preceded it? After my recent return visit I fear that it did.

At the top of the brae where our little road joined the circular road around the parish was the site of a property which must have been a sizeable place in its day. Called "Breck", the original building was no more and one house had been built on the kitchen and another on the hall with a road between the two. They had become known then as the Ha' o' Breck and the Kitchen o' Breck, or just the Ha' and the Kitchen. They were all Cloustons who lived there, and we were always assured a welcome at both these houses. Isobel lived at the Kitchen with her mother, and for a long time her brother Jackie and his family lived there as well. Isobel taught at the school, and later Jackie worked there as well as janitor, and proved to be very popular with the kids. At the Ha' was old Tom with his two sisters, all in their 80s. This was another traditional old croft where you were welcomed in the traditional way. Of the three, the two sisters were frail and hardly ever ventured out, but Tom was as fit as a fiddle and could often be seen walking up the brae past our house with a bale of hay on his back, and would always stop and pass the time of day. In the end it was his eyes that let him down. Cataracts started to affect his vision more and more until he could see little more than the difference between night and day. Clearly this interfered with his driving, so he limited his outings in the car to going to the Post Office once a week to collect his pension. That far presented no problems since, after a lifetime of making the trip, he could drive there from memory. The little road that ran around past Greentoft, turned back on itself and came out by the Deerness Stores was little frequented. If he met anybody it would be a local and they would recognise Tom and keep out of his way. Other locals might be someone like the twelve-year-old from a nearby farm, driving a tractor and towing a trailer loaded down with hay. He clearly knew how to manage a load like that, so Tom's weekly outing could pass without risk!

Tom still kept a few cattle and also owned an old bull. It was the mangiest old bull you have ever seen. Its best days were long past and it could not have caught even the most desirable of cows, not even a bovine supermodel. It had reached those declining years in which it felt that what was needed from a relationship was friendship rather than sex. From the herd's point of view, one might imagine that this made it somewhat superfluous - a sort of supernumerary bull. However, Tom needed friendship as well, and was very attached to the old beast. One might walk past and see him with his arm over its still ample neck, talking into its ear. The demise of the bull coincided with the time when Tom had to cease his lifetime of work and went off to have operations on his eyes. Sadly, these failed to restore his sight, and at around the same time the bull was carried away to the knackery. I felt sad to witness the failing of the bull, but most especially the failing of old Tom o' the Ha', after a lifetime of toil and endeavour. He was a nice man, and I shall always appreciate his willingness to stop and talk to me, an incomer from a background so totally different to his own. His life continued into a very old age, but I am sore of heart when I think what it must have meant to him to be deprived of the view of life around him, and the broad open vistas of the Isles.

I could go on spreading the net ever wider, meeting more and more neighbours. At "Greentoft" were the Bruces, a great family of crofters. Thelma was a cook of great talent, the sons followed the father on the land, and Billy junior played a mean fiddle. There were the Eunsons of Halley who were the biggest landowners of the parish, and were unfailingly kind and helpful. David was to meet a very sad end after we left Orkney, victim of a tragic shotgun accident as he appeared to catch the trigger in a fence as he climbed over it. A kinder man it would have been hard to meet. How very tragic! Then there were the other Eunsons at Keigar, Mary and Kenny, who were also good friends, and remain so to this day. Mary was a large lady with a heart to match, and a zest for life. Perhaps it is she who best illustrates this constant theme of humour that runs through the tales of our ferry, because Mary loved to laugh. She revelled in the eccentricities, the tricks, the jokes, the unusual and the unexpected, and would greet any revelation with obvious glee and merriment. Perhaps when your horizons, beautiful though they may be, are limited by a vista of sea and island and a limited populace, this love of life and of people is best expressed through humour and an appreciation of the odd and unexpected. I remember one memorable dinner party at "Keigar", and a story that illustrates what I mean. There lived in the parish a wag called Jim. He was out on his land one day digging a ditch, when up came an incomer and joined him. This chap was also called Chris, and it must be said that he was less well accepted in the parish than we had felt ourselves to be. There was just something about him which occasioned comment and sideways glances. He was different. He was eccentric. He walked about in the middle of the night, and was known to peer into empty crofts, except sometimes they weren't empty. My belief was that this was perfectly innocent and brought about by curiosity and perhaps even the search for another dwelling place. However, if you want to be accepted in a small community, odd behaviour is one thing likely to count against you, even if there are home grown eccentrics enough. People can be comfortable with a home-grown eccentric, having been brought up with their strange ways, while finding an imported eccentric more than their capacity to assimilate. His partner and mother of his child was a European lady who occasioned no such comment and was thus widely liked. I never found him to be anything other than perfectly pleasant, and I suppose that I must have an appreciation for the eccentric, because I got along with him well enough when we met. Anyway, this was the man who approached Jim and engaged him in conversation. Chris was a willing enough chap, and even joined Jim in the ditch and took a turn with the pick and shovel.

"Are you married?" Chris enquired, making polite small talk.

"Ah am that," was the response.

"What about family? Do you have any children?" came the next enquiry. It was all pretty mundane stuff; straight from the 'How to engage a stranger in conversation' manual. It was the straight-faced response which departed from the normal.

"Aye. Theer's een tae me and three tae Geordie the postman."

To fully appreciate the humour behind this, the reader must imagine Geordie, lifelong bachelor, and a man so unlikely to have engaged in the activity indicated by Jim's reply as to beggar all belief. Now up until that day, Geordie had always been welcome at Chris's croft and had often been proffered a cup of tea while he paused on his rounds of remote dwellings. It must have greatly exercised his mind to find that this welcome was thereafter withdrawn. You might imagine the great glee with which this tale was repeated that night of the dinner at "Keigar", though it was from a surprising source that I heard another tale of Jim the following day.

Ada was the postmistress, and was everybody's idea of a favourite Granny, petite, demure and Granny-like. She too had heard the story about Jim and told me one of her own. Many of the Orkney worthies had decided to go on a charter flight to Aberdeen to the Royal Agricultural Show and organised by the National Farmers' Union. This was an event that was attended by many of those who had progressed beyond crofting to be true farmers, and pillars of their communities. The NFU was a powerful and influential body on the local scene, as indeed it is in many rural areas. Furthermore, this was an event of some significance, one for getting out the Sunday best. One did not wear one's farm clothes on such a trip. Jim was going, for one, and also from the parish was another chap called Sydney. Sydney, in certain respects, had many of the attributes of Geordie, insofar as that he was no philanderer by nature. Instead, he was bespectacled, shy and earnest, the very last person to be guilty of riotous or loose behaviour. Jim agreed that the two of them should go in Jim's car to the airport to cut down on the parking, but, when nearly there, Sydney suddenly realised that he had left his wallet behind. Fortunately, Kirkwall airport is on the road that leads to Deerness. There was nothing for it but to turn the car around and head back the eight miles or so to Sydney's farm and collect it. As a result, they were late. By the time they had made it to the British

Airways plane, everybody else had boarded, and as they entered the door and headed down the aisle looking for empty seats, they were confronted by all the faces of local farming dignitaries and their wives, each one in their Sunday finery. Many must have been saying to themselves, "Typical, those eens thit lives nearest aye arrives last," and other appropriate thoughts. Every eye was on them.

"Ah'm awfu' sorry we're late," said Jim, so all could hear, "but Sydney fergot his condoms!"

Perhaps Ada wasn't the conventional Granny figure after all.

Another topic of conversation that night at "Keigar" was the spherical object that had pride of place in Kenny and Mary's living room. Kenny had won a ba'. What is more, he had done so only recently, and not in the first flush of youth, as would normally be the case. The Kirkwall Ba' is a ball game, the origins of which are lost in antiquity. One story has it that the severed head that killed Earl Sigurd by banging against his calf and causing septicaemia was thrown to a crowd to fight over. The game is not entirely unique, and similar exists in England. The hard cork-filled ball or ba' is thrown into a crowd in front of the Cathedral in Kirkwall, and one team tries to get it into the harbour and another tries to get it against a wall at the other end of the town. One side are the Uppies, the other the Doonies. Which side you are on depends on what part of Orkney you come from. The principal rule is that there are no rules, and each team is limited in number to as many people as can be persuaded to turn out. Thus, the ball frequently spends long periods lost in a vast mêlée of people, stuck at the entrance to one of the small lanes or Wynds in Kirkwall, or trapped in some entrance way. Suddenly, the ball comes free and the braying mob tears after it. Windows must be boarded. Injuries are not uncommon, and Kenny himself was to be rushed to hospital in a later year when the crush of the multitude almost caused his untimely demise. The game is not all brute force and ignorance. Tactics do exist, and one of the main ways of gaining ground is through the smuggle. With such a throng, half the time no-one really knows where the ba' is. If you can just stuff it up your jumper, sidle to the edge of the crowd, stand up looking as though you are stopping for a rest, and then stroll off as though to get a second wind, you might just meander quietly to your goal while everyone else stays in a great scrum, wandering just exactly where under all the bodies the sphere might be. The Doonies had had a long run of victories, partly because of demographic changes in Kirkwall. If a Doonie scored by getting the ba' into the harbour, he had the added honour of following in after it. As the events take place on Christmas Day and New Year's Day, this was a little more than a pleasant cooling dunk. The best player on the winning side is then decided by a group of adjudicators, and the ba' is awarded to them to keep. And Kenny had got one - a great honour.

As for the aforementioned Chris, the tale of Geordie the postman was not the only one connected with his brief tenure in Deerness. Another incident involving him happened one year at the Women's Institute annual children's Christmas party. This event was eagerly anticipated. Christmas is a feast that stems originally from the pagan wish to fill the long winter's nights with festivities and merry making, the better to withstand the short days, the poor weather and the gloom of the winter solstice. For the children of Deerness, the WI party certainly set the scene. For days beforehand they would be busy preparing entries for the fancy dress competition. Mothers were roped in to help, and some very ambitious results ensued. There were prizes in many different categories, and even one for parents. Few adults entered, however. The fun was in helping the bairns. Come the big day, early in the evening all the children and most of the parents would foregather in the parish hall, a plain and unadorned building, similar to thousands of parish halls all over the land. After food and many a party game and great excitement, the fancy dress judging would take place, followed by a visit from Santa, who often seemed to have that same weather-beaten visage with pallid white balding head that I have already associated with many a farmer. He would bear a gift for every child in the parish, and would often preface the presentation with words such as, "Ho, ho, ho. Hid's nae very nice oot. Theer's even a peedie bit o' snow in Birsay," thereby showing a wonderful ability to imitate any accent that he might find in his trip around the world. On this occasion, there was an empty seat on one side of me, and I was joined by this Chris, who was a latecomer. To mark the occasion he had clearly decided that a certain amount of physiognomic decoration was called for, so he wore face paint in the shape of some scrolls and hieroglyphics on cheeks and forehead.

"Hello, Chris," I welcomed him as he approached and sat down next to me. "I see you've decided to go in for the fancy dress," I added, not without some admiration at his willingness to throw himself into the fun. He looked at me strangely, clearly wondering what on earth I was talking about. "No," was all he said! I curled up and pretended that the exchange hadn't taken place at all.

Later that evening it was his turn to be embarrassed. He had incurred the wrath of Mrs Cooper-White, the WI president. This lady was a great organiser, ideal for her role; but she was not a person to suffer fools or put up with any unacceptable behaviour. You incurred her wrath at your peril. She approached Chris later that evening, and clearly was displeased. "I've confiscated your home brew," she stated, in a manner that brooked no argument. "You've no right to bring home brew to a children's party," she said.

"But… … " Chris tried vainly to interject.

"There's no but," she continued. "It's disgraceful. A children's gathering is no place for such behaviour."

"But… … "

"You can have it back when you leave. I've no idea what you were thinking of, bringing that stuff here of all places." Her dander was clearly up, and it must be said that she was making a fair point. What excuse could he have for bringing home brew to the children's party?

"But… … But it's not for me. I brought it for the baby!" So that was all right, then.

Before the proceedings started, there was a sumptuous repast. Earlier in the day every Mum had been baking and preparing sandwiches, and before the games, the fancy dress judging and Santa's arrival and departure, benches erected along the middle of the hall were bowed down by plate upon plate of food. Everyone dived in. The scene would not be unfamiliar to many a country dweller, and the fare would have not been dissimilar to that being prepared at many a similar event in the land. True there might be the odd plate of traditional fare - some Scots tablet perhaps, but no bere bannocks. However, there were oodles off egg sandwiches, tomato sandwiches, fruit cakes, sponges, trifles and home-made biscuits; but there was one thing that we never discovered. Who was it who year after year made date and sardine sandwiches?

This Chris subsequently moved to a parish in the West Mainland, but news of him still filtered back. Grace Wylie in the shop told that two old ladies, both in their seventies, went to take the air and took a stroll past Harray Kirkyard. To their considerable surprise, Chris was sitting on a gravestone there as naked as the day he was born, thereby frightening the two old dears out of their wits. "They wis that skeered, they've vowed they'll ne'er go theer agin," Grace said. "They'd heerd o' this strange English fellow, but ne'er seed him afore," she added. "Well they have now, with knobs on," I replied.

Before we return to the sea, I can't move on without introducing you to another Jim, also a great character. Jim was the Deerness haulier. He hauled anything, but mainly it was cattle or feed. Such was the activity of the parish that Jim was hard put to manage all the work that came his way. All he wanted to do was to get on with it and he possessed a great capacity for work, but he was constantly hampered by the need to fill in forms and bits of paper, and comply with certain legal requirements. Jim found this very irksome, and who are we to criticise him? From dawn to dusk, he could be seen flying along the highways and byways of Deerness and off into Kirkwall. His vehicles had an unusual characteristic. Whereas most trucks have some form of progressive acceleration, Jim's seemed only to possess two engine speeds -flat out and stop. His war with officialdom led to a most curious state of affairs. Knowing something about the regulations connected with operating commercial vehicles, I noticed in the paper that he had been convicted of driving one lorry with the operator's licence of another. This surprised me somewhat, as it is not illegal. Unlike the road tax, the commercial licence is designed so as not to discourage an operator from taking his vehicle out of service for regular maintenance, or so he can undertake a contract even if his vehicle breaks down. In Jim's war with bureaucracy, he had neither the desire nor the means to hire expensive legal support, and so had conducted his own defence. When I asked him how he had been convicted when it wasn't even against the law, he said, "That's whit ah kept tellin' them, but they wuildn'a believe me!" He had achieved the equivalent of being fined for walking on the cracks in a pavement, or for loitering in a shop with intent to purchase.

Anyway, you may judge from this that Jim and officials just didn't get on, so when he disagreed with his rates from Orkney Islands Council, he withheld part of the payment. In turn, they got on their high horse, and it all led eventually to a sheriff's officer going to his house with a view to impounding his second truck. When the official arrived, the house was empty, but Jim was in the back garden. On seeing that someone was out the front sniffing around his lorries, Jim crept through the garage at the side of the house and peered surreptitiously out to see what was happening. Unfortunately, Jim's collie had no such reservations about meeting the visitor, and rushed over, wagging its tail. Not realising that he was being observed, the sheriff's officer turned and swung his right boot at the poor dog, kicking it in the bum. The dog ran off yelping. Jim was so incensed at this that he broke cover with an enraged yell and swung his own right boot right at the sheriff's officer and caught him four square on his bum. The official retreated yelling threats and imprecations at Jim to the effect that he would be back and would take the second truck. This idea did not please Jim, so to immobilise it he took the wheels off and kept it on blocks. Unfortunately, when the sheriff's men returned, deprived of their primary target, they took his main truck instead!

Another tale of Jim and his truck also stemmed from his impetuosity. His eldest lad was driving his Ford Cortina home from Kirkwall one night. As he went over the Wideford Brae out of Kirkwall, he lost all electrical power - ignition, lights, horn, starter, everything. Getting to a nearby house, he phoned home and inveigled Jim into coming out to get him. Into the truck leapt Jim, chucking a rope in by the side of him, started the engine, selected his usual flat-out position of the throttle and hared off at high speed - through Deerness, down the brae at Grind, across the peninsula at Dingieshowe, past St. Andrew's school, past the Toab shop, out by the Quoyburray Inn, down by the airport, up the Wideford Brae, and screeched to a halt when he spotted Bruce and the car. He did a three-point turn in the truck that would have been the envy of any learner in a mini and pulled in in front of the broken-down vehicle. Within moments the rope was made fast to the front axle of the Cortina and also attached to the rear of the truck. Scarcely pausing for breath, Jim leapt back into the cab, selected flat out again, and hared back off to Deerness. Making no concessions to the fact that Bruce was following him on the end of a tether, he raced homewards at his usual breakneck speed. He turned off the main road through Deerness, drove up the brae and into his yard. As he pulled to a halt he could hear the phone ringing in the house, so he leapt from the cab, thinking to leave his son to untie the tow rope. He sprinted through the unlocked door. (No-one in Deerness locked their doors, of course.) Grabbing the phone before it stopped ringing, he intoned, "Deerness three - twa- seven. Wha is hid?"

"Hid's me!" said the son. " Ah'm phonin' frae the Quoyburray. Didst thoo no ken the tow rope brakked afore we got tae the top o' the brae past the airport?"

Jim had been towing no more than a frayed end for seven miles! The parish had many a chuckle over that one in the ensuing days.

Eventually in later years someone in Kirkwall had the great good sense to spot the tremendous capacity for hard work of all the members of Jim's family, and they called a truce to the war and instead put them to work, and I believe that they have never looked back.

I will return to life in Deerness again before the end.

# What a Burke!

Well, four of them, that is. Burkes, I mean. North Isles Burkes. Burkes from the North Isles. The four sons from the Burke family - all of them seamen in one guise or another. They were not alike. Indeed, between them they covered the full gamut of alcohol consumption. As for the eldest, I never once saw him sober. The second son was abstemious and never drank. He was a fine family man, and mate on one of the tugs in Scapa Flow. He often travelled with us to see his relatives in the North Isles. Third son Erik, was a man of few words, but disliked tedium, so, like many in society, was sometimes drunk. Ian, the youngest, was carefree and, except when working, usually drunk. He was a quick witted, happy-go-lucky handsome young daredevil, with a shock of curly hair, and he earned his living working on the fishing boats. I sailed with Erik later and could write a whole chapter about him, because he had the endearing habit of hating life to get too boring. As for the eldest, he had been deep sea in the prestigious Ben Line, and never ceased to talk about it. His days deep sea had clearly been the highlight of his life. However, I suspect that he was not the success he would have liked to have thought himself, and his failure to live up to his own desired view of himself may have contributed to his relationship with the bottle. It is to Ian that we turn for this brief tale. At the time he was sailing on board the Shapinsay based "Our Catherine".

Jeff Popplewell had retired to Eday where he lived looking out over Calf Sound and spent his days painting delicate water colours of the beautiful scenes that surrounded him. When we first started operating, he soon approached me when he was travelling with us and volunteered to paint for us a sailing board. I accepted his kind proposal with alacrity, and in due course it appeared. It was a board of some 3 foot by 2 foot, had a painting of the "Golden Mariana" set against an island scene, had the name in fancy lettering, and had two patches of blackboard paint. One patch was labelled *Sailing for:* and the other said *Departing at:*. All we had to do was take some chalk and fill in our destination and the time of the next departure. It was a very practical piece of help and we used it with pleasure and pride for a while, until one day it just went missing - disappeared off the face of the earth. We searched around the pier in Kirkwall, but someone had clearly made off with it, and I suspected that it had floated away, having been helped by some passer-by who was the worse for drink. We thought no more of it. Not wishing to presume upon Jeff Popplewell again, I got Marvin Elliott, the celebrated wood carver on Shapinsay, to do another one, and that was very nice too. Our original one faded from our recollection, though we were from then on very careful not to leave the sign lying around when not in use.

It was two years later, and Ian came aboard in Shapinsay, in his cups, and headed for Kirkwall. He stood in the wheelhouse and chatted to us, but he wasn't really making a lot of sense. This was unusual for Ian, because one thing that I had noticed about him was that, however drunk he became, and however much his speech was slurred, what he said still made sense. He was a rare example of a quick-witted drunk. However, on this occasion he seemed to ramble, and the subject about which he was rambling was, strangely enough, sailing boards. This surprised us more than a little as it is an unusual preoccupation for the tipsy, and our lost board had by then been completely forgotten. Slowly the conversation became more specific.

"Didst thoo nae have anither boord afore this een thoo has noo?" he asked.

"Yes," I replied, "but that went missing a couple of years back."

"What woodst thoo do if thoo kenst wha it was thit nicked hid?"

"Well, I would be curious to know where it went, but that's about it. That's water that long since passed under the bridge," I told him.

"Weel. Suppose this fellow thit nicked hid didn'a mean tae nick hid, and meant tae give hid back, but ne'er got the chance?" Ian clearly knew more than he was letting on, yet.

"Why, do you know where it went, Ian?" I prompted.

"Ah might jist ken wheer it is noo," he said, "but if ah tells thee, will thee tek action against him what tekked hid?"

"Of course not," I assured him. "It was a nice sailing board, but it wasn't the Mona Lisa."

"Weel, " he said. "Hid happened like this." and launched himself into the tale. "Ah wis cummin' back frae the toon tae gang aboord the "Oor Catherine" this nicht, hind ahd tekked a few peedie drams. We wis berthed at the Kirkwall pier afore settin' oot fer the fishin'. Whin ah seed this lovely paintin' ah wis jist overcummed. Ah cuildna jist believe a body cuild paint summat sae beautiful. Whit a paintin' hid wis. Hid wis that guid ah cuildna leave hid theer wi'oot showin' the lads on boord, so ah picked hid up hind carried hid back wi' me tae the boat. Ah didna mean tae kep it, jist show everybody hind then put hid back. Whin ah got on boord, the lads wis a' turned in, so ah jist sat theer luikin' at this paintin', hind thinkin' whit a grand job hid wis, thoo ken. Jist at that moment, wha shuild come intae sight but the skipper, hind he wis in a powerful hurry. He wis jist bawlin' tae let gae the lines fer we wis tae be aff tae sea that very minute. I didna dare tell him that ah had yon boord, fer thoo kenst the man. He wuildna have bin best pleased. Ah jist turned hid o'er hind laid hid on the deck so the skipper cuildna see hid, hind the nixt thing ah kenned we wis in The String hind headed fer the Fair Isle. Anyhoo, ah wis dead skeered fer days fer I wis feared thit the skipper wuild ask whit this boord wis doin' on the deck, and ah cuildna bring mesell tae throw hid o'er the side. Eventually, ah wis tekkin' a watch hind the skipper wis kipped doon below, sae ah grabbed me chance hind carried hid doon intae the fore peak hind put hid face inwards agin the after bulkhead, and fer a' ah ken, t'is theer yet. Ah've bin feared tae tell thee ever since.

Thoo'll nea be tekkin hid oot on me fer tellin' the truth after a' this time?"

What could I say? The matter of our sailing board must have been praying on his mind for two years. I laughed and thanked him for the information. Next time we did a castle trip to Shapinsay the "Our Catherine" was alongside the pier there. I jumped aboard. Nobody was about, so I prized open the hatch into the fore peak and climbed down the ladder. It was dark and musty and full of nets and floats and mooring lines. I made my way gingerly aft and peered in the gloom along the after bulkhead. There was indeed some sort of board lying up against it. I turned it over, and, in a beam of light that filtered down through the open hatch, I made out the words "Golden Mariana - Sailing for: - Departing at:"

Erik was a talented engineer. In common with many islanders, he had a tremendous ability to keep machinery running without ready access to spares or any of the normal equipment that would be normally found in garages or machine shops. He would work for me later on our Shetland vessel and you will meet him again.

You will also meet Ian again when he hitched a ride back from Shetland.

# IT'S A HARD LIFE SELLING

Rod Wylie was a business man, and he wanted nothing more than to foster good relations with his clients in the isles. It was not chicken feed that he sold, either literally or metaphorically, nor did he peddle any minor item of household ware. No indeed, Rod sold nothing less than John Deere tractors, great big green monstrous things with wheels the size of a small car. His problem was that selling in the isles had to follow certain traditional and well-worn procedures that took up a great deal of time and involved not a little consumption of Highland Park, Orkney's own brand of peaty single malt nectar, quite possibly in combination with a peedie glass o' the home-bru. If you wanted any further evidence of the success of some of the most successful toilers of the land in the Isles, the fact that Rod deemed it worthwhile to journey there to visit clients, existing and prospective, should be the proof that you seek. Normally, as a businessman, he would travel out to Westray on the Loganair Islander service, where the little ten-seater passenger plane would land in a rough paddock, euphemistically known as an airport, weather and waterlogged fields permitting. (Nowadays they have laid hardcore.) On this occasion, it being a Saturday, Rod had nowhere near enough time to visit his Westray contacts and get back on the last flight, so he devised a different routing. He would return on the "Mariana". It was, however, a Saturday, and the "Mariana" was not scheduled to go anywhere near Westray that day. Saturday meant that Eday and Sanday were our destinations. Rod would hire a boat to take him to Eday, and there he would await our return last thing in the evening.

Let us pause for a moment and look a little more closely at the inter-island air service. It was a lifesaver for the outer isles. With the steamer route taking so long and being so cumbersome, their main contact with the outside world had been taken over by these small aircraft, flying backwards and forwards among the isles, with an occasional interruption to collect a sick person and deposit them in Kirkwall for the Balfour Hospital, or even to Aberdeen for more serious cases. One of their scheduled stops actually justifies an entry in the Guiness Book of Records - the shortest scheduled flight in the world. The route between Westray and Papay was scheduled to be covered in 2 minutes, though Captain Andy Alsop had got it down to under a minute in favourable conditions. It was no more than a hop off the ground from the field at the north end of Westray, and then straight down again on Papay just over the water. There is another strange fact about flights around the isles. One of the main landing places was London Airport -no, not Heathrow or Gatwick, nor yet Stansted or Luton. This one is the real McCoy. It is the only London Airport in the land, and it is on Eday, just adjacent to the Bay of London. I would be the first to admit, however, that there is none but the most cursory similarity between Heathrow's Terminal 1 and the little shack that represented the airport building on Eday.

One farmer on Stronsay owned a field that doubled up as the landing strip, though it was one that had little similarity with the tarmacked strips of other airports. His strip was on a field that required the pilot to land the aircraft with a sideways tilt of some 10 degrees. About the only thing that identified it as a landing strip was a windsock. The farmer was paid an annual fee for the use of his land, but it carried with it certain responsibilities for its upkeep. He confided in me that its main advantage was to bring with it a classier type of junk mail. In amongst circulars advertising ency-clopaedias, cattle cake or the latest cure for the staggers, which is a disease in cattle, he would find a glossy brochure that told him that for the modest expenditure of millions of pounds, his airport could be the proud possessor of the latest all-weather, all-singing, all-dancing landing system. The problem with the maintenance of the air strip was that it did not always coincide with the priorities for work about the farm. This gave rise to a rather odd CB conversation that we had one day. A woman's voice came across the CB air waves.

"Three three fer the "Golden Mariana". "Golden Mariana" are thoo on channel?"

We were steaming down the Westray Firth at the time somewhere off the East side of Egilsay. The voice was not familiar. What did the caller want, I enquired?

""Golden Mariana", wouldst thoo no ca' by Stronsay , fer ah must git tae the toon."

"I'm afraid I can't. Our schedule today takes us to Westray."

"Ah ken that, but ah'm booked oot o' Kirkwall on the plane the morn's morn fer oor holidays, and theer's nae plane fer Stronsay today."

"But why don't you speak to Loganair," I enquired. "There certainly should be a flight to Stronsay sometime today, I'm sure."

"Aye. Ah ken, but hid's bin cancelled."

"Why is that?" I asked. After all, the weather was fine and there was no fog. "Has it been called away for an ambulance flight?"

"No. Tis nothin' the like o hid. Hid cannae land, fer the farmer hasnae cut the grass!"

On reflection, I have never seen a sign at Heathrow that said: "Flight cancelled. Grass not cut!"

Let me return to the plans of Rod Wylie after his day of visiting customers on Westray. He phoned up Jamie Sigurdson. Jamie's croft looked out over Calf Sound at the north end of Eday and he went to the creels. In other words, he laid creels, which is the Scottish term for lobster pots. From the croft window he could see his little creel boat moored in the flowing tide near the jetty by the pub. Calf Sound is a beautiful and mysterious spot, about which you will learn more if you persevere with these idle scribblings. Jamie also did hires with his boat and agreed that he would be happy to go round to Rapness and meet Rod when his work was complete and take him back to Eday, ready to catch the "Mariana" later that evening.

Jamie was a character who one was bound to come across if one had any dealings at all with Eday. He was a large, florid faced man, with a large, but not florid faced, wife. He habitually wore the crofter's normal attire of shapeless trousers, thick shirt, covered by a jumper of indeterminate age, shape and colour. However, Jamie had a great affliction, which was of such a handicap to him that it soured and impeded his whole life. He had an awful stutter. The other affliction that had been sent to upset Jamie's equilibrium was incomers. A great traditionalist himself, exponent of the island way of life, he could not understand anyone who came to live on Eday and refused to live in the old way and honour the old traditions. It must be said that his frustration was not without foundation. Some incomers had a terrible habit of coming in and imposing their ideas on those whose families had lived there for centuries, and on Eday incomers were sufficiently numerous that they almost equalled Orcadians in number. This meant that there was ample opportunity for the incomers to propagate their alien ideas, and ample opportunity for Jamie to be frustrated. That is not to say that the incomers were anything other than very nice people as well. It was just that the lines of communication between incomer and Orcadian were not always very good. Jamie was a man of strong character, and not prepared to let things wash over him when he didn't agree with them. The trouble was, the more he was frustrated, the more he stuttered, and the more he stuttered, the more furious he was wont to become, fuelled by his inability to express himself with ease.

Jamie's *bête noir* was one particular incomer who had one of the larger farms towards the southern end of the island. They were chalk and cheese, cautious and impetuous, stolid and mercurial, North ender and Sooth ender, Orcadian and incomer. This incomer would try his hand at anything. A man of action, he would get stuck in first and work out the details later. In an island community which existed on the knife edge of viability, his characteristics and ideas could bring great benefits, but he failed in one important area. He didn't bring others along with him, and he certainly didn't bring Jamie Sigurdson. Together the two of them would have made a formidable team; separate, they created a corrosive influence. Relations on Eday had reached a state of affairs in which folk tolerated each other, but barely, and any idea that was put forward from any faction was immediately and automatically shot down by most of the others. What a shame. They were all nice folks, and some were very nice. I wish them well.

This phenomenon of a split community was not confined to Eday, and the incomer versus Orcadian aspect was just a convenient peg upon which to hang a hat that had appeared in many different guises down through the years. It seems that when the population of a small isle drops below a certain critical mass, the day-to-day concerns of people become concentrated in an unhealthy manner on those few people that are their fellow islanders. Arguments arise from any of a number of potential flash points. Religion might be one. Papay was split between the Plymouth Brethren and the Kirk. Egilsay was split in so many ways that it was hard for an outsider to comprehend, and Eday, as we have seen, was split between the new and the traditional. However, 'twas not always thus. Eday had been split before ever an incomer first arrived "frae Sooth." Bitter arguments had long characterised relations on Eday. Many surrounded perceived injustices over the location of the shop, the distance from the pier, and things had settled down to a split between the north enders and the sooth enders. With the numbers on the island decreasing, families were very worried about the viability of keeping their own doctor, their own school, a profitable shop. Thus, the first incomers were welcomed with open arms, especially if they brought children. Young people of marriageable age were also in great demand. It didn't take long, however, for relations between the newcomers and the existing folk to deteriorate, and the old north end/south end conflict changed. I am persuaded that the old habit of conflict is now so ingrained that, when the incomers have been assimilated, conflict will break out between the tall and the short or the dark and the fair! One day as we headed toward the island, there lurking at the back of the Green Holms was a rather evil looking Danish Navy patrol boat, inexplicably called the "Shadowfax", on annual manoeuvres. "I see the Eday 'eens has started hiring mercenaries," Stuart commented. Life in Arcadia, as in Orcadia, is not always what it seems.

I mention this problem with sadness and affection. Individually they were kind and friendly folk, and Eday, as the other islands, is a beautiful place. The views from high ground across Sanday and Stronsay on the one side, and Westray, Egilsay, Rousay and all the smaller islands on the other were breath-taking. What is more, a day out on Eday was a culinary highlight of any holiday. We arranged farmhouse meals, and there was scarcely a taker who failed to comment on the sumptuous nature of them. Mrs Popplewell, wife of the artist, was a cordon bleu; Ellie Sigurdson, Jamie wife, was famous for her Orkney repasts. Many others excited comment as well. I would not want the reader to think that the underlying tensions were visible to the casual observer, nor that they would spoil a visit. On the surface all appeared normal.

Relations between the Sigurdsons and the afore-mentioned incomer family reached their nadir over taxis. It all came about when the taxi driver for the island retired and moved to Kirkwall. He had run the island taxi for years, collecting folk from the pier or from London Airport. Over the final weeks of his sojourn on Eday he talked seriously to Jamie about Jamie's son, buying up the business. This would be an invaluable chance for the son; one that would help him to continue to stay on Eday and not find employment in some strange and far off place like Kirkwall. Negotiations continued in the Orkney manner, at a calm pace, with extended discussion, and when the retiring driver left, the discussions continued by telephone. There was the consideration to be agreed, and legal matters to be formalised. The trouble was, meanwhile Eday was left without a taxi. I did tell you that our incomer friend was a man of action, and so, true to character, he acted. In no time he had got a license and was running a taxi himself, and shortly afterwards there were two taxi operators for an island of 150 people. This was seen by Jamie as being the ultimate betrayal. Things just were not done that way. From that moment forwards it was war. He refused to deliver people to the other one's farm and would have nothing to do with folks that might be innocently accepting accommodation with the incomer. Woe betide a guest of the incomer if they wanted to hire Jamie's boat to go over to look at the Calf, across Calf Sound. Raymond Lamb, the County archaeologist, found himself faced with organising transport and accommodation for a very senior personage. It was a nightmare. How could he do it without offending one party or the other? He decided that compromise was the best option, and asked Jamie to collect the man from Sanday when he had finished there, and then hired a taxi from the incomer. This all sounded very equitable until Jamie found out about the taxi and refused to have anything more to do with the deal, stranding the man on Sanday for the whole weekend.

Jamie had battles to fight on other fronts as well. He fought and lost the battle over Heglie Ber jetty. No wonder he was cross. To be honest, I was cross about this battle on his behalf when I heard what had happened. Jamie didn't do a lot of hires with his boat, but in the summer there was always a smattering of folk who wanted to cross Calf Sound and be put on the Calf; archaeologists mainly. However, there was one regular call on his services. Eday had no vet, whereas Sanday did. (We will meet Bill Carstairs later.) To plough across Sanday Sound to reach Kettletoft in a tiny boat was out of the question, and far too time consuming, especially when Sanday was just opposite on the far side of the Sound of Eday. The shoreline of Sanday at this point was universally rocky, but Jamie had all the knowledge he needed to be able to manoeuvre his little creel boat into those rocks and pick people up from there. Nonetheless, it was not an easy task, either for Jamie or for the passenger. A call for the vet was no respecter of tides, and it would often happen when the tide was low and Bill had to scramble over rocks wet with the sea and slippery with the seaweed. Meanwhile,

Jamie, having struggled to get his boat alongside the rocks, had to hold her there with no place to tie a rope. What was needed was a small jetty, and a campaign, strongly supported by Bill Carstairs, was launched. With strong support from the Community Councils on both Eday and Sanday, a motion was finally passed by the OIC (Orkney Islands Council) to allocate some funds for the purpose. The planning department were given the job of designing the structure and getting it built. Perhaps my view of this matter is over simplistic, but, as a seaman, I would not dream of building a jetty on a rocky, tide-wracked shore without making sure that I knew every nuance of conditions that had to be faced. Since I do not have that knowledge of the coast of Sanday at Heglie Ber, the first thing I would do would be to seek someone who did have that knowledge. There was but one - Jamie. Imagine, therefore, the annoyance, nay anger, that came across Jamie when he heard that some fellow from the Council had already designed the jetty and put its construction up to tender without once asking him, who was to be its sole user. In common with authorities the world over, the council were about to break my second law of boat operations. They were going to build a jetty without ensuring that the user would have his say in its design. Greatly concerned, Jamie phoned the Council. He was sufficiently angered at the rumour that his speech impediment troubled him greatly, and what he heard troubled him still more and his speech deteriorated further. The rumour was clearly true. They had designed the jetty without consulting Jamie, and from what he could make out, the design was completely useless. He spluttered at the man from the Council, but the latter clearly took his inability to speak clearly as meaning that he didn't have anything worth saying and took absolutely no notice of Jamie's complaints. They went ahead and built Heglie Ber jetty. It would not be fair to say that it was a complete white elephant. True, it did not serve its design purpose of landing and collecting passengers. One glance at the rocks alongside it and the swirl of tide was enough to persuade a visitor of that. However, it was a very fine vantage point from which one might view Bill Carstairs, scrambling across the wet and slippery rocks, trying to board Jamie's boat to get to a veterinary emergency on Eday.

The arrangements were all made. Rod arrived in Westray and conducted his affairs with John Deere customers on that island. Meanwhile, with plenty of time in hand, Jamie set out for Rapness, taking his son, along as crew. They made a nice trip out through the Heads at the northern entrance to Calf Sound, cut across the northern end of the Sound of Faray, through Weatherness, and arrived with more than enough time to spare. Rather than lie alongside and be subjected to constant surging, they threw the anchor over the side and lay quietly at anchor in the little bay just beyond the jetty. It was a fine and pleasant afternoon, with only a few white clouds scudding across a brilliant blue sky. They had nothing to do and nowhere to go, so the pair of them settled down in the boat and cracked a half bottle. What a pleasant afternoon - a warm sun on their backs, a bottle of Scotland's finest, the gentle lapping of the water and the swaying of the boat. It was very relaxing, and Jamie was very relaxed - relaxed as a newt, one might say!

In due course Rod had prized himself away from the hearth of his last customer, who proceeded to drive him down to the jetty. Rod was also pleased with life. He had sold no tractors that day, but had had a great deal of enjoyment not selling any. As they neared Rapness, he could see Jamie's small boat anchored by the jetty waiting for him, and when it became clear that he was on his way, he saw them preparing to weigh anchor and come alongside. Jamie's son started the engine and took the helm while Jamie himself went onto the fore deck and grabbed the anchor chain. It was only a small boat - no need for a winch to heave in the anchor. One just caught hold of the chain and pulled. What happened next would make a good problem for a maths test. The anchor weighed $x$ kilos, Jamie exerted a pull of $y$ kilos, Jamie's fulcrum was at $A$. What would happen if $x$ exceeded $y$? Whatever the precise answer, the conclusion was that the anchor would fail to move. Instead, Jamie's force exerted on the cable merely caused him to pull himself into the water headfirst with a great splash. Like many a seaman, Jamie could not swim. There was a mighty threshing, and a flailing of arms and legs. Try as he might Jamie's frenzied efforts did not suffice to enable him to grab hold and heave himself on board. His son watched in horror as his Dad's struggles became weaker. "Jist hang on tae thit anchor chain," he yelled at his Dad, and Jamie did. The son was a big block of a lad; solid. He grabbed hold where Jamie had grabbed hold a moment or two before, but with a super-human effort, he gave a mighty heave and dragged cable, Jamie and anchor all on board together. By the time Rod got on board at the jetty, it was a wet, exhausted and sobered boatman who met him. To keep out the chill from the water, the son handed Jamie the half bottle. Relief at the happy outcome mixed with the fiery sprits and a warm glow came over Jamie. There was surely a need for a wee dram to mark his safe return from the brink of disaster, and Rod produced a bottle of his own from an inner recess of his suit. A mood of euphoria exerted itself aboard the small boat, and the return journey turned into a mighty celebration.

In due course the trio arrived back on Eday and retired to Jamie's croft to continue the impromptu party. "Whit ever hast thoo bin doin'?" asked Ellie when she saw her husband enter the house with a beatific smile on his face, and clothes still dripping over everything; but both the son and Rod were well briefed, and their lips were sealed. It so happened that the return run of the "Mariana" that night was not at the usual time of around 9 o'clock. Because of an extra run in the afternoon, we were not due to get to Eday until gone 10 o'clock. Jamie and Rod didn't care; the more time to celebrate, and out came the beer chasers to follow the whisky. It was the son that maintained his composure, and in due course he herded the two celebrants into the car and drove them down the little road that led from north to south of the island, depositing them at the pier. Over the top of the Holms of Spurness they could see the "Mariana" coming. "Hid'll be a peedie blink yet afore she's here," slurred Rod. "Pass oot more beer frae the car. We'll tak anither drink while we're waitin' " And Rod and Jamie stood side by side on Backaland pier, their legs wide apart to combat the swaying, and supped ale while they watched us steam ever nearer.

We found them thus on the edge of the pier; two large men, side by side, their legs spread wide apart for balance, a pint glass of beer in their hand, and swaying gently in the breeze. On their faces was a look of serenity and good cheer. Jamie had had a narrow escape; all was for the best in the best of all worlds. Rod busied himself about boarding, but his legs had ceased to obey the signals that his brain was trying to send them. It was like pulling a brick with a piece of elastic. Nothing happened when he first tried to move, so he tried harder and suddenly the leg shot away twice as far and twice as fast as he had intended. He fell aboard, and lurched into the wheelhouse, leaving Jamie still standing in the same position with the same stance on the jetty. I could not fail to notice that Jamie was giving a fine exposition of the beer glass dance. What, do I hear the reader ask, is the beer glass dance? It is based on a similar principle to the gyroscope. In the latter case, the centre of gravity maintains an equilibrium created by the gyroscopic motion. In the case of the beer glass dance, the centre of gravity is replaced by the glass of beer. The glass remains rock steady, and never a drop is spilled, while the body gyrates about it in what, to the uninitiated, may appear to be an alarming manner. It is this phenomenon that permits the very drunk to continue to drink even more without spilling any, despite a complete inability to do any other action that might require even half as much co-ordination. I stood at the wheelhouse door and, slack-jawed with admiration, watched Jamie. His stocky frame was swaying like an erratic pendulum, his rather detached, not to say inane, grin beamed down at us. The beer glass was held straight-armed downwards, and stayed totally still - not a slop, not a waver. One just had the feeling that if the centre of the gyroscope, namely the beer glass, was removed from his hand, the equilibrium could not be maintained, and his position on the edge of the pier would immediately become untenable. Rod was by now on board, as were other passengers, and as we cast off again, the son led Jamie quietly away, and they drove wearily homewards to the north end. The pier was left in peace for another day.

Not so our wheelhouse, however. It now possessed an out-of-control salesman. Rod tried to acquaint us with the not uninteresting happenings of his day, but his speech was interrupted at regular intervals by the elastic effect that I have already mentioned. When he least expected it, the pressure to make some minor readjustment of his position would build up to the level at which it would suddenly take effect, causing him to rocket without warning across the wheelhouse until prevented from so doing by coming up against an obstruction. If this obstruction happened to be one of the crew, the result was somewhat painful. He was, after all, a big man, and he had the advantage of having lost all sensation, so the resultant collision seemed to bother him not a jot. I was seriously concerned. If he should have an argument with the radar, for example, it was clear that Robbie would win. Besides which, steering a ship is rendered difficult when the helmsman is being periodically hit by an intercontinental ballistic tractor dealer. How was I to control this force of nature that had come unbidden among us? Fortunately, Rod took care of the situation all by himself. The force of nature was tamed by a call of nature. What goes down must come out, and Rod badly needed to vacate some space in his bladder. He rocketed from the wheelhouse through the door of the port toilet. Calm returned to the wheelhouse once more. However, after a while we became concerned. Rod failed to materialise again. Was he alright? At the risk of stirring things up and setting them off once more, we went and had a look; or tried to have a look. The door of the toilet was not locked, but refused to budge. A rather large object was slumped on its far side and was blocking it. The object snored stentoriously. All told, it seemed a good solution, so we let the sleeping salesman lie, and continued quietly across Greentoft Bay, past the Green Holms, down the West side of Shapinsay and into Kirkwall.

In due course we entered the Basin and came alongside the steps. One by one our passengers left us. The passenger cabin was empty. Unfortunately, the port toilet was not. There on the quay a car was waiting, its doors open, to pick up the managing director; but he was ensconced in the bog, snoring like a hippopotamus. We pushed against the door, we shouted, we pushed some more. Our efforts were rewarded by an incoherent muttering and the sound of movement. The door slowly opened, revealing a dishevelled businessman. There was a pause as the first instructions to his legs were ignored, but, of a sudden, the cumulative effect reached the critical level, and Rod launched himself back into the wheelhouse. We took him in charge and helped him on deck and over the side onto the steps. Indicating the car above was akin to lighting the blue touch paper. There was a pause while the fuse burned, and then Rod careered up the steps and into the waiting car, for all the world like a rugby forward charging for the line with the ball at his feet. The door closed behind him and he was wafted away homewards. It's a hard life selling!

Ellie Sigurdson came into Kirkwall with us a week later. Did I know how Jamie got all wet? But I was well briefed and my lips were sealed.

# CARGOES

I am conscious of the fact that this chapter shares its title with that of the wonderfully evocative poem of John Masefield.

*Dirty British coaster with a salt-caked smokestack,*
*Butting through the channel in the mad March days,*
*With a cargo of Tyne coal,*
*Road-rail, pig-lead,*
*Firewood, ironware, and cheap tin trays.*

How perfectly Masefield made the staccato effect of the short syllables mirror the image of a small vessel punching into short seas. with spray flying periodically from the bow back over the decks and the wheelhouse. It is the more suggestive by comparison with the colour and exoticism of the 'Quinquireme of Ninevah' in the first verse and the grace of the 'Stately Spanish galleon' that follows. Oh that I could convey a similar picture in words, but, try as I might, any thoughts I have had on the subject have been doomed by the prosaic nature of our cargoes - groceries, car spares, a cage bird, goats, tractor tyres, an old anorak someone had left behind.

It didn't take Isles folk more than five minutes to cotton on to the potential for moving small urgent items around by using the "Golden Mariana". Indeed, our first ever paying passenger was a day-old calf, orphaned on the Mainland and being sent to a foster mother on Rousay. I think it was the informality that was attractive. Someone on Westray, for example, could telephone one of the

Kirkwall stores in the afternoon, order some items and ask them to take the package down to the boat just before sailing time. We asked for no forms to be filled in, no delivery notes to be signed. Later the same evening the person could drive down to Rapness and collect their goods. We didn't even make a formal charge, using the service as a sort of loss leader, a goodwill gesture. In any case, we would be recompensed by the generosity of the Isles folk, who never failed to make some small donation for our trouble. Davey Hewison of the large farm of Greentoft on Eday used to take advantage of the service. For example, he would put a punctured tractor tyre on board in the morning and get it back, repaired, on the evening run. One day we were pulling away from Backaland pier when his Land Rover raced onto the jetty and he leapt out, a package wrapped in old newspapers in his hand. Moments before we were out of reach, he chucked the parcel across to me. "T'is a peedie gift fer a' thee help, fer we're mighty gratefu' fer sich a fine service." He took me by surprise and I spluttered some thanks without having the first idea what the present was. Inquisitively, I unwrapped the newspapers, and there inside was a massive joint of pork from a freshly butchered pig - a joint to feed a family for some days. I was touched by this kindness. After all, I was an incomer, an interloper, a ferry louper, a sooth-moother who had dared to come among these island folk and do something that they themselves considered themselves to be expert at.

I think our CB carried almost as much traffic about parcels as it did about humans. Having ordered something, the person concerned would be loath to drive to the pier without some confirmation that the parcel had indeed been delivered to the boat. "Three three fer the "Golden Mariana". Dost thoo hae a package aboord fer Harcus?" would be a typical call. With good will and good sense this added facet to our operation worked well, and nobody abused it. There were no mammoth crates arriving at the jetty, just everyday items. In one respect only did we have any difficulties - living cargo!

What would Masefield have made of it.

*Dirty British passenger vessel with a salt-caked smokestack,*
*Butting through the Firth in the mad summer days,*
*With a cargo of calves in a sack, a goat that needs milking,*
*Three bags of groceries, a Ford starter motor,*
*Two lambs a-bleating and a parrot in a cage.*

It lacks something! JM, you are safe from competition still.

This trade in day-old calves got quite brisk. There was always urgency about matching an orphaned calf with a bereaved cow. However, when the match was made with one of the Isles, urgency in the delivery became paramount. What could be simpler. The calf was bundled into a sack and the sack tied about its neck. We placed the animal on the after deck where the smell could waft away astern, and within a couple of hours it was united with its new mother. If the weather was poor we had little choice but to keep the sack in the passenger cabin. Although the waste products were more or less enclosed within, there would nonetheless be the inevitable pong of dung. Isles folk just accepted it because they understood the importance of the item. Tourists put it all down to quaintness, and it enhanced the voyage for them rather than the contrary. They had come a long way and spent a lot of money to see life in the raw. Unfortunately, what constituted a day-old calf seemed to be a matter of greater conjecture than one might have imagined. Being no farmer, I could not tell if the day-old animal was really a day old, or three days old, and it made little enough difference. However, having been assured that the beast that was to be delivered was a "tiny peedie thing", even I would be suspicious when half a bull turned up. Sometimes we found ourselves grasping some large, frisky and frightened animal by the neck and having to tug and push it unwillingly through the passenger cabin to the after deck, where this bovine leviathan would be tethered to the after rails and then given a wide berth by all and sundry. I would remonstrate sternly with senders and recipients alike, but by then the damage was done.

Other live cargoes were less troublesome. We even speculated on having our own sheep on board and training it to utter one prolonged bleat every two minutes in poor visibility, as required by the Collision Regulations. However, as those regulations do not specify what action should be taken if one finds oneself on a collision course with a farmyard, we decided that it could lead to confusion. It was a cargo of ducklings that gave rise to a bizarre incident that nearly floored the skipper from shock. They had also been placed inside a sack so that they would stay dormant in the darkness. One of the crew had received it and placed it in the space in front of the rows of seat on the port side of the cabin where we normally loaded bags and cargo items. It lay there among the other packages with nothing to distinguish it from any other mundane item, and nobody warned me as to its existence. All proceeded normally until we were up off the north end of Egilsay, bound for Rapness, when the CB burst into life.

"Three three fer the "Golden Mariana". "Golden Mariana" are thoo on channel?"

"On channel," I responded.

""Golden Mariana". Dost thoo hae a peedie package fer Pottinger? T'is spare parts fer me tractor, but ah dinna ken if the garage managed tae put them on boord."

"Stand by. I'll go and check."

I left the wheelhouse and went into the cabin, where I was faced with quite a heap of packages of various types and sizes. To find one marked for Pottinger, I started to rummage around, thereby inadvertently disturbing the occupants of the sack. Imagine my amazement and consternation when, before my very eyes, one of the items of cargo suddenly proceeded to walk across the deck of its own accord! I jumped backwards. "What the heck," I called into the wheelhouse. "There's a package here walking about all by itself." The helmsman had to be relieved from his duties as his paroxysms of mirth were not commensurate with steering a straight course.

# FOG

Fog comes to Orkney on a southeast wind. Southeast winds blow around the anticyclones over Scandinavia that bring the Northern Isles fine summer weather. So, unlike the English summer which consists of three fine days and a thunderstorm, Orkney's summer comprises one fine day and fog. You can sometimes stand on the piece of high ground in the centre of Deerness and see the fog billow in from the North Sea like a tide. It flows into the Stronsay Firth, and a finger pokes into Deer Sound. Another creeps inexorably up the String and fills Kirkwall Bay and the Wide Firth, while yet more goes up around the Green Holms and surrounds Shapinsay. Bit by bit every metre of shoreline is blanketed in grey cotton wool. The observer will, in due course, find themselves on an unfamiliar island set in a sea of grey, looking out at other unfamiliar islands that are the areas of high ground elsewhere. Before too long the southeast wind will freshen, and before you know it, you have one of Orkney's less desirable specialities - gale force fog! As the observer returns towards sea level, they leave the sunny uplands and enter a grey, dank and drear world in which every colour has been leached from view, every landmark has lost its familiarity and become mere shadows in a grey and formless world. And once the fog has set in, it can last for days.

It would be to exaggerate to say that we dreaded fog, but fog definitely made our work hard. Worse still, it drove away the passengers. What tourist wanted to take a trip to sea when visibility was down to a few yards? At Kirkwall Pier grey cars emerged from the fog and disgorged grey passengers. Their voices were muffled; the sounds of the town were muted. At sailing time, we blew three prolonged blasts on the whistle to indicate that we were coming astern, turned around amid the moored fishing vessels, and slowly poked our nose outside the Basin. The radar would long since have been warmed up and tuned in, and we set out for sea with one eye on the amorphous masses that were ships at the pier and one eye on the radar to see if any other vessel was approaching. From then on our eyes were glued firmly to the radar, and the echoes of islands and rocks became as familiar to us as the sights of the land on a clear day. We knew what Vasa Skerry looked like on the screen when the tide was high, we knew which blob was a buoy and which was a fishing vessel, we could even tell how rough it was at the Green Holms by spotting the waves on the radar in the form of what is known as clutter.

I sometimes think it must have seemed miraculous to the uninitiated. Once we had left Kirkwall behind, we entered a closed world. The vessel appeared to move, but nothing beyond the vessel seemed to change. The engine turned, the wash of the propellers trailed out astern, the horn sounded every two minutes, but the outside world was nothing but a grey void. If the passengers were lucky, they might suddenly and momentarily see the shadow of land close to as we went through Vasa or around Strombery, but otherwise their voyage was featureless. Then the engines died away, the speed dropped and the vessel crept slowly through the water towards an unseen and un-guessed at goal. As if by magic, a grey shape would first appear, slowly materialising into a pier, with people and cars. With no sense of movement they had left one pier and arrived at another. Had they travelled across the sea, or had they stayed still and the island had come to them? Meanwhile, cocooned in cotton wool, the people waiting on the pier had no inkling of our approach until the muffled noise of a motor reached them, dulled by the fog. We loomed up out of the murk, and the skipper's face would peer upwards from the wheelhouse. "Would this be Westray or Eday?" I would quip.

These final few metres of our trip could be the hardest to negotiate for the crew. Some piers made a good target and were easy to spot on the radar. Rapness, however, would almost disappear when the tide was high, and we somehow had to find it on an otherwise featureless strip of coast. Perhaps we would suddenly see a momentary echo from Ian Burgher's little creel boat, and then we would creep in ever so slowly and hope to see the grey shape of the jetty. Sometimes even that would be missing and I would call Billy Stout on the CB in one of the buses. "Billy. Do us a favour and blow your horn. There's no echo at all from the jetty today!"

"Aye," might come back the response. "Thoo're nae far aff fer we can hear thee." Then we would creep in, all eyes peeled, hoping to see the little strip of concrete. Sometimes we were right alongside it before we had spotted it. There was a brief period of relaxation while we let folks ashore and others boarded, but before you knew it, sailing time had arrived and it all started again. By the end of a trip in thick fog, I felt as though I had been through the wringer.

And as if all that wasn't enough, there is a local Orkney saying, "The fog raises the sea!" And it was true. When there was fog the wind was almost always in the southeast, and the wind blew more than seemed reasonable in such visibility, or lack thereof. Only on the Grand Banks does the phenomenon of gale force fog exist in the same way as it does in the Northern Isles, and if there is one thing that is worse than a lump of tide, it's a lump of tide that you can't see! (You may recall that the expression 'lump of tide' refers to the steep dangerous seas that form when seas travelling in one direction meet a fast-flowing tide coming against it from the opposite direction.) In a southeast wind, one of the worst places was passing through the Falls of Warness. The Point of Warness formed the southwest tip of Eday, and the full rush of tide squeezed between there and the Muckle Green Holm just opposite. To make things worse, rocks extend to the south from the point, so it has to be given a wide berth. When the tide was on the flood in a southeasterly direction, and it met a heavy motion blown on a southeast wind, the resultant seas were appalling, and the association between the southeast wind and fog meant that one often had to tackle them at a time when they were lost from view in poor visibility. An ancient mariner who had spent years on the old island steamers told me that there was no need to worry about The Falls of Warness. They could easily be avoided, he told me. "T'is like this, boy," he said. "Thoo crosses o'er frae the Green Holm tae the Eday shore way oop tae the north, almost oop by the Seal Skerry hand then thoo comes doon alang the Eday shore, and thoo jist keeps close in by the Point of Warness, and thoo looks doon at the rocks o'er the port side, hind thoo looks hup at the seas on the starboard side, hind thoo're dead right, boy!" Well, it was fine in theory, but the idea of glancing over the port side and seeing the rocks was not one that I fancied much for our passengers, so we used his route, but kept out in the seas - bumpier, but easier on the nerves.

How had seamen managed in the days before radar? What did the Vikings do when they couldn't line up the cathedral with Strombery to find their way through the Wide Firth? How did they find the low flat land of Sanday in fog when they were coming down from Hjaltland? (Shetland) Much the same question was asked of the ocean voyaging Polynesians. How did they find their way over vast tracts of the Pacific without navigational instruments? Well, for a start, seamen of old read the surface of the waters much more carefully than we need to today. Just as we recognised the place where we moved from slack water into the mill race of tide flowing between the Green Holms and Eday, so they recognised far more. Each change of direction of the tide, each change of colour in the water, the passage of weed, guillemots feeding, all were noted and the information was bracketed away so that the seafarer with years of experience could compute all the information and make an informed and sensible decision as to how the vessel should proceed. Then again, he might send a man up the mast so that he may see over the top of any low-lying fog. Another would sound the depths with a line and a weight. The Viking skipper might call "Oars" to his men so they would cease their rowing, and all would listen. Was that the sound of waves lapping on the rocks? Did they hear the lowing of an animal on a cliff top? And if all else failed, he would have no choice but to throw over an anchor and wait until visibility improved.

It is not so long ago that the Shetlanders went miles out to sea to fish in the summer háf (the ocean fishery) in sixerns or sexærings. As the name suggests, these were six oared and were lightly constructed double ended rowing skiffs. They were a development of even smaller skiffs with which the Shetlanders, and to a lesser extent the Orcadians, wrested fish from the sea. If they had not a well-developed sense of reading the seas, how could they have returned to shore when fog rolled up and engulfed them? Or what about the Foula islander who had rowed his frail craft to the Burra Isle to get messages (shopping) and then found himself blanketed in a damp and pervading murk that hid his lonely home from view? (There is an evocative piece of Shetland music called Rowin' Foula Doon.) But what was possible in a small craft could not be done in a larger vessel. Sailing ships and early steamers could not be allowed to risk passengers and crew by taking risks and, in the days before radar, when visibility closed in, the Isles steamers just stayed tied up until conditions improved. The old "Earl Sigurd" once took 48 hours to sail from Westray to Kirkwall, with enforced stops at Sanday and Stronsay on the way. Doubtless the passengers were less than enthralled. Nowadays we have become blasé. With radar to help us, bad visibility has become no more than an inconvenience. Does that mean that we are any the less skilful as seamen? How would we fare if we in turn were faced with making these difficult journeys without our electronic eyes? There came a day when we were tested and not found wanting.

It was the last week of our summer schedules in September 1984; the final week of our service that summer before packing up for the year. The service was well established, passenger numbers were mounting, but at the back end of the summer it remained to eke out our last scheduled runs. Most of the tourists had gone, and from the beginning of August onwards the weather became increasingly uncertain. The first of the equinoctial gales might arrive early, but at least the fog was less likely to disturb our passages, gone with the summer anti-cyclones. By then we knew the waters of the North Isles like the backs of our hands. Each summer we crossed one or other of the Firths four times a day, six days a week for half of the year, and by then we had been at it for three years. That made over eighteen hundred crossings. It amounted in all to a voyage of nearly 9000 nautical miles each summer. At the beginning of April, if we had just headed out past Eynhallow, made a course for Cape Wrath, through the Minches, down the Irish Sea, and headed southwest for the West Indies and Panama, the same length of journey would have taken us all the way to Tahiti. By then there was little enough that I didn't know about navigation in the North Isles, or so I hoped. Then our radar packed up!

Without delay I telephoned Ian Nelson, our friendly neighbourhood radar repair man. At the slightest sign of trouble, Ian would appear on board in a trice and restore our sight. He had gone away on holiday, the summer over and summer activities on the water done. I was left with some awkward choices. The season of the midnight sun was over. No longer could we watch the blood red orb sink behind the northern horizon, only to be able to follow its progress briefly from the glow and see it reappear scarcely more than a couple of hours later. By this time of the year we returned home the last few miles in the dark. Still, I argued, there was unlikely to be fog. As long as the weather stayed fine, we would carry on and see the season out, just a few days to go.

Most of us live in towns. A generation of young people have grown up to see orange streetlights come on at the first sign of dusk and believing that the natural colour of night is a diffuse orange glow. Even those who live in the country find that the skies are patterned with a number of these glows around and about. We have come to live in a lonely firmament in which only the brightest of stars and planets shine through. To see the real glory of a night sky is a privilege no longer afforded to everybody. It is, however, afforded to many inhabitants of the Northern Isles. And even when it is cloudy without the benefit of star shine, there is always some light on the darkest of nights. For us navigators, we were aided, moreover, by selected navigation marks - the buoy at the Galt flashed twice every twelve seconds. Another buoy marked the Broad Shoal and helped us through the narrow channel of Vasa. The lighthouse on Helliar Holm aided entry into Elwick Bay for Shapinsay, and the light at the head of Kirkwall Pier changed colour depending on whether or not you were approaching from the correct sector. Doubtless, I thought, we can eke out the final few days and see the service through for another year.

All went well at first. On the Tuesday morning there was no question of us sailing. The wind blew at 40 knots from the west-northwest. It abated during the day and we managed to fit in an uncomfortable evening run to take the ten people to Eday and Stronsay who simply had to go. The day of storm was followed by a day of perfect conditions, a day of light airs. There was a pale blue sky. The sea was a similar delicate shade with a surface unruffled by any breeze. It was like sailing on a mirror. Every island had a double, perfectly reproduced upside down beneath it. Even a bird on the water had its exact mirrored twin. Who needed a radar? In the evenings, as dusk fell, we extinguished all the lights on board except the navigation lights to show other ship's our presence. As it got darker slowly, so our eyes became keener. The scene was no longer one of pastel colours, but one of fine shades of black. Stars would appear, first a few, and then a display of breath-taking mag-nificence. The flashing lights of the buoys became prominent, and on each inhabited isle, the lights came on in the crofts. We could no longer see the old gun emplacement on Salt Ness as we came down the side of Shapinsay, nor yet the shingle bank on the Point of Vasa, but the silhouettes were there, and there was the light in the farm at Furrowend, and the black shape of Strombery was easy to make out where it cut off the lights of Kirkwall at the head of the bay. In latter years I have sailed in African rivers where there were no lights, no silhouettes of headlands, no shades of black, and I have marvelled at the local man who navigated the twists and turns of a creek with sureness and confidence. It is a phenomenon that is even mentioned in the Admiralty Sailing Directions; *"There is a channel used by pilots, but the marks used by them cannot be identified by strangers!"* Our task of bringing the "Mariana" home without radar was child's play by comparison. Even when the weather was no longer quite so clement, with concentration we always knew precisely where we were.

The following day also dawned fine, and the breeze returned and went into the southeast!

We had two more days to go. I was reminded of the Orkney summer that was one fine day followed by fog. Would this still apply so late in the year? We did our final run to Rapness without incident, navigating at night by the familiar outlines of the Kili Holm and Mae Ness. With greater avidness than usual we listened in as Orkney Harbour Radio broadcast the weather forecast for the following day.

"All stations, all stations, all stations. This is Orkney Harbour Radio, Orkney Harbour Radio, Orkney Harbour Radio. Here is the weather forecast for Scapa Flow, Pentland Firth and the North Isles. There is an area of high pressure becoming established over Scandinavia leading to a flow of south-easterly air across the region … …." Visibility the following day was to be moderate, with the possibility of some fog banks later in the night. The following morning I phoned up the Met Office. In those days the ethos of service to the community still rained among public servants, and the meteorologists at Kirkwall Airport were conscious of the need for people like me to have as precise a knowledge as possible of what the weather might have in store for us. Nowadays everything must pay for itself and the seaman has to have a contract before he can get a personal service. Either that or he phones a special number and gets a pre-recorded message. The decade of monetarism that followed has changed everything. Be that as it may, I was able to have a long chat with the Met boys and they came to the conclusion that any fog would be strictly localised and unlikely to bother us until on into the night, by which time we would be back home and tied up, our season over.

The morning run went well. There was a late flurry of traffic. Knowing it was to be our last run of the summer, many folks on Eday and Sanday would come into Kirkwall for a last opportunity of doing some shopping before the long, dark days of winter set in. When we left Kirkwall just after 5:30 that evening we remained hopeful that we would have an uneventful voyage before we could enjoy some well-earned rest after some months of working long hours. We negotiated the Wide Firth without incident, but when we rounded the Galt it was clear that our troubles were not over. There, between us and the Green Holms was a swirling bank of thick white fog. To make things worse, the tides were big and flowing strongly, making the potential for being pushed off course all the greater. It was time for some serious navigation. We had the echo sounder running. I got the chart out and the parallel rules and laid off a course so we entered the fog with a well-formed plan of action. It was not to be needed. After a few minutes of being engulfed in the murk, the Muckle Green Holm suddenly materialised off to port, followed by Eday, and we had sailed clean through the bank into clear visibility beyond. At Backaland Pier we said our farewells for another year to our Eday friends, and carried on without let or hin-drance towards Kettletoft. The pier stayed in view all the way, but I couldn't help but notice with some trepidation that Eday astern of us had disappeared from view. Another bank of fog was closing in behind us. It rolled up the Stronsay Firth and was busy spreading out into every cove and channel.

There were more farewells to the Sanday folk. We welcomed back on board the handful of late season trippers, and I headed out to the Holm of Elsness and set a course on the chart that would take us through the channel past the Holms of Spurness. Once again we entered a world of cotton wool in which we were cut off from everything but the beat of the engine and a small grey area of sea. In no time everything on deck was dripping wet and we had to turn on the windscreen wipers to keep the wheelhouse windows clear. I was by now seriously concerned. Finding my way back to the pier on Eday and then crossing the Firth past the Green Holms to turn down through the tortuous channels of the Wide Firth without ever seeing a thing was not a task that I undertook with any relish. On the other hand, if anyone could do it, I argued, he who had made the self-same trip so many times in the previous months should be the one.

We were to be granted a respite. Right on cue the Holm of Huip loomed out of the fog on the port side, right where it was supposed to be. My satisfaction at seeing it turned to delight when suddenly the gloom cleared, and there ahead I saw the lights on Backaland pier, still some way off. We headed towards them and not once did we lose them from view as we headed through Spurness Sound and crossed the Sound of Eday. We came alongside the pier again. Charlie Tulloch took our line. Charlie was the pier master, and he took his duties very seriously. He never missed. Whenever we arrived, Charlie would be there to catch a rope and put it on a bollard for us. After the first couple of years he actually retired, but that didn't stop him. Coming down to the pier when a boat came in was the habit of a lifetime. He was a stolid and friendly man with a great deal of knowledge about local waters and always had time for a friendly chat and a laugh and a joke. This time we were in no mood for banter and idle chatter, and Charlie's news was scarcely encouraging. From his house he thought that the fog was becoming quite generalised, and he feared we would not cross the Firth without becoming enmeshed.

He was right. We left Eday again and followed the coast around towards Veness on the Southeast corner of the island. We had not gone far before the land, some 15 to 20 metres away on our starboard side, was at the extreme limit of our visibility. We were to cross the Firth blind. Stuart Ryrie was at the wheel. Roger was sailing as purser. I nominated him as lookout, while I manned the echo sounder and the chart. The task that faced me was daunting. First I had to cross Greentoft Bay where there was no tide running. Then we would enter an area of strong flowing flood tide that would be pushing us sideways to port at a speed of up to eight knots. As we reached the far side of the Falls of Warness, we entered slacker water, that soon became replaced with more tide coming at us on our starboard bow as it flowed around the end of the Little Green Holm. Further on and the flow of water changed yet again as we reached a place where the tide started to rush down to the South past the Galt. How could we calculate the drift, the influence of this tide, on our course? It was too complicated and too imprecise to be able to work out the navigator's triangle of course steamed, direction and speed of the current, and course made good. The speed and direction of the tide were changing so rapidly and so frequently as to make any such calculation meaningless. It all came down to experience, instinct and local knowledge. The penalty for failure would be to pay an unscheduled visit to the rocks that constituted the Galt, a long stratum that stuck out a good distance from the land, or else to become irretrievably lost, cocooned in a dank and dreary world with no longer the first idea of where land was. In the words of a friend from latter years when faced with impossible complications, "Let's make a plan!"

The plan was this. Clearly, I had to keep to the north of the Galt or I would run ashore. However, if I was too far to the north I would miss it altogether, and I wouldn't know when to turn to the south to come down through the Wide Firth along the west side of Shapinsay. On the other hand, I knew our speed, so if I missed seeing the Galt, I could continue on for a few more minutes until sure that I had passed it. Furthermore, the echo sounder would show the depth to be decreasing as we passed the Galt and then starting to increase again on the far side. Then, by heading east by south, I could work my way slowly towards the cliffs to the north of Salt Ness. The bottom shelved gradually there and I would have warning of when I approached the shore. Inching in until I picked up the land, I could then follow it down past Salt Ness and on through Vasa.

Leaving Veness behind, we entered a closed world. The crew and me had all worked together now for some while and we slipped into action like a well-oiled machine. Roger went out on the fore deck as lookout. Stuart at the wheel had strict instructions to concentrate and not to deviate one jot from his course. I divided my time between peering at the echo sounder, peering out of the wheel-house door, and pouring over the chart, checking and rechecking every move. A passenger wanted to chat in the wheelhouse. For once we were not sociable. He was banished to the passenger cabin and the doors were closed. Crossing Greentoft Bay, I allowed no drift from the tide whatsoever. With my watch in my hand, I calculated how long it would take us to reach the fast-flowing tide coming past Warness. We waited, we watched, and there it was. Suddenly the water was flowing sideways past us. Stuart felt the tug on the wheel as we left the slack water behind. I marked the time and position on the chart. Now I allowed for the sideways sweep of the vessel as it was pushed along at right angles to the course we were steaming, and then, there it was again - a change in the flow of water. We moved out of the fast-flowing river and into the slacker tide behind the Green Holms. As if to reward us for our work so far, Roger suddenly shouted, and there, in a momentary respite, the hazy but familiar shape of the Muckle Holm appeared briefly to starboard, before the fog descended like a blanket once more. I marked the time and position again. The course now assumed a certain push from the tide, but not so much, I hoped, that we would be left a long way to the north of the Galt, but with at least enough allowance to make sure that we weren't pushed too far South so that we ended up ashore on the rocks.

For some while we carried on our way, lost in our private world of concentration and concern. How I longed to see the Galt Buoy's light flashing. What delight it would have been for our blindness to be transformed and for the lights of the farms on Shapinsay to suddenly gleam out in the dusk. The engine continued its steady beat. There was Roger up in the eyes of the boat, Stuart stood at the wheel - no pilot's chair today. His eyes were glued to the compass that hung from the deckhead. (That's a ceiling on board a ship.) Outside our world was bounded by an impenetrable wall of gloom. Just a few minutes to go, I calculated, and we would either be past the Galt or suddenly, with no warning, the depth indicated on the echo sounder would come down to almost nothing and we would be careering into the rocks. As expected, the depth did come down slowly. "Roger," I called out. "We should be almost there. Look all around. The Galt Buoy could be anywhere." My nerves were as taut as the strings of an Orkney fiddle. Nothing. Any moment now. I peered out to port. I peered ahead. I peered to starboard. Nothing. My eyes kept turning to the echo sounder. No signs of the depth reducing dangerously. I joined John out in the bows and together we scanned the gloom until our eyes ached with the effort and we had to blink to see clearly again. I looked ahead. I looked to starboard in case we were passing it on the wrong side. I looked to port where it should be, and then I looked astern to port as well. There! Like the briefest flicker of a candle. There was a tiny flash. I blinked and stared again. It flashed again, and I made out the slightly darker shape of the buoy. It was exactly where it should have been. Closer, and we would have been too close for comfort. Further off and we would never have seen it. Phew!

The tension was released in an instant. With a feeling of euphoria, I told Stuart to bring her round and head South. We still had to feel our way down along the Shapinsay shore, negotiate the narrow channel through Vasa, round Strombery, and find our way into Elwick Bay to stop at Shapinsay, but after our feat in crossing from Eday, this seemed no more than a minor task. Before long we picked up the gloomy shape of the cliffs to the north of Salt Ness, and we coasted down the shoreline and shot through Vasa with a strong flood pushing us onwards. In due course we recognised the silhouette of Strombery and turned along the Southern shoreline of Shapinsay and into Elwick Bay. The shape of the Douche and the lights on the pier only materialised when we were almost on top of them. We picked up some late-night travellers and returned to the fray. I had no intention of trying to locate Thieves Holm on a night like that, so I set out into Kirkwall Bay and turned to steer a course towards home. Still watching the echo sounder like a hawk, we were rewarded by an orange light suffusing the gloom ahead of us, telling us where the streetlights of Kirkwall were. In due time the light at the head of the pier came into sight right ahead. We rounded the pier end, slipped into the Basin, and tied up at the steps. Our last passengers of the season appeared from the cabin and said their farewells, unaware of the drama that had been enacted around them. As for me, I had been through the wringer. I slumped with relief in the cabin and rewarded myself with a coffee. We had been tested but not found wanting.

# LOOKING FOR SEALS

A week or two after our ordeal by fog, with our radar repaired, a group of naturalists hired us to take them around to the homes of the Atlantic Grey Seals. This was a pleasant task. Our licence for the outer waters continued until the end of October - strange when you consider that some of the worst gales are in that month. Anyway, we didn't need to worry about the weather. If it was poor we just wouldn't go. As such these trips were very relaxed and they gave us the chance to go and look around islands that we didn't normally visit. Duncan, my second lad, had by then purchased his own inflatable with a 25 hp outboard motor, which was powerful enough to get it up onto the plane when it would really fly. We tied it astern and set off on a couple of visits. It behoved us to treat the seals with respect and we never approached them too closely so as not to frighten them when they had young. On this occasion we were in the hands of experts and were guided by them.

Our first trip took us to the Muckle Green Holm. We had passed it by so many times, seen it from every angle and in every type of weather, but we had never set foot there. Few people have, as there is no natural landing place. We looked forward to rectifying the situation. The weather was clement or else a landing would have been out of the question. First, we tried landing on the South end of the Holm, as well as looking at the much smaller Little Green Holm, but there were few seals around and the rocks made landing difficult for anyone not prepared to risk a ducking. Most of the seals, with their pups, were on a shingle beach in a bay at the north end of the Muckle Holm, opposite the appropriately named

173

Seal Skerry on the Eday shore. Since landing at the South end and walking over the steep slopes of the Holm was not going to prove to be an easy task, we pootled on up to the north end and tried again there. The trouble was, the tide was quite low, and spreading down the little bay from the seals' beach were strata of rock which left fingers of sea along which we could approach in the dinghy. Guided by the naturalists, we approached. We cut the engine on the dinghy and paddled in quietly so as not to disturb the seals, but they are nervous of humans, especially when there are pups to protect. First the cows with the larger pups shepherded them down from the shingle beach and made off along another of the fingers of water. We had a wonderful view of these massive marine beasts as they shot past very close to us, setting up considerable waves in the neighbouring channel. Eventually, only the big bulls and some of the small pups were left. The bulls were less inclined to be intimidated. We inched forward again, but then even the bulls started to get nervous, and one by one they too came down the beach with their slug-like motion and made off. At last there was one particularly big bull left. How large is a big bull Atlantic Grey seal? Let me tell you, they are very big. This one seemed as long as the 12 foot dinghy, but was probably more like six or seven feet long and it must have weighed the best part of a third of a ton. I have seen seals close to before, but we were about to see one closer than we had expected. Suddenly, he decided it was time to make himself scarce, and he made his break for freedom - along the very channel that we were paddling up. He came at us like an express train, and I could see no way of preventing the dinghy from being hurled to one side, occupants and all. There was no room for him to pass on either side - we filled the channel, and the bottom seemed no more than inches beneath us. With no time for us to take any avoiding action, his massive frame arrowed through the water in our direction, and dived right beneath the boat. The amazing thing was that this large cumbersome looking beast not only managed to go through the tiny space, but he did so without even touching the dinghy, and we were left rocking gently in the waves that his passage had created.

There was nothing left on the beach for us to see except one or two cubs that had been left behind and I was concerned about their welfare. If we continued along the route we had chosen, we would prevent the mothers from returning, so we went back to the "Mariana" and sought a better landing place. We found it nearby where a rock formed a perfect natural jetty, and our naturalists were able to step ashore and walk to the bay from another direction. There they inspected the pups to their hearts' content and to their great satisfaction.

The Green Holms seem to have been the centre of world events twice during the centuries. In the historical section that I have added at the end I have recounted Asleifsson's famous contretemps when he hid in a cave from the Earl's men. Thereafter the Holms slumbered on for generations before next they made the news. There seems little enough known about them. We judge from the Saga that monks lived there. It was a suitably austere spot. Lashed by storms, surrounded by ferocious tides, beaten by the sea, it was no place for the faint hearted to dwell. There is nowhere that lends itself to agriculture - just a mound of rough grassland on which sheep can graze. Both islands came up for sale while we lived in Orkney. The Little Green Holm was purchased by Sea Shepherd, the environmental group, and the Muckle Holm was auctioned off to an Englishman who had never seen it. There were stories that he intended to build an island retreat on it. The costs of landing all the building materials by helicopter would have put paid to that rather silly idea. Either that or he would have had to wait for fine weather and land every brick by dinghy.

Eventually, in the mid-eighties, a seal cull caused the Green Holms to pass briefly across the world stage once more. I don't propose to tackle the pros and cons of culling seals. It is one of those subjects about which everyone talks and nobody listens.

"They shouldn't cull those poor seals. It's cruel to bash them over the head." (Orkney seals were not culled by bashing them over the head. Rifles were used by licensed hunters.)

"I think it's cruel killing those poor little seals!"

"Hang on. Don't you hand round the stirrup cup to the local hunt?"

"Yes; but that's different!" (From a conversation I had with someoe.)

"The poor islanders say that they need the extra revenue to help them last through the winter!" (From a news cast. The poor islanders with the licences were mainly Westray men, who could have bought and sold me before breakfast!)

Then again, at the drop of a hat, fishermen blamed lack of fish on the seals, and it seems somewhat unreasonable to expect seals to become vegetarian.

I suppose it is natural for us to see things in black and white. Unfortunately, the seal culling issue was, like the Atlantic seals themselves, in various shades of grey. There was a moral issue involved - does man have any right to kill animals for profit? There was a humanitarian issue involved - the seal colonies were getting over-populated, leading to fights among the bulls and suffering among the injured. There was an ecological argument involved - man, being a hunter, kills seals. If he ceases to kill seals, he upsets the balance, therefore allowing the seal population to increase at the expense of the prey that the seals themselves live on. If seals destroy too many sand eels, for example, there will be nothing for the terns to feed on. What I wish to convey is that the issues are complex, and there is scope for many different, but honourably held, views. Unfortunately, this was not the way the argument was conducted at the time. Anti-cullers were all portrayed as long-haired, lefty lay-abouts by their opponents. Pro-cullers were portrayed as evil, monstrous baby slayers. I confess to a feeling of frustration, as with other similar issues, at mankind's inability to reason and discuss any type of emotive subject without descending into stereotyping and abuse.

The news coverage at the time did nothing to restore my faith in the powers of reason. The anti-cull brigade in their boats circled the Green Holms, the police circled the Green Holms, the hunters went about their bloody business; but something was lacking. It seemed that everyone was waiting for a starting pistol, some mysterious sign to begin their activities. A fresh boat hove into view bearing the news teams and the cameras. The moment that they had readied themselves, mayhem commenced. The hunters hunted, the protesters protested, the police policed, the TV teams produced TV. However, it soon became clear that the driving force behind all this activity was not the seal cull, because the moment the TV producers yelled "Cut," everybody stopped, not just the film crews. The importance of the film crew was clear from footage shown on the national news that night. A hunter went about his business on the Little Green Holm, while a protester ambled around the grassy knoll, enjoying the air and the pleasant surroundings, and completely ignoring the cull. Off camera someone attracted her attention and she raised her head in their direction to hear what they were saying. Clearly she was being told that she was being filmed, because she immediately turned and saw the camera. With a start, she suddenly changed her whole demeanour and raced across to a nearby hunter shrieking "Murderer, murderer!"

There was no cull the next year. I would like to think that somewhere serious people sat down together and discussed the moral arguments, the ecological, the humane, balanced all the views and made a calm and rational decision. I say I would like to think that. What I suspect, however, is that on the year of the cull it was the fishermen who shouted loudest, and in following years the decision was based on nothing more than the fact that a seal pup is indisputably more cuddly looking than a licensed Westray hunter. Come on, people; that's not the way we should make important decisions.

After that, the Green Holms receded again into anonymity. Still, making news twice down through the centuries isn't bad.

The next day dawned with perfect weather. We set out in the "Mariana" just after ten o'clock and made our way over to the jetty at Tingwall on the Rendall shore where some fifty minutes later we collected our naturalists and took them to the little island of

Eynhallow. We anchored in the bay where there is a hut that is used as a refuge for shipwrecked mariners or as accommodation for visiting naturalists and ran them in the dinghy to the pleasant beach in front of it. There followed a perfect day. While our passengers went hunting for more seals, we took it in turns to stroll around the island in the late summer sun. Those left on board got out the fishing lines and we caught sillocks. In English I think that's a young pollock, and on the way home Roger went below into our little cabin and fried them. After a day out in the fresh air we were famished and they tasted wonderful. It was one of those perfect days. We were under no pressure, and we had a whole island to ourselves. The sound of waves breaking lazily on the shore, or ripples lapping on a beach; the sound of the sea birds crying; the views across the water to the high land of Rousay on one side and the West Mainland on the other; what a perfect place Eynhallow was that day. It has been considered a holy island. Like Egilsay, it exuded an air of peace and tranquillity.

# THE PUB CRAWL

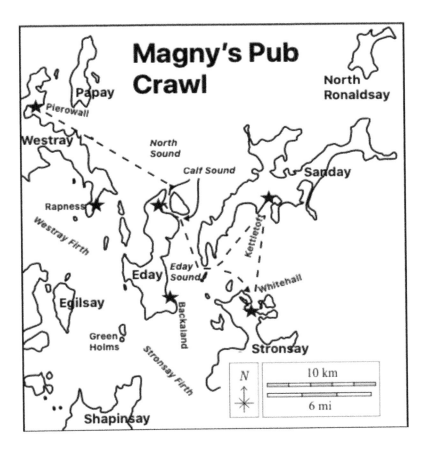

*Map 4: The Pub Crawl*

R osemary, my wife, once overheard an intriguing conversation. A man and a woman were talking in those informal moments when a meeting had just finished and the participants were starting to relax. One, smartly dressed and known for his eco-friendly views and lifestyle, turned to the woman next to him.

"I had a blackbird for my tea," was his introductory gambit. The recipient of this unsolicited and somewhat surprising piece of information looked rather bemused, so by way of explanation the chap continued. "The cat brought it in, and I didn't like to let it go to waste."

"Just as well it wasn't a rat it brought in," thought Rosemary, and waited for more revelations. Mind you, in later life in the Mozambique civil war, street vendors sold a cooked rat on a stick and it was viewed as a delicacy! Further revelations were not long in coming.

"Yes. I deep fried it. Mind you, there wasn't a lot of meat on it!" Well, there wouldn't have been, would there? It takes quite a few blackbirds to make a meal. Four and twenty for a pie, for a start.

We all had a chuckle later. I suppose most people would dismiss this man as an eccentric. I will not. Rather, I treasure him as an eccentric. There are all too few of them around these days. It is as if society has ironed out all the differences, the idiosyncrasies from modern man. When I thought about it, I realised how much I had missed tales of this nature. Here in the middle of England they are all too few, whereas in Orkney in those years they had been meat and drink, a valuable and valued part of everyday life.

One of my favourite characters was a 19th. century cleric from my native North Cornwall. The Rev. Robert Hawker, better known under his title of Vicar of Morwenstowe, has gone down in history as an eccentric of the first order. He was a poet of some repute, and was the author of *The Song of the Western Men*, Cornwall's National Anthem.

*A good sword and a trusty hand,*
*A merry heart and true!*
*King James's men shall understand*
*What Cornish lads can do!*

He wrote many of his works in a small hut built from driftwood in a nook at the top of magnificent cliffs. I can picture him, high on laudanum, the west wind whipping the seas to fury far below, the seabirds swooping by on the wind, as he sat and wrote *The Quest of the Sangraal*. Right from his youth he played practical jokes on people that showed great originality. For example, he swam to an offshore rock off Bude several days running and sat there combing his long hair and singing until folks came from miles around to see the mermaid. Then again, he painted the doctor's grey horse with black stripes so it looked like a zebra, and called him out on a spurious visit that entailed him passing the church when all the august parishioners were leaving after the Sunday morning worship. As he got older he battled with his fertile imagination. Having taught his flock not to disrespect drowning sailors, but to save them where they could and to give them a Christian burial when they could not, he lived in mortal fear of the spirits of these unfortunates. The bodies awaiting burial were brought to the Manse that he built in this glorious out-of-the-way place. Until they were safely buried he went around in a state of abject terror. His religious beliefs were extreme and now seem bizarrely medieval, and yet he lived sufficiently recently in the 19th. century to have been able to travel by train to London from Exeter. Mind you, evangelical pastors in the US are identifying witches among their congregations, so little has changed since the witches of Salem in 1692 and others are blaming autism and even rheumatoid arthritis on demons. Bizarre religious views were not the exclusive privilege of the 19th. century.

I fear for the Orkney eccentric. You have met one or two in these pages, and will meet some more. How long can they last, however, under the onslaught of TV, modern telecommunications and the internet? I fear they may go the way of Hawker, to become footnotes in history. If I honour them in this book, I make no apologies for it. The world has been the richer with them and will be the poorer when they are gone. Returning to visit Orkney after so many years only tends to confirm this fear.

To meet such a larger-than-life character, you go to an island that we have not yet visited - Stronsay. Magny was pier master, publican and boatman, so if you needed to know what was going on on Stronsay, who better to go to? (Magny is the familiar form of Magnus; that popular name that comes from the Norse era.) This was a larger-than-life character. He loved rough weather, he loved a laugh, he loved booze, he loved life. It was said that he had brought about the demise of the Stronsay lifeboat. On the night of the Longhope lifeboat disaster in 1969, he had also put to sea as the cox'n of the Stronsay lifeboat as they went in search of the missing Liberian vessel, the Irene. So appalling had been the conditions that Magny took them through that Stronsay could never raise a crew for the lifeboat again and it was disbanded.

Stronsay's heyday has gone. That had been in the days when the herring fishing fleet followed the shoals up and down the North Sea, and was in turn followed by all the ancillary workers, the fisher lasses who gutted and salted and packed the herring that the fleet brought home, the coopers who made the barrels for the fish to be packed in. It is hard for us today to imagine the life that surrounded the fishing fleets of those days. There was great danger; there was back-breaking toil; there was a nomadic way of life; there was a camaraderie; there was great sorrow when lives were lost, as they were with terrible frequency; but the arrival of the herring shoals followed by the herring fleet brought a life and colour to many an East Coast port. The herring fishing started off Shetland in May and followed the shoals South until they reached East Anglia at the end of the year. Early in the 19th. Century nearly all Scottish fishing was undertaken in open boats, but first the decked Fifies and Skaffies took over in the '50s, 60s and 70s. Then in 1879 a boat builder in Lossiemouth, faced with building a boat for a man who favoured Skaffies using dowry money from a family who preferred Fifies, combined the two designs and came up with something new. It was named a Zulu after the wars then going on in Southern Africa. This hybrid combined the best points of both earlier types, and became the prominent design of boat at the end of the century and on into the 1900s. Heavily constructed in 2 inch larch planks on oak beams, they would be up to 70 feet long and had a fore mast that was almost as high as the boat was long. The interiors were heavily tarred, and a fisherman sleeping in his bunk whose head might come up against the bulkhead in hot weather was in danger of finding himself attached by the hair to his ship. He would not turn in without having a knife at hand to cut himself free.

In the early days of the 19th. Century the boats were too small to be able to undertake the substantial voyages needed to follow the shoals, and the fishery was carried on by many smaller local craft. Deerness, without a single proper harbour or jetty, nonetheless had some 50 or 60 boats, each employing four men. There were curing stations set up at what today scarcely seem propitious landing sites. Those communities that were the closest to the North Sea were in the most favourable locations, and Stronsay not only enjoyed an ideal proximity to the fish, but also possessed a good harbour that was developed for the purpose. As the newer, larger craft came into service, their crews were able to move up and down the coast in pursuit of a living, and they sold off the smaller Fifies and Skaffies which ended up in the hands of the local fishermen. In like manner the Zulus ended up in Orkney when they were being replaced further south by a new generation of steam drifters. So it was that in the month of June up to 500 boats were based on Whitehall. The womenfolk of visiting sailors had followed them and joined locals in unloading the fish, gutting them, salting them and packing them into barrels. At the weekend the fleet would return to harbour, not only to observe the Sabbath, (or to visit the pub; or both), but also because it was widely believed that a day off gave the shoals time to reform. The vessels would crowd into the harbour and fill it, and then moor at other curing stations on Papa Stronsay, a small island opposite. On these occasions, so great was the throng of ships that it was possible to walk from one side of the sizeable harbour to the other by stepping from boat to boat, and even to reach Papa Stronsay by the same method. What a hubbub, what colour, what endeavour! Each vessel would have had up to eight crew, meaning that there would be some 2500 fishermen alone on Stronsay, without even starting to count the fisher lasses, who would have numbered as many again; and this on an island which now slumbers with fewer than four hundred inhabitants. What a change the years have wrought. Nowadays, when the forecast is poor and the winter storms are blowing, ships still make their way into Whitehall harbour and shelter until the gale is past. Magny's pub was right at the head of the pier, and there was ne'er a policeman to impose licensing laws. What better spot to escape for a while from the rigours of the ocean? And when it is time to sail again, the skipper knows exactly where all his crew have gone. Just for a while there is the faintest of echo of those wild, noisy, colourful days of yesteryear when the herring fleet was based on Stronsay.

For all that frenetic activity in the past, that vast fleet of craft, that army of fishermen, today's few craft catch almost twice as many fish. However, that is not true of herring. The herring catch has, not surprisingly, reduced considerably since the heady days in the early years of the last century. The catching power of the largest modern fishing vessels is immense compared to that of the old Fifies, perhaps one hundred times as great. No wonder there are worries about the sustainability of the fish stocks. No wonder the Canadians, with ample help from Europeans, destroyed their fishing, and at times we watch almost powerless to prevent the same from happening here; and that assumes that we haven't killed off species with microplastics. Thus those families who have risked the lives of their menfolk for generations at an honourable trade, now find themselves caught up in arguments over quotas. I have sometimes been critical of the slipshod seamanship and navigational practices aboard fishing vessels. However, they do a job that I, who know the sea, would not do. They fish in conditions which I, who know the sea, would not accept. The world over they provide food for people, many of whom would otherwise not have enough. It is a dangerous trade, but it has been an honourable trade and it's a shame for the fisherman that we now see more clearly the problems of over-fishing. It was after all only just in time that most of the world banned whaling.

The entrance to Whitehall is a tortuous one which is now well buoyed to guide the mariner, though at night I often felt that a visiting seaman who didn't know the port would have some difficulty in negotiating the entrance. Being a smaller vessel, we were able to take a short cut from the main channel. Appropriately, this involved us lining up the roof of the Masonic lodge with a house on the top of a hill beyond. In the days of our time there Stronsay remained a hot bed of Masonry and we carried parties of Masons out from Kirkwall for visits from time to time. They were royally entertained, as was evidenced by the condition of one worthy burgher on his return. He retired at once to the toilets and could be heard calling for Hughey, as the graphic Glaswegian slang puts it. He reappeared a little later with an inane grin on his face, vomit on his waistcoat and his false teeth in his left hand!

Just as the visitor to the port thinks he has negotiated all the twists and turns of the approach, he finds one last obstacle in his way. A buoy marks one of the more unusual obstructions to navigation that I have come across. It is not a rock, nor a wreck, nor any form of natural impediment. Instead, it owes its existence to all those Fifies and Zulus that came in and out of the port in past years. To make sure that they are suitably stable, ships carry what is known as ballast which weighs them down. Ballast takes many forms. It can be sand, it can be iron ingots, it can be water, pumped into special tanks. In the case of the old fishing vessels, it was stones. The larger Zulus carried about 40 tons of them. Sometimes they would be left too deep in the water to be able to get into harbour on a low tide, so as they approached the piers at Whitehall, the skippers would jettison a number of their stones to lighten the ship. With so many boats doing the same thing in the same place, a ledge of stones built up and built up, until today it forms a hazard to ships entering the port, and the spot has had to be marked with the buoy.

Papa Stronsay, which, confusingly enough, is also abbreviated to Papay, as is Papa Westray, also rang to the cries of the fisher lasses and the seamen from the fleet. There were even 32 permanent residents living there once, but over the years the island population has ebbed and flowed. Nowadays it is home to a monastic order called

The Sons of the Most Holy Redeemer. This continues a tradition that links the island to holy orders back into the Viking days.

In our day the Romain family were often in residence in a large two-storied dwelling by the Papay pier. They owned the whole of the island and peopled it on occasion with their large family of adopted children, mixed with their own. These were smashing kids from many different backgrounds, some of whom had defied all the efforts of local authorities in the South to impose some order into their young lives, and so sent them to Papay as a last resort. There, in the freedom of the Isles, and guided by the wise heads of Robin and Jill, they prospered. They also travelled. When the shearing and lambing were over on Papay, the whole family would crowd onto a bus and set off overseas. They travelled all over Europe, to North Africa, and one year they went to the US where they bought another bus and drove to Mexico and back. From time to time when they were in residence they would call us on the CB and ask if we could collect them from Papay pier, so we would make that small extra journey and pick them up. These youngsters, some of whom had been viewed as problem children, were perfect passengers. They would produce a set of French Monopoly and play together with no greater fuss than the occasional exclamation of, "You've landed on Champs Elysées. That will be Fr.10,000."

Eventually they set off in the bus - and just kept on going. In due course we got a card from them showing the bus being loaded onto a dhow to cross the Straits of Hormuz, and they ended up in New Zealand where they took the bus to country fares and charged admission to see the vehicle that they had driven halfway around the world. Someone once asked them how they could leave Papa Stronsay, their own island, and they replied, "We've done that!"

Talk of French francs reminds me of the strange failure of the French to come to terms for many years with the devaluation of their currency that took place in 1960, when the franc was divided by one hundred. Twenty-five years later they were continuing to talk at times in old francs, thereby giving rise to a great deal of confusion, often necessitating the question, "Is that new francs or old francs?". A car priced at FFr.100,000 was still referred to as being worth ten million. A Scots friend of mine had the relatively unusual job of driving big French articulated lorries. Stopping at a truck stop in Northern France, he gathered round a table with a number of colleagues, and the talk turned to the size of the town that they found themselves in.

"Combien d'habitants est ce qui'il y a dans ce bled?" he asked - How many people are there in this one-horse town?

"J' sais pas," was the reply. "Il doit en être dans les cent milles." - Dunno. There must be around 100,000.

Irked by the Gallic illogicality in continuing to use such a grossly outmoded currency value, my friend made his point rather well. He replied laconically, "Ouai. Mais est ce que ça c'est des habitants nouveaux ou des habitants anciens?" - Yeah; but is that new inhabitants or old inhabitants?

But I digress. Stronsay today is a quiet place with a lot of lovely beaches and the usual Orkney supply of remains from ancient times. It did not attract as many tourists as some of the other islands, though there was an Orkney weaver of great repute to visit, and nestling around the pier was what could be described as the only small town in the North Isles. When we arrived there on Tuesdays we would pass the entrance of the harbour and make our way to steps that were half way along the outside of the main pier in the direction of the old lifeboat station. There Magny would meet us, along with any curious person with time on their hands. Unlike Sanday folk, the Stronsay ones came down to see the boat arrive, but were more or less silent. Even at two o'clock in the morning a constant stream of cars would pull up, the occupants would peer down at us, and then, after a minute or two, the driver would gun the engine and the car would go on its way. However, amidst the more taciturn folk, Magny would make his way down the pier from the pub and take our lines for us. He was a large man who had kept all his own tooth. It was in the middle on the top. As soon as he arrived he stood out from the crowd. Dressed in a sloppy old fisherman's jersey, his weather-beaten face possessed copious laughter lines, and when something appealed to his catholic sense of humour, the lines deepened, his eyes narrowed, his head remained steady and his chest and shoulders heaved up and down, though no noise emanated from his frame other than a wheezing sound. Some may recall that Ted Heath had a similar laugh.

"Whit like, boy?" he would shout down to us. "Hid's a grand day fer a trip tae sea. Ah'll mebbe awa tae the creels in a peedie blink." This requires some translation. Linguistically he was saying that it was a good day for a trip and he would be going to tend the lobster pots a bit later; but in Magny's parlance, a grand day to be at sea meant that the wind was blowing at least a Force 5. There was nothing he loved more than to take a boat to sea on a poor day. The more it bounced around and the more he was buffeted, the better pleased he was. Magny possessed two boats, both of which were rather small. He had what he called his speed boat, which was a little thing with a powerful outboard engine. Being quite fast, this suited Magny perfectly, for when there was a bit of a chop he could leap off the top of one wave and career into the next one. Magny offered a floating taxi service. If someone was desperate to travel to Sanday on a Tuesday, we would take them to Stronsay and Magny would run them across to Kettletoft. Furthermore, he would frequently bring Stronsay folk out and meet us to the north of the Holm of Huip when we were bound to and from Sanday on a Saturday. When it got too rough for the speed boat, he would revert to his little creel boat called the "Bella". He took someone to Sanday for us one morning and at night I asked him how he had got on, as the weather was none too calm.

"Och, theer wis nae bother, boy," he told me. "Ah jist wint up tae the Point o' Comely, put the sea on the starn, hind eased her doon tae Kettletoft wi' nae bother at a', hind the passinger wisna even damp whin we got theer. Mind," he continued, and his eyes shone out with delight at remembering. "Ah didnae bother wi' a' that on the way back. Ah jist pointed her at Whiteha' hind boonced aff o' wan wave onto the next," and the chest heaved, the shoulders went up and down, and a noise like escaping air reached my ears.

Although Magny was very good at coming down to meet us, even if we should arrive on some special run in the middle of the night, he was not to be relied on in the same way that we could rely on Charlie Tulloch on Eday. Magny would always be there - if he was sober and if he was about. He was somewhat inclined to go on mighty benders, when he would drink himself to incoherence, and was said by Stronsay folk to be "aff" (off). I needed to speak to him one day, but after trying for some hours and finding the phone constantly engaged, I gave up and contacted a neighbour, who was the councillor for Stronsay. "Ah must see Magny mesell, sae ah'll gie him a message fer thee." Half an hour later he called me back. "Magny's aff today hind he's falled asleep on top o' the phone, hind theer's nae a body on Stronsay kin sheft en. Thoo'll mebe need tae try agin the morn's morn." With that, and going to the creels, and the chance that he might have got itchy feet and taken it into his head to go to sea on a visiting trawler, you couldn't rely on Magny being about. Next time we went to Stronsay, there he would be again with some tail to tell which invariably involved a great display of his half-concealed mirth somewhere in the telling.

One Tuesday he was there at the pier with a perplexed look on his face. "Mighty, boy," he said to me. "Ah dinna ken whit tae do, fer ah wis awa fer the weekend hind whin ah got back ah had ten poond in me pocket which wis moor than ah had afore ah left hame. Some puir body must hae lent me hid, but ah dinna ken wha hid wis hind noo ah cannae pay them back."

"So where did you go, Magny?" I asked him.

"Boy, boy, hid wis sum do," he replied, and there went his shoulders, heaving up and down with a "Hee, hee, hee, heee." "'Twas like this." and he launched himself into the tale of his weekend pub crawl.

Magny and a friend set out on the Saturday morning to haul some creels out by the Holm of Huip. It was a nice day and the sun was warm on their backs as they heaved in creel after creel. They didn't have much luck, and by late morning they had little to show for their endeavours but sweat on their brows. "By heck," said

Magny, wiping his forehead with his forearm. "Ah cuild fairly gae a beer."

"Aye," responded his companion with feeling. "That cuild I too!"

Magny stood up. The little craft was bobbing up and down. The grass covered holm was nearby, bright and green in the summer sun. Off to the north was a line along the horizon that was Sanday, and in the distance, nearly four nautical miles away, they could make out Kettletoft. The buildings seemed to float between the sea and the sky, like some desert mirage. "Ah kens, whit we'll do," said Magny, and his face lit up. "We'll awa tae the Kettletoft Hotel fer a peedie drink," and without another thought the pair of them settled down in the small craft. Magny grasped the throttle on the tiller and twisted it hard round with a determination that seemed to convey itself to the motor. In no time the bow rose up in the air and the speed boat was flying off to the east northeast. The Holm of Huip slipped steadily astern and the mirage of the buildings at Kettletoft slowly took on a more permanent shape. Boat and crew were as one as they arrowed towards the first beers for the day. In the rest of the land, folks were returning from their Saturday morning shopping, or heading for the coast, or maybe they were taking out their whites for a cricket match on the village green.

The speed boat shot towards Kettletoft Pier, its engine wailing like a banshee, and leaving a wake that led straight as a dye behind them. Then it turned around the pier end like a racing car, the noise came down both in decibels and in octaves, the bow settled back in the water, and in moments they were safely alongside. With the grace and economy of movement of a lifelong seaman which was incongruous in a big man like Magny, he was out of the small boat and ashore in a trice, a painter in his hand. With one fluid motion that distinguished the sailor from the boy scout, he tied a bowline in the painter and made the craft fast, and then turned and the pair of them headed for the Hotel, a single-minded gleam on their faces. They pushed open the door to the bar.

"By heck. Luik wha t'is!" cried the publican. "T'is Magny frae Stronsay," answering his own question. "Whit like, boy? Whit are thoo drinkin'?" and in no time at all two cold glasses of Special Brew were laid in front of the visitors and a hubbub filled the bar. Imagine what it is like to go to the pub throughout the year and never see a strange face other than the occasional tourist. Whatever the conversation, it always seems remarkably like the same one that you had last week. Suddenly, a well-known character appears, a different character, a character known for his wit and repartee, his tales of yore. What excitement! In no time, the drinks were flowing freely. Folk queued up to buy rounds for Magny and his colleague. On through that Saturday afternoon beers and whiskeys followed in rapid succession. Tales were told, jokes were made, Orkney islands Council was slagged off, the world was set to rights, and the publican rubbed his hands gleefully as he saw the afternoon's takings sore to new heights. Come teatime, folks down South were heading home from their day out, or took tea after an afternoon playing cricket or watching sport on the TV. Gardeners came indoors for sustenance; but on Sanday Magny was by now just getting started. "Thoo kens whit, boy?" he said to his friend with a gleam in his eye. "We've ne'er bin tae thit new pub on Eday. Ah've a mind tae gae up theer and gi' hid a try. We'll mak an evenin' o' hid!" No sooner thought than done. With hearty farewells to all their Sanday friends, the pair took their leave of the Kettletoft Hotel, and in the light of a summer's evening, they returned to the speed boat, their gait a little less steady than it had been those hours before when they had arrived. With a heave on the starting cord, the outboard roared into life once more, and the happy pair were soon headed Southwest towards the Holms of Spurness on the next leg of their journey - a mere eight nautical miles. In no time an observer on the pier would have seen nothing more than a dot in the distance, as they shielded their eyes against a setting sun. The ear-splitting roar of the outboard also dwindled until it was no more than the drone of a mosquito, and then that too disappeared and quiet reigned once more on Sanday.

The Rugmans were incomers who had come to live on Eday. They had bought the little croft of Furrowend up on Calf Sound.

It was a beautiful spot that I will tell you more about in a subsequent chapter. Just by their house was the little jetty by which Jamie Sigurdson moored his creel boat. To open a pub there was a stroke of genius. What better way for incomers to supply a need, earn a living and integrate themselves into the community, all at the same time? It was not a big place, but there were few enough regular drinkers on an island of little more than 100 souls. By taking in visitors and doing meals, they had assured themselves of a valuable and valued role in the life of the community. The opening had occurred just a week or two before that day of Magny's escapade, which is why he was so keen to go and have a look - a sort of professional interest, one might say. The little craft passed through The Keld and headed north across Eday Sound, entered the Calf Sound, and coasted to a halt at the jetty. After a heavy afternoon session, Magny was less fluid in his movements than earlier in the day. Had he fallen as he alighted from the boat, however, so near was the pub that he could have been at the bar by the time he stood up.

By now, people elsewhere were readying themselves for an evening out - a couple of swift halves at the pub and then on to a party or a disco. Or perhaps they were donning evening wear and were about to head for the theatre. Nothing so mundane for Magny and friend. With eager anticipation they burst through the door of Furrowend and took a couple of paces to the bar.

John Rugman knew everyone on Eday, but he did not at first recognise the newcomers. They were clearly Orcadian. No tourist would be dressed in such baggy trousers and fisherman's jerseys. Nor would their faces be stained by the winds to the colour of mahogany. Furthermore, most visitors were not orthodontically challenged. Here was a puzzle. Two Orcadians had arrived, but not from Eday. "Good evening, gentlemen," said John. "What can I get you?" Before he could answer, an Orcadian voice from the far end of the bar called out, "By heck. Luik wha t'is! T'is Magny frae Stronsay," answering its own question. "Whit like, boy? Whit are thoo drinkin'?" and before long John Rugman knew only to well who his unexpected visitor was. As the evening progressed

Lord Magny held court. Other folks called in and stayed. There was many a quip, many a tale, many a Special Brew quaffed and many a Highland Park supped. In the twinkling of an eye it was closing time, and John Rugman called "Time Gentlemen, please!" in traditional fashion. He was after all a law-abiding citizen and saw no reason to extend his working day beyond the normal limits of the licensing laws. However, it was a novel concept for Magny - an Isles pub that closed at closing time. By now his brain was somewhat befuddled, and it found it hard to take in the idea that he still wanted more drams, but the pub was closing. As the Eday folks finished their glasses and said their farewells, Magny remained deep in thought, considering this alien situation. Suddenly, his face brightened again. A beatific look spread across his visage. "Ah ken whit we'll dae," he said to his companion. "Let's head awa' fer Pierowall. The hotel'll no be closin' on a Saturday nicht. Come on, boy. Git a move on. We'em missin' oot on guid drinkin' time!" And the pair of them made their unsteady way back to the jetty, fell into the speed boat, and before long the whine of the motor could be heard shattering the peace of the Calf Sound's tranquillity. By now the sun was an orange ball, low on the horizon to the northwest. The sky was a vivid tangerine and the sea was aflame in the glow. Out between the Grey Head and the Red Head they went, their little cockleshell craft dwarfed by the immense cliffs, and they started to rise and fall gently. They had entered the North Sound, and they were no longer within the shelter of the Isles. This next leg of their day out was nearly ten nautical miles long, and most was on the open ocean. The day was coming to its close. Theatre goers had gone on to the restaurant, parties were in full swing, revellers were leaving the pubs and going to seek entertainment elsewhere. Magny headed steadily north, watching the last of the sun set behind Westray. It was the 'simmer dim'; that light that comes to the Northern Isles when the sun passes only briefly below the horizon bringing a night that never gets dark.

By the time the speed boat reached the harbour at Pierowall, its occupants were getting a little chilly and the worst effects of their efforts to drink both Sanday and Eday dry had worn off. Fresh supplies were as yet some way off as it is no five-minute stroll from the harbour at Pierowall to the Hotel. As Magny and his friend strode out around the bay only the hardiest of revellers were still at it in the rest of the land. Discos were starting to empty, noisy youngsters spewed out onto the streets outside clubs, the staid were already long since abed. Finally the pair of them at last came in sight of the Hotel. Its lights still shone out brightly like a beacon. Magny's estimation that it would still be open was proved right. The Holy Grail was only separated from them by a few more strides and a door. They opened it and stepped inside. For a moment all conversation ceased as heads turned to see who the newcomers were. Then, as though rehearsed, half the voices in the room united in a single cry of amazement. "By heck. Luik wha t'is! T'is Magny frae Stronsay," answering their own question. "Whit like, boy? Whit are thoo drinkin'?"

Magny's arrival was an excuse for much celebration. Many of the late-night drinkers were fishermen from Westray boats that were home for the weekend. They had often been welcomed at Magny's bar. Now it was their turn to reciprocate. The liquor flowed free, yarns were spun, the world was put to rights - again, and a great party went on throughout the night into the hours of the Sunday morning. One by one the Westray drinkers had had enough and disappeared homewards or into some quiet corner to sleep it off. At the last, Magny was still there, still going strong, but the Hotel could not stay open for ever. Eventually even an isles landlord must away to his bed. A local worthy led Magny back to his own hearth, where food was served, and washed down with home brew! Rare were those in the land who had not gone to their beds from the night before, and the nation's early risers were already abroad, but Magny supped on. His mighty appetite was dulled, but not sated. His brain was no longer in control of every faculty, but it still managed to keep his body upright, his eyes open and liquid pouring down his throat.

What happened at this stage, Magny was no longer very clear about. As he stood on Stronsay pier and recounted the events of the weekend with a twinkle in his eye, his account of his epic binge became somewhat vague; probably because Jimmy himself was rather vague about what happened. Did he doze during the morning? He thought not. Later, though, he was back at the Hotel holding court again, and a whole new set of acquaintances appeared, only to swell the chorus. "By heck. Luik wha t'is! T'is Magny frae Stronsay," answering their own question once again. "Whit like, boy? Whit are thoo drinkin'?" The afternoon came round. In the South people were back in their gardens again, or off playing tennis, or tramping the hills, or sat in traffic jams on their way to the coast. For Magny, though, yesterday had not yet ended. His Saturday outing was still going strong. As teatime came round and people's minds turned to Monday morning and work, Magny's mind turned to a further ambition. "Now we've started, how boot we gaes tae a' the pubs in the North Isles? We'll jist cross the Firth tae Rousay and git a few drinks theer, and then we kin carry on tae The Gatehoose on Shapinsay hind tak a few peedie drams theer. We''ll jist be needin' sum fuel fer the ootboard. Is theer a body cuild lend us a gallon or twa o' two stroke." Well, Magny might have been full of ambition, made brave by the effects of the Special Brew, the home brew and the Highland Park; but thank goodness there were more sober heads on Westray. A benefactor replied, "Whit. Are thoo stone mad, Magny? I wuildna be responsible fer sendin' thee across the Firth in thit peedie tub o' a boat. Ah kens thoo likes hid fine when hids a peedie bit humpty-dumpty, but thoo're in nae state to be gaein' acrass the Firth, and especially no in thit shoe box. Ah tell thee whit. Ah'll gie thee some fuel, but jist enough tae git back tae Stronsay hind nae further." There was a flaw in this logic. If he had enough fuel to get to Stronsay, he also had more than enough to get to Rousay. Fortunately, Jimmy was not strong on logic by this time on Sunday evening, and he failed to spot the deliberate mistake. Perhaps, deep down inside his seaman's soul, a part of him realised that enough was enough.

And so it was on the Sunday evening, as folks walked home from evensong, and settled down for a quiet Sunday evening at home, Magny and his crewman made their way back down to the pier, replenished their fuel, and set off on a long and weary journey back to Stronsay. They made their way down through the North Sound in their frail craft, passed between the mighty cliffs and were dwarfed by nature. The boat droned through Calf Sound with a noise like an angry hornet, and more than one crofter looked out with surprise to see two figures, seated like statues in a craft scarce big enough for the pair of them. Down Eday Sound they continued, through Spurness, and at last they rounded the Point of Comely, came to Jack's Reef Buoy, and wound up the entrance channel to the pier. Gone were the grace and economy of movement of the lifelong seaman. Jimmy fell ashore. The speedboat was tied with a knot that would have embarrassed a boy scout, and Jimmy staggered down the pier, in through the door of the pub, and collapsed in his bed. He arose again on Tuesday morning in time to welcome us and take our lines, and so the tale unfolded:

"Mighty, boy," he said to me. "Ah dinna ken whit tae do, fer ah wis awa fer the weekend hind whin ah got back ah had ten poond in me pocket which wis moor than ah had afore ah left hame. Some puir body must hae lent me hid, but ah dinna ken wha hid wis hind noo ah cannae pay them back." .........

By the time he finished, our passengers had left and those for Kirkwall had come aboard. It was time to go. He slung our lines off for us, and I looked up with a grin. His eyes lit up, his shoulders heaved, his eyes narrowed, and his whole frame shook with glee. It had indeed been "sum do". Magny went back down the pier, a spring in his step. Boredom had been banished for another day or two.

There was another tale of Magny's escapades. One Saturday he contacted me and told me that his wife had broken her arm and been medevacced by aircraft to the hospital in Kirkwall. She was going to take advantage of her unexpected visit to the metropolis and would do some shopping and then join us on our evening run to Sanday. Magny would then come and meet us and collect her in the usual place off the Holm of Huip as we passed by. It was a choppy day and Magny enjoyed bouncing from wave to wave as he came out to the rendez-vous. By the time he came alongside there was a copious amount of ocean slopping about in the speedboat. We put the shopping bags into the boat first and then helped his wife to transfer. Given that one arm was in plaster, she was clearly hampered. Nonetheless, Magny set off back to Whitehall with gay abandon, bouncing from one wave and crashing into the next. By the time he got alongside half the shopping was floating about in the bilge. A packet of butter floated around joining Brussels sprouts and the like. Magny's wife was far from being a shy and retiring woman and she made her feelings known in a stentorian voice that could be heard halfway round Stronsay. Magny decided that discretion was the better part of valour; took twenty pounds from the safe in the pub and went to sea for a week on a Stromness fishing boat that happened to be just about to sail.

# A Status Symbol

When I was younger I much appreciated the rock music of Status Quo. You may wish to ridicule that because it is no longer fashionable, but in their day they had developed a type of rock music that had a driving force to it, coming from a strong and very distinctive beat. It was a beat that was not conducive to safe driving, since I am convinced that there was a tendency to drive five miles an hour faster when one had a Quo tape on in the car. I discussed this phenomenon one day with a man from Papay, (Papa Westray, that is; not Papa Stronsay), and he agreed with me and said that he was the same.

This Papay man was the brother of the owner of the "Our Catherine" who had had trouble with the freezer. They were both Papay men originally, and the parents still lived there. The one who was our passenger was a contractor, and he had obtained a contract to dig drains on Shapinsay. For the whole of one summer he was on board almost every day that we ran a Westray service. On a Friday he would leave work and return home to Papay, and on Monday we would get him back again. He was a cheerful, friendly chap, but unlike his brother, who looked like the Army boxing champ he had once been, this brother was bespectacled and looked more like an accountant. He passed the trips in the wheelhouse with us, chatting away about anything that was in the news and much that was not. As we came down along the Egilsay shore on our way South from Rapness, we decided that having a Quo tape on a ship would be a very useful thing when faced with a strong tide, since an extra knot would come in very handy. Furthermore, we decided, the effect would be enhanced if at the same time we wore our caps backwards to simulate the extra speed. We dropped him in Shapinsay on our way in, and thought we had seen the last of him until Friday. Our rather inane conversation was forgotten.

That night we wended our way up to Rapness again against a strong flood tide, collected our day trippers, most of whom had been on to Papay for the day. Then, as we headed back across the Firth, the tide came behind us and we were fairly flying. As I looked across the Firth to the Eday shore and the Muckle Green Holm, I espied a fishing vessel close to the shore and creeping up against the tide. One glance of the binoculars was enough to confirm at once that it was the 'Our Catherine'. "Wherever is she off to?" I speculated. "That's not their normal route to the fishing grounds," and then forgot about it as we carried on our way. A few minutes later a call came for us on the CB. 'Three, three fer the "Golden Mariana". Are thoo on channel?"

"On channel," I responded. "Who's that calling?"

"Hid's me frae Papay here whit cummed in with thee this morn. Ah'm aboord the 'Oor Catherine' o'er by the Green Holms. Ah seed thee across the Firth sae ah thought ah'd gie thee a ca' ". It was him all right, and he had been drinking, that was clear.

"Whatever are you doing on there. I thought you'd be hard at work in Shapinsay."

"Ah kens. Ah shuild be, but mi brother has tae gang hame tae Papay fer sum personal business, but we bin drinkin' a' day and he's fast asleep, so ah must tek her mesel'. Ah can tell thee, ah'm nae best pleased at it, either, fer ah've mare then enough work tae do that I dinna want tae be backwards and forwards frae Papay ivery five minutes."

"So when will you be back in again then?" I asked, more to make polite conversation than anything else.

"Hid'll be the morn's morn, hind ah'll hae lost a whole day. Tae think thit ah left Papay this morn, and tonight ah'll be right back wheer ah started. Boy, boy. Here," he continued. "Theer's a mighty rumble o' tide oer here at the Green Holms. She's gaein' flat oot and we're pretty damn near standin' still. Jist wait a peedie blink," and he went off the air for a second or two. "Thit's better," he came on the air again. "Ah've jist put me cap on me heed backwards, but thoo kens ah dinna think hid works, fer we're nae gaein' any faster."

"It won't work unless you're playing a Quo tape," I informed him.

"Likely that's hid," he replied. "Will, boy. Hid's grand tae chat. Ah'll likely see thee on Friday. Hae a guid week. Thit's me gone," and he signed off, and we saw no more of him until Friday, as he had promised. But a minute or two later, there was a crackling; not on the CB, but on Channel 16 of the VHF. That's the marine safety frequency, the channel that is sacrosanct - only to be used to make contact with another station, or to call for help. It's the channel that is never to be used frivolously. It's the channel on which, if you talk for too long, the coast radio station cuts in and tells you off. We listened with one ear to the spluttering, waiting to see what call was being made, but instead of someone trying to contact the Coastguard, or wanting to make a link call over the phone, music started to issue unexpectedly from the radio. It took us a moment to work out what was happening, but then we all recognised the driving beat. It was Stutus Quo, singing *Whatever you Want*. Doubtless, if we could have but seen it, across the Firth was a skipper with his cap on backwards, trying to find an extra knot to combat the fast-running tide.

# I'M SPARTACUS - OR SHOULD THAT BE WILLIAM JOHNSON?

I always remember a scene from the film *Spartacus*. The Romans were trying to identify Spartacus from among a great throng. Spartacus himself stepped forward and said "I'm Spartacus," upon which, to protect him from himself, another stepped forward, quickly followed by a horde of others. "I'm Spartacus," said the second one, or rather he actually said "Oi'm Spoitacus," in a broad Brooklyn accent, thereby creating hilarity at a very serious moment. We once had an incident packed day when all the main players could have stepped forward and said, "Oi'm William Johnson!" To be precise, there were two of them, and both from Westray. I have already mentioned the confusion that might arise when two people on the same island have the same name, and how this is often resolved by calling them after their property. However, neither of the two William Johnsons were as yet old enough to have become associated with any particular dwelling. The Westray folk had fallen upon a good way of not confusing the two. They called one Willy and the other William. Both were young men in their twenties, and therefore both were very interested to learn that the "Golden Mariana" was to make a special run from Westray to Eday to go to a dance that the Eday folk had laid on for the coming Friday. What we had agreed to do was to return from our usual Friday evening service from Rapness, through Calf Sound to Backaland Pier on Eday, having warned all passengers through press and radio that our subsequent return to Kirkwall would be later than usual. Then, having finished our scheduled runs, we would go back out to Eday and collect the Westray folk to take them home after the dance. It was to prove to be not without incident.

At 5:30 we set sail from Kirkwall. On board we had a smattering of regulars who would normally be returning to Westray for the weekend, and of these, one or two had heard about the dance and were going to accompany us right the way round, via Rapness, to Eday. One of these was a rather shy, diffident fellow of around twenty, who was known as Willy Johnson to distinguish him from his namesake, who was known as William. Willy didn't say very much, but when pressed would answer with a mutter and an embarrassed grin. Another passenger wasn't a regular for Westray. He was an Eday man who had joined the Army, brother of the owner of a large farm overlooking the south end of Eday. Here was the typical soldier, home on leave, handing out bonhomie in the form of beer for all and sundry, and he had got to hear of the sailing for Eday that very night. My, and there was to be a ceilidh as well. It must have seemed like a welcome home laid on specially for him. His arrival on board was accompanied by the snap, hiisss of opening cans. He installed himself in the passenger cabin, turned his ghetto blaster on at full volume and held court, dispensing largesse in the shape of Special Brew to all and sundry. Willy muttered, gave of his embarrassed grin, and sipped the ale.

Closing our ears to the sound of punk rock that emanated from the passenger cabin, the crew followed their well-oiled routine. The "Mariana" steamed steadily northwards, left Shapinsay behind, and slowly turned the grey line ahead into the familiar shape of Westray. As we went about our business, checked tides, decided on routes, answered the CB and the VHF radio, steered and drank coffee, the court of our soldier continued in session. In common with many a drinker, he shared that objectionable habit of wishing to dictate exactly how much everyone else drank, as well as how much he drank himself. "Johnson. Dinna tell me thoo hae an empty can, boy. Only a soft idiot wuild sit wi' an empty can whin theer's guild beer tae be supped still." And Willy muttered, gave of his embarrassed grin, accepted another can, and the punk rock was accompanied once more by a snap and a hiss.

In due time, we cut our engines and coasted in towards Rapness Jetty. There were rows of cars parked up in Jim Burgher's field, and a good percentage of the youth of Westray were making their way down onto the concrete slip, dressed ready for the dance. With them came the day trippers who had been to Papay and a good sprinkling of older folks who were also keen to trip the light fantastic on Eday. The Westray folk all greeted Willy, who replied by muttering and giving them his embarrassed grin, only the influence of the ale had added two new features to his response. The grin was now accompanied by a nervous giggle and his eyes had become very bulbous. Does anyone know why some people's eyes stick out like gob stoppers when they have had a few drinks? Is it pressure that has built up from the excess of booze? Anyway, the fresh faced Westray folks took their seats around him and chattered among themselves, having quickly realised that Willy was already beyond the possibility of coherent conversation. Indeed, as they animatedly discussed the coming dance, Willy's grin suddenly collapsed, his bulbous eyes snapped shut, and he fell into the arms of Morphius. As we steamed out through Weatherness into the North Sound and made a course for the Heads on Eday, Willy snored and snuffled, quite oblivious of his surroundings, and stayed that way all down through Calf Sound and along the East shore of Eday until we arrived at Backaland Pier.

Holding a dance was a noteworthy event on Eday, and holding a dance to which Westray folk came in profusion was noteworthy among noteworthy events. As a result, the Eday folk were not content to open the hall and get started in their own good time. They came as a person to the pier to meet and greet their visitors, not least so that the Westray folk all had transport. So it was that Backaland Pier was crowded with grinning islanders who started to call out to people they knew as soon as we came within hailing distance. There was a very festive air about the place. Out through the wheelhouse filed the dance goers, onto the fore deck, where they at once looked up to the top of the steps on the pier above and saw scrubbed and smiling faces beaming down at them. "Whit like, Jimmy?" "By heck, Billy, whit are thoo doin' here, boy? Are thoo nae a peedie bit old fer a' this dancin'?" "Thoo Westray eens hae sum cheek if thoo thinks thoo can last oot at a dance on Eday!" The banter flowed freely.

After a minute or two the crocodile of departing dance-goers ceased, leaving the passenger cabin in relative calm. There remained some fifteen day trippers who had been to Papay, and had soaked up the atmosphere of the Isles - and then there was Willy Johnson, who had soaked up the Special Brew. Instead of sleeping in the middle of a chattering throng, he had been left in splendid isolation, seated by himself, upright, head lolling backwards, and his mouth wide open. I approached him and shook him gently by the shoulder. "Willy, we're here at Eday. Up you get now." He snuffled to wakefulness and peered around with a surprised look on his face, and clearly had no idea which way was up, let alone where he was and what he was doing there. I took him by the arm, encouraged him to his feet and led him out on deck. The surprised look did not abate and no hint of recollection or realisation came across his visage. He allowed himself to be guided over the boarding point of the vessel onto the steps. Grins of amusement rained down on him and a few encouraging shouts wafted from the crowd, who were amused to see that Willy seemed to have arrived at the condition they themselves only aspired to achieve when the dance was over. In their eyes, to be like it before it had even started must be thought a considerable accomplishment. I left Willy to make his own way and he stumbled up the first couple of steps, and then stopped again. Turning in my direction, the first signs of awareness started to dawn across his features. The old shy and nervous grin returned to his face, but for once he failed to mutter. Instead he looked straight at me, and spoke out loudly and clearly, for all to hear. "Will thoo marry me?" he said! A great bellow of laughter erupted above, swelling to fresh heights as people further away enquired. "Whit did he say?"and were informed of the proposal. We cast off our lines, put the engine astern, turned and made our way towards Kirkwall, leaving Willy to be caught up in a laughing throng. He had got the evening's proceedings off to a first class start.

You may recall reading that on an earlier occasion a certain Eday character had also proposed marriage to me, but as I was aware that he only wanted to marry into a connection with the "Golden Mariana", I declined to take the offer personally. However, this second incident, occurring as it did just a few weeks later, did give me pause for thought, and as we rounded the Point of Veness and headed for The Galt, I risked a speculative glance at my reflection in the wheelhouse window. Had I inadvertently taken on any effeminate mannerisms, I wondered? Was my curly, but greying hair too long? Would I accept? What would Rosemary say? As for poor Willy, he lived to rue that moment. It was his lot to travel with us quite frequently as he worked in Kirkwall and returned to Westray at the weekends. Thus I had ample opportunity to tell him that, if he failed to name the day, I would sue him for breach of promise. After all, I would remind him with some glee, I had half of Eday as witnesses!

Duncan, Stuart and I tied up to the steps in the Basin in Kirkwall. Duncan plugged in our drinks dispensing machine to a power point and topped up the water in it, while Stuart went up to the chippie at the head of the pier and bought us all some supper. We relaxed long enough to munch the chips before we cast off our lines and made our weary way back out to Eday. Fortunately, it was a fine enough night, and the trip was quiet and pleasant. We took it in turns to go and stretch out on one of the passenger benches and get some sleep. In due course we reached Eday where we closed the engine down, switched off everything but the VHF, and settled down quietly to await the return of our passengers. At two o'clock in the morning the first car lights could be seen coming down the road towards the pier, soon to be followed by a convoy of vehicles which stopped in random fashion and disgorged the Westray folk, together with the Eday people who had come to bid them farewell. In no time at all the pier was a mass of revellers, in high spirits. Inspired by Willy's example, as he had been before the dance, so were they now. On a scale of inebriation from 0 to 10, there were no zeros or ones, a couple of twos, and a majority of over five. As usual, there was the occasional 9 or 10! Who was the worst? No, it was not Willy. He had achieved the unusual feat of returning less drunk from a dance than he had been when he arrived. As he had sobered, others had caught him up and then leapt ahead, and well in the lead was – William Johnson.

William had come on board earlier that night looking forward to a good knees-up, a few bevvies, and a pleasant evening's association with his lady friend, who accompanied him. She still accompanied him on the voyage to Eday, and they left the boat together. However, sometime during the intervening period, they had ceased to be together. The lady in question had found that there were other fish to fry, and that this other species of fish was an exotic foreign, Eday sort of fish. In short, she had spent the evening dancing with someone else. William had retired to the bar, sick in his soul and angry at the perfidy of the human race, and of the female of the species in particular. However, he was not really a vengeful man, and he did no more than watch the interloper dancing with his girl, albeit with an understandable degree of ill will that left a bad taste in his mouth that could only be assuaged by the quaffing of copious glasses of beer with whisky chasers. As the evening wore on the dancing followed the usual frantic pattern of a Scottish ceilidh - reel upon reel, two-step followed two-step, waltzes were waltzed at a speed and energy that would leave a lambada specialist breathless. The dancers repaired periodically to the bar where they quenched their copious thirsts and kept dehydration at bay despite the sweat that dripped from every brow by the end of the night. William, however, refrained from partaking of any terpsichory, and the effects of the home brew and single malt were undiluted. He became morose, and so he remained when the otherwise happy Westray crowd were brought back to the pier for the journey home.

At first the voyage home was a happy affair. The weather was fine, but it was a dark and moonless night by the standard of an Orkney summer. We wound our way northwards through the Calf Sound. Despite the hour, there were still a good few lights on in the crofts as we passed where Eday dance-goers had just returned to their homes and had yet to collapse in their beds. Back in the passenger cabin there was a happy chattering of excitement from people who had had a good night out and were still bathing in that warm glow brought on by the combination of violent exercise and a liberal supply of booze. In the wheelhouse Billy Stout joined Duncan and myself and we chatted happily. Stuart had taken his turn to descend into the forward cabin and had gone to sleep on one of the bunks. The engine thrummed steadily, the bow wave swished by, the islands were outlined against the night sky, and we were at peace with the world - or so we thought!

Electricity had come to the islands by the laying of undersea cables. One cable went around the Eastern islands, and another supplied the Western ones. Any break anywhere in either of the lines effectively cut off everybody who was supplied by that cable. It was put to me that the work that was going on in the Bay of Rapness was to join the two cables so as to turn the islands into a sort of gigantic ring main. Thus everybody would be protected from a catastrophic failure. Lest electricians laugh at this doubtless simplistic view of the work that was going on, let me hasten to say that I take no responsibility for the accuracy of this information. I merely mention it to explain that a cable layer had been at work for some while in the middle of the Bay of Rapness, and, to mark the location of their work, they had laid two large buoys. Unfortunately, the combination of the shape of these buoys and a complete lack of any radar reflector thereon meant that they were exceedingly hard to spot on the radar, and as they had no lights there was also no chance of spotting them with the naked eye. Furthermore, one of them lay right in our path as we crossed the bay from Fersness towards the jetty. The conversation in the wheelhouse slowed and then ceased as I became more and more absorbed with peering at the radar to try and spot the slightest flicker of an echo. Duncan was despatched to the eyes of the boat where he peered ahead into the gloom. I confess to a certain amazement that such a large steel object could become so invisible. From time to time I adjusted the radar set. I changed range. I tried to reduce the clutter, those echoes that come back from the surface of the water. I stared ahead through the wheelhouse window. Billy had also given up chatter and tried to make out where the buoy might be. My concentration was so intense that I completely failed to notice a change in the tone of the happy chatter that was coming from the passenger cabin astern of us. It was Billy who was alerted to the fact that something was not as it should be. One glance through the door into the cabin was enough to explain the change in the noise from our throng of passengers. He turned back towards me, and in a quiet, calm voice mentioned, almost in passing, "Theer's a peedie fight gaein' on back theer!"

My mind was so much on the buoy and its failure to materialise that his words washed over me without impact. I was the husband who says, "Yes, dear," and carries on reading his paper when his wife has just told him that the house is on fire. It was several moments before his words conveyed any meaning to me, and even then it was with some disbelief that I dragged my attention away from the radar and also turned and glanced over my shoulder. The sight that greeted me caused me to forget completely the problem of the buoy. Instead of benches filled with chattering people, or dozing people, or drunken staggering about people, I saw what I can only describe as a pile of humanity that looked like a gigantic rugby scrum! After a moment more of being mesmerised by this unexpected sight, I thrust the wheel at Billy and said, "Take the wheel for me, would you Billy. Hold her steady on 246 degrees," and proceeded sternly towards the scene of the fray. Entering the cabin, I wasted no time in niceties. "What the hell do you think you are all doing," I bawled at the top of my voice. "You should be ashamed of yourselves. Stop it at once and return to your seats!" To my surprise, the scrum collapsed at once and turned back into individual Westray folk, who meekly dusted themselves down and sat quietly again, with an abashed and shamefaced look on their faces. What had caused this unexpected departure from the norms of decorum? As far as I could later ascertain, William's ire had finally risen to the surface, and he wished to fight the world. The trouble was, he was too drunk to hurt anyone, but no-one else was sober enough to stop him. A sort of impasse had been reached, with everyone joining in and nobody capable of calling a halt to the ensuing fracas.

There was no time for feeling satisfied at the ease with which the conflagration had been doused. Freed from the one worry, my mind returned at once to the other. Where, oh where was the buoy that lay on our route? I stepped back into the wheelhouse, where it took a moment or two for my eyes to reaccustom themselves to the dark. The sight that slowly came to me was scarcely encouraging. The vessel was heeling over to port. Billy was frantically twiddling with the wheel, while he appeared to be searching for something. "Wheer's the compass?" he wailed. "Ah canna see the compass anywheer!" It was not surprising that he hadn't found it. He was searching among the engine instruments on the panel in front of the helmsman, whereas the compass was set on the roof of the wheelhouse and was viewed through a periscope that came down through the deckhead (which is nautical parlance for a ceiling). While he conducted an ever more frantic search for it, the "Mariana" had chosen its own course, and was now going round and round in circles in the middle of the Bay of Rapness. Instead of showing the outlines of the peninsula of Rapness and the islands of Faray and the Holm of Faray, the radar now showed continuous circles of colour as the echoes also rotated rapidly around the screen. The unusual course changes had somewhat surprised Duncan as he stood alone in the bow. At first he thought we had spotted the buoy on the radar and were taking avoiding action, but when we continued to go round and round he started to suspect that all was not well. "Did you not realise that it's up in the deckhead?" I asked Billy as I grabbed the helm back from him and started to steady her up on the right course again. After a moment or two the outline of the islands steadied again, the radar echoes cleared, and a white face peered through the wheelhouse window, its eyes wide with surprise. "Whatever's happening?" Duncan mouthed. We never did see the buoy that night. In a minute or two it was clear that we had passed it by in the dark and we were preparing to come alongside the jetty.

The night's happenings were not over. Calm though the night was, there was still some motion coming in from the Atlantic, and when we tied up to the outer end of the jetty the boat, as so often happened, was ranging backwards and forwards. The revellers were now suitably abashed after their previous boisterous behaviour, and they filed quietly out of the passenger cabin, through the wheelhouse, and onto the jetty. I stood at the departure point and supported them as they stepped over the side and onto the rough concrete, warning them where appropriate to watch out for any slippery patches as they made their subdued way up the slope to the cars that awaited them in the field. Eventually the crocodile of departing folks had wound its way ashore until the person who staggered from the cabin was a by now very drunk William Johnson. Eschewing any help, he stood back and eyed the step as though preparing for a long jump in the North Isles sports. He paused, swayed towards the side of the boat and, timing his approach to perfection, he stepped unsteadily forwards, gathering speed as he went. His calculations were more or less correct, and his legs carried him out of wheelhouse, onto the step, and he launched himself with perfection onto the waiting pier. The trouble was that, in his befuddled state, his brain had proved capable of controlling his departure from the boat, but had failed to think ahead and work out how he would stop himself before careering onwards across the jetty and straight into the sea on the far side. Fortunately for him, I was somewhat quicker on the uptake, and, as he went past me at the trot, I could clearly see that his destination would be the cold waters of the Bay of Rapness, unless I could do something to stop him. I grabbed a handful of clothing as he careered by, only to have it snatched from my hand by the momentum of his precipitate departure. It was just enough to slow him down. He teetered to the brink of the far side of the jetty, and just managed to halt his forward flight in the nick of time. Thinking that the worst was over, I breathed a sigh of relief, realising that I also had just missed a ducking as it would have been me that would have had to go in after him.

Next in line to step ashore was the sober Louse Stout, Billy's wife. I took the upper part of her arm in one hand and supported her forearm with my other, preparatory to helping her onto the jetty as we ranged back and forth. Her left leg reached the jetty, but she got no further. My eyes were drawn to the sight of William as he progressed up the pier. To my amazement, he proceeded with drunken gait to stagger right over the side of the concrete. Just when a ducking appeared yet again to be inevitable, the guardian angel of drunks took charge, thus enabling him to defy the laws of gravity. I watched, slack mouthed, as he appeared to change direction when already suspended over the abyss, and staggered right back onto terra firma once more. My gaze continued to follow him as he lurched from side to side of the narrow strip of concrete, making his unsteady way to safety in the field. So bizarre was the whole scene, and so unlikely, that I had completely forgotten about Louise. I was brought back to my senses by a small cry of "Chris!" Turning back towards her to ascertain the reason for her apparent alarm, I was appraised of a further bizarre episode, brought about by my own lack of attentiveness. Louise was straddling the bulwark of the boat. Her left leg was already ashore, but her right leg remained firmly implanted on the deck. Lacking any movement from my guiding and supporting hands, she stayed where she was, but the vessel continued to surge up and down along the jetty. This meant that while her left leg stayed still on the pier, her right one moved first ahead so that she found herself doing the splits, and then moved astern causing her legs to cross alarmingly like a child desperate to go to the loo. It took her a moment or two to appraise herself of this unusual situation, but after a few such leg movements she eventually realised that my attention was elsewhere and she let out the cry that had brought me back to life. Quickly moving her onwards to safety, I helped the remaining folk ashore, while remaining perplexed at the feat of aerial acrobatics that I had witnessed from William. To this day I have no idea what combination of convulsive movements made it possible for him to change direction in mid-air so as to return him to safety.

Our night's entertainment was almost at an end, but a final curtain call was yet to take place. Just when we thought that we had finally finished with the passengers for the night, I became aware of a last lonely figure seated in the passenger cabin, weeping quietly to itself. It was our aforementioned Eday alcoholic friend. He had boarded with all the rest and had enjoyed the voyage. The only trouble was - he was an Eday man. He had come aboard chanting, "Ah've ne'er been tae Westray. Whit a grand chance. Ah've ne'er been tae Westray." There was an air of suppressed excitement about him. In all his fifty odd years, he had never yet managed to visit the neighbouring island, and here he was, headed off into the night on a great adventure. While the fight had gone on around him, he had stayed quite still, a small smile on his lips, occasionally commenting on what a fine opportunity fate had brought his way. Suddenly, as soon as we had reached Rapness, all his Westray friends from the dance had deserted him and were making their way to their own hearths and their own beds, abandoning him. Suddenly Westray was not the Shangri-La he had thought it such a short while before. Instead, a dark, lonely and unknown island lay before him. His enthusiasm evaporated in an instant. "Ah dinna ken wheer tae go!" he wailed. "Ah dinna ken anybody on Westray. Ah've naewheer tae go. Ah dinna ken anybody on Westray!" The tears coursed down his weather-beaten island face as he started on his new incantation. He was inconsolable. I had assumed from the first that he had arranged to stay with someone, never imagining that he was launching himself into the unknown, and I had happily allowed him to travel with us, despite not paying any fare. Now that I realised his plight, I felt duty bound to make sure he was looked after. A quick call on the CB to Billy Stout was instantly rewarded by the traditional Isles hospitality. "Thit'll be nae bother," said Billy. "He kin jist cum hame wi' us tae oor hoose," and he came back to the boat to collect him. We last saw him being led, still weeping copiously, up the jetty and into Billy's car. Another problem had been solved.

Duncan cast off our lines, we came astern into the dark, and in no time we were bumping our way across the Westray Firth, bound for home. Stuart Ryrie, meanwhile, had been taking his turn to have a break, and had been asleep in our forward cabin throughout all the recent proceedings. We had let him sleep on at Rapness, quite capable as we were of handling the boat with two people. Somewhere off Rusk Holm his tousled head appeared in the hatch. "Whit like?" he asked. "So theer wis nae bother wi' the Westray eens, then?" Little did he know!

# A Peedie Word or Twa
## aboot Peedie Words

A small word or two about small words.

Do you feel as I do that life is far too short? Do you, as you go about your daily life, often think to yourself, "If only I had time to study this or do that"? For my part, one of the things that I find fascinating, but have never had time to study, is philology, the study of language, especially in its historical and comparative context. In other words, "Where did this word come from, and why?" Orkney is a fertile ground for the study of comparative language, as was my native Cornwall. I was brought up in an area where it is said,

*By Tre-, Pol- and Pen-,*
*Thou shalt know the Cornishmen.*

Why do so many Cornish people's names commence with the suffix Tre, for example? Simply that they are named after the place that they come from, and tre means a village. When Dan first went to a new primary school in Berkshire, his teacher was a Mrs Chynoweth. She was delighted when I addressed her one day as Mrs Newhouse, and was surprised to find someone in the Home Counties who recognised her Cornish name and its meaning.

In this book I have tried to represent the Orkney words and accent in the speech quotations. Somehow putting them into received pronunciation loses some of the impact, but where that makes it hard to understand I have put a translation afterwards. Thus you may see, "Ah dinna ken," for "I don't know". Often people will recognise this because of similarities with known words used by the Scots. What may be less obvious is using the word 'hid' for it and 'whit' for what and other peculiarities of the Orkney accent.

When I went to live in Orkney, I lacked the knowledge of the Norse languages to be able to recognise the origins of so many of the dialect words. Clearly most of them are taken almost directly from the Norse tongue that was still talked in the islands in the Middle Ages, and represented the last vestiges of Norn, the old language of Orkney and Zetland. The one exception to this was the word for small or little - *peedie* if you lived in the East Mainland, or *peerie* if you lived in the West Mainland or Shetland. It doesn't sound Norse, and has a clear phonetic association with the French word *petit*. I have often asked if this association represents a reflection of the origin of the word, or whether it is just coincidence. So far nobody has been able to give me a definitive answer. If it does come from the French, how did it get to Orkney and Shetland? With the "auld alliance" between France and Scotland, the importing of a French word would not have been surprising, but instead of appearing in the language of the Lowland Scot, why does it crop up in the far reaches of the realm? I suppose I will never know the answer, but such is my curiosity that I would love to find out, and can thus understand those people who do make philology the subject of their life's study. Furthermore, were I one of the Scandinavian races, what would be more interesting and natural than to study the derivations from their tongue that still exist in areas of Norse influence within the United Kingdom? Thus it was that one of the more interesting groups of people that we carried on the "Golden Mariana" was a party of Swedish philologists. For their annual holiday, some forty of them had organised a tour of Orkney, and came with us on a day trip to Westray and Papay. They hung on every dialect word that was uttered.

That fine summer's day we deposited the party at Rapness and saw them off in a fleet of minibuses. In due course they boarded Tommy Rendall's boat and went on to Papay, and they had a great time. Whereas most visitors rummaged around in the cairns and other prehistoric remains, or else hunted birds with their binoculars, or walked around with their eyes to the ground in search of the rare *primula scotica,* our Swedish friends went hunting with their ears and rummaged around for words. They were not interested in incomers or schoolteachers, but made a beeline for the oldest inhabitant, or the crofter or farm labourer, and instead of binoculars, they carried tape recorders and microphones. There was many a *roust* and *noust* recorded, and they were delighted if they heard that the sea was "a peedie bit chabblie"; (a little bit choppy).

That evening, a farmer from Holm (pronounced Ham) stepped aboard for an evening's cruise. He was quite a regular passenger, and just travelled for the pleasure of it. I don't think I have recorded his name, and I wouldn't repeat it if I had. He was a very friendly fellow, and often came up to chat to us in the wheelhouse. He looked like any other farmer, and when he spoke, he sounded at first like any other farmer. It was only after a moment or two that it slowly dawned on the listener that they couldn't understand a word that he said. It was doubtless partly due to the fact that he spoke rather like a machine gun, with rapid staccato bursts of sound, but try as the listener may, converting that sound into intelligible and coherent language proved impossible. One might recognise individual words, but they were rarely placed next to other words that complemented them. Was it a speech impediment? Was it that our farmer friend was on a slightly different plain to the rest of us? Was it both? None of us knew, but he was a nice chap and interested in everything that went on, and we just got used to holding rather disjointed and frustrating conversations with him. On the way to Rapness he enjoyed the scenery, the birds, the majesty of the islands, the seals. Imagine his delight when we reached Rapness to find that he also had a boat load of Swedes to chat to for the return journey.

The philologists returned on board, chattering away to each other, and, being Swedes, they also chatted in English to the rest of us. Everyone was a linguist. The leader of the group came up into the wheelhouse and expressed his satisfaction with all the rare linguistic finds they had made during the day. I even asked where the word *peedie* came from, but received little in the way of elucidation. Our conversation was interrupted in mid-flow by another of the party, who rushed into the wheelhouse, excused himself in English for butting in, and proceeded to talk excitedly in Swedish. After a moment or two, the group leader picked up his recorder and microphone, said, "Excuse me. Somesing very important has cropped up," and disappeared back into the passenger cabin at speed. I saw him push his way down the central isle between the seats and out onto the small after deck where our farmer friend was enjoying the summer sun and the view. After a few moments the leader put the microphone in front of our Holm worthy and engaged him in earnest conversation. I put two and two together. Someone had been chatting to the farmer, and had also completely failed to understand a word that he was saying. However, it had a good Orkney intonation to it, and there was clearly a mixture of English, Scots and dialect words. "Aha!" thought the Swede. "Zis sounds to me like ze missing linguistic link. Here ve haf a man in the later years of ze tventieth century who is still speaking ze last vestiges of ze old Norn langvage." For all I know, he could have been right, and it was not for me to pour scorn on a man whose speech was, shall we say, different. However, after a few minutes, the head of the party returned sadly to the wheelhouse and packed his tape recorder away. "It vas a false alarm," was all that he said.

# Maggie Watson's Farewell to Blackhammer

What can this be about, I hear you ask. It's about music. Orkney and Shetland are part of a North Atlantic network that eschews modern popular music for the traditional folk music based on the fiddle. The network includes Iceland, the Faeroes, parts of Ireland, Norway and of course Orkney and Shetland. Maggie Watson's Farewell to Blackhammer was written in the 20th century by a neighbour of hers to mark Maggie Watson's departure from Rousay, and it has become a standard for Orkney fiddle bands. It is also on an album of the Faeroese band Spælimenninir í Hoydølum. Blackhammer is a croft which takes its name from a chambered cairn that dates from neolithic times. It is one of my favourite pieces of music of the region, and many years ago I could play it on the accordion.

Periodically we did extra runs for bands and groups and on our scheduled services we often let them travel free if they played en route. As a result we had some wonderful impromptu concerts. I remember bringing the Orkney Strathspey and Reel Society back from Westray. It was a bumpy night and some of them stayed further aft where the movement was slightly less, but one of the best fiddle players stayed in the wheelhouse and a drummer used the wheelhouse door as a set of drums. As they played, I held the button open on the CB so the concert could be heard around the islands. It was appreciated. An anonymous voice on the CB commented, "Boy, boy! Thit was mighty fine music."

After the traditional music, the next most popular genre was Country & Western and the islands had their own performers. The best known of these was Ruby Rendall who even went on to perform at The Grand Ole Opry, mecca for country singers in Nashville. We did a tour of the islands for Ruby and her band. After gigs they would be psyched up and not ready to stop on their voyage home or to the next island. Consequently we were privileged to have our own private concerts as we plied our trade between the islands. Country music made great use of the fiddle skills taught around the islands and Ruby was equally able to turn her hand to the traditional music.

The traditional instruments most associated with Scotland are, of course, the bagpipes. However, they are part of the Scots tradition and not that of Orkney and Shetland. Nonetheless, the pipes were not unknown. My home parish of Deerness had a piper – Innes Wylie, husband of Grace at the Deerness shop. It fell to him each year to pipe in the haggis in the traditional manner on Burns night. Fortunately we didn't have a profusion of pipers as passengers. I say fortunately, not from any dislike of the pipes, but because they are just so loud. However, we did once have a drunken piper who came on board in Shapinsay to go to Kirkwall and insisted on playing all the way. The noise seemed enough to blow the deckhead (roof) off the passenger cabin. Furthermore, his inebriation was affecting his playing and it wasn't all in tune. Ships in foggy weather are obliged to advertise their position with signals on the ship's whistle, but I am not sure that a skirl of the pipes is a permitted alternative, even if when out of tune it would certainly warn other vessels to keep out of the way!

Later you will read how traditional music played a big role in the celebrations of reopening the old link between Orkney and Shetland.

# Meanwhile, Back at the Ranch –

You will have seen how widespread use of the CB was. Those who had listened to the fine music as I held the mic open to the Orkney Strathspey and Reel Society were joined also by Rosemary back at the house. The CB wasn't only used by Isles folk to communicate with us. It was also an important business tool for us. At Horries I had the CB located so that Rosemary could hear it as she went about the house. People without CBs would phone her and ask the same type of questions as those with CBs were wont to do. "Whit time will the Mariana be in?" or perhaps, "Is that reet that thoo're makkin' an extra trip fer the dance on Eday the morn?" (Is that right that you're making an extra trip for the dance on Eday tomorrow?) It was then Rosemary's task if she didn't know the answer to relay the question via the CB to us while the person enquiring hung on the line. It worked the other way as well. I would call her on behalf of a passenger and get her to get a taxi to meet us. There were also enquiries from 'sooth' from tourists thinking about coming to the Isles – all the myriad types of enquiry that a ferry operator might receive.

Rosemary's day was as frenetic as mine. For a start, there were five children or young people, with all the corresponding washing and ironing, bed making, cleaning and tidying. She has always been a stickler for cleanliness and order anyway and would have been overcome with shame if anyone visited and found a house that was anything but immaculate or if a child went to school with an unironed shirt or blouse.

Earlier I described the glorious location that we found ourselves in with Halley Beach, a beautiful unspoiled length of sand,
directly below us and rare was the occasion when we saw more than
a couple of people on it. To get to it we walked down the small road
that ended at "Horries" and "Bishops". As mentioned, the lane then
turned 90 degrees left, but a rough track carried on down right to
the entrance to the beach. We once saw about five people on this
long unspoiled strand and I commented that the place was getting
like Brighton.

In term time the day started with the kids getting to the Kitchen
o'Breck to catch the school bus. As they became old enough, they
had little bikes and could cycle there, their satchels on their backs.
We could watch them for much of the way until they disappeared
behind "Midhouse". Once at the Kitchen they could just leave their
bikes unlocked, but quite safe, at the side of the road, to be collected on their return in the afternoon. However, cycling became
ill-advised when a gale was blowing, and then they would walk.

Periodically we might receive a phone call from the school.
"The forecast is awfu' bad, so we've decided tae send the bairns
hame early. The school bus is leaving noo." From your home in
suburbia it may be hard to understand that this required action
on our part. The children were too small to be out when the wind
was blowing violently. There was one such occasion when I went to
meet the bus at the Kitchen. It pulled up at the junction with our
road and Tammy appeared at the top of the two steps down from
the bus. The moment that she went to take the final step coincided
with a violent gust and I managed to reach out and catch her as she
was blown from the step and was about to take flight.

Other communications from the school are noteworthy and
would have been unheard of elsewhere. The tarmacked playground
was relatively small, but next to it was a field where the children
could play when it was dry enough. However, in order to bolster the
school's finances, a local farmer was allowed to graze his sheep on
it. The children once brought home a letter from the headmaster

in which he apologised because there had been a number of complaints from parents that their child who had been playing in the field had returned home 'sheep-soiled'!

School concerts were well worth attending. They did Grease one year and Dan, with his hair slicked flat with Brylcream, was in it and Tammy played Gretel in Handsel and Gretel on another occasion. Strangely, rather like Santa, all the characters spoke with broad Orkney accents. Tam's friend, Kelly, was a witch and had to speak the line, "It's only the wind!" However, she said it with such an outrageous accent as to make it funny. There was one young lad in Deerness called David who was a particularly gifted cornet/trumpet player, and he had been allocated a spot for a solo at one concert, and this was shown on the Programme that we were all given on arrival. However, when it came to his slot – nothing. It later transpired that he had been practicing while his dad had been watching football on the TV and it was his favourite club, Aberdeen, who were playing. The two things, rehearsing and football, were deemed incompatible and football had won. The cornet had been confiscated and not returned, even for the concert.

All the children were getting good reports, which was very satisfying.

The winters were certainly wild, and I have memories of Rosemary and I lying awake at night listening to hurricane force winds whistling around the house. The croft was in need of modernisation, but our money had all gone into the ferries. However, at least it was built to withstand Orkney weather. Our only heating came from the Rayburn stove and a back boiler also heated our water. One winter we disappeared under feet of snow and leaving by car was unthinkable. Sandy and I traipsed to the shop together for supplies, ploughing our way through drifts. At least the wind blew the snow away from flat surfaces, but created very deep banks up against any obstruction.

Our operating season was still prone to some wild days. Then it was waiting for the shipping forecast that kept me awake at night. It was broadcast on Radio 4 each night after the midnight news.

Weather forecasting in those days had not reached the level of accuracy that it has today, but it was nonetheless a valuable indication. I slept better if the forecast was good and I have little doubt that Rosemary did as well. She may have been able to listen in on the CB to what was happening on board, but she knew well enough that there would be no time for radio or CB calls if and when an emergency occurred.

# A Last and Timeless Journey

It was a good day; not much wind, blue sky in between the cumulus. If you had to go on one last voyage among the islands, you could choose a far worse day than this one. We made our way steadily out to Sanday Sound, and now we were nearing the pier at Kettletoft. Our passengers were already standing there in a group waiting. The men were dressed in their black Sunday suits with all three buttons firmly affixed. Most of the suits were just that bit too tight. They had hung in their owners' crofts for years and were just brought out on special occasions, like today, and the owners had spread just that little bit, despite the back-breaking toil of trying to wrest a living from the sea or the fields. Above the suits were rusty hued faces, testament to many years out on the land in all weathers, or hauling creels in fresh winds. Many were topped off by a flat cap, which hid a balding head of a stark paleness against the complexion of the features. The women folk were also soberly attired, with their Sunday church-going sensible suits, covered with warm overcoats and topped with cheap, old-fashioned hats. They stood and watched us arrive, showing no emotion. There was no waving, no ribald comment, no friendly shout. They were all subdued.

We eased back the throttle and the bow lowered itself in the water. Past the pier end we went and came hard a'port, the engine kicking first astern, then ahead, and we were soon drifting alongside at the back of the pier and making her fast. With no more than the occasional word, the lines were taken from us and placed on bollards. Then we opened the rear door of the passenger cabin wide and hooked it against the after bulkhead. Some of the men disappeared into the small store on the pier, and reappeared shortly afterwards carrying the coffin. We had quite a job manoeuvring it across the rails and then turning it so that it lay fore and aft and we could pass it into the passenger cabin. At length it was done, and it stood in the alleyway between the rows of seats. The mourners boarded on the fore deck, passed through the wheelhouse, and sat quietly on the old bus seats in the cabin. Then we cast off the lines again and headed astern, cleared Kettletoft Pier, and set off on the final trip of a Westray man, bound home at last to be buried on his own island among the graves of his own family.

Every mile through Sanday Sound was a poignant one. The deceased had lived nearly all his life on Sanday and had been married to a Sanday wife, but he was still a Westray man, and that was why, in death, he was returning home. Still, that did not, could not, wipe out all those years that he had lived on Sanday, through good times and bad, seed time and harvest, tempest and calm, all the sound and fury of a man's life. I could not guess at all the events that had led inexorably to this moment. The births and deaths that he himself had lived through, the laughter and tears that he had endured. I knew little of him, but that he was elderly. It would have been around the time of the First World War when he had first been at the school on Westray, and the great depression had stamped itself on the Western world when he courted a lass from Sanday, married and moved away to the island that was to be his home for so long. He had lived through momentous times, seen the first electricity come to Sanday, the first telephone, the first car, the first tractor, the first television; yet in most respects the life he had led was not vastly different to that of his ancestors who had farmed and fished down through the centuries.

The funeral party talked, but quietly. Some came up into the wheelhouse. For islanders, who had often owned their own boats, to stand up in the wheelhouse with the crew was as natural as screwing one's eyes up against a bright sun. They chatted with us about day-to-day things, and there was little talk of the dead friend who accompanied them, but there was a quietness about everyone that spoke of a respect and an acknowledgement of the finality of this last trip that he was making. There was Spur Ness coming up on our starboard side. We passed Hacks Ness close to and looked into the Bay of Stove and saw the farm at its head, the last dwelling on Sanday. Nowadays things have changed and there is a ro-ro terminal on this Southeast corner of the island, but that would be well in the future. Each name that we passed had been as familiar to the deceased as every other farm and croft name on the island. How many times had he passed the Bay and looked up and seen the self-same sight as he left Sanday, or as he returned to his adopted home? But this was the final farewell. Then we were in The Keld and turning north into the Sound of Eday. From this point we would head steadily away from the Sanday side of the Sound. Each mile was taking us further from his home of so many decades and back to his ancestors. Ahead of us was Lashy Sound, and every now and then we could see a splash of white as a pinnacle of tide, created by who knows what forces, rose from the sea around it into a wave, and then collapsed foaming; but long ere we reached that spot, a much narrower waterway opened up to port, a channel through which the tide swirled and eddied like a fast flowing stream, and we eased the helm over and turned into Calf Sound.

What a beautiful place it is! What grandeur! What a timeless and wonderful route for one's last trip. I always loved the passage through Calf Sound, but passing through on our way to someone's last resting place seemed to compress time and put life into a new perspective. It was easy to look back and see it down through the ages. I had no special knowledge of the history of this wild and impressive place, but in my mind I could see the scenes that must have taken place there down through the ages. We followed the Eday side of the channel and looked across the 300 metres to the uninhabited island on the other side. It is known as The Calf of Eday, the child of the parent, and was a green and pleasant isle, with rocky outcroppings, birds nesting. On the Eday side the land rises towards hills, covered with rough vegetation and with many a rocky crag. There is The Stone of Setter, yet another of Orkney's standing stones, and a line of chambered cairns. Up there, out of sight from sea level, is the Mill Loch, nesting site of the red-throated diver. Lower down was grazing land, and lower still were fields and agriculture. A small road came over a hill from the south end of the island. Closer to the vessel, down near the shore were scattered crofts and houses, a little stone jetty with Jamie Sigurdson's creel boat moored just off it. His croft was nearby. Right there was Furrow End, now the new pub run by the Rugmans. There was Blett where Mr Popplewell had a studio and did his delicate water colours of Eday. And that was Mounthoolie that was the shop for many years until the island co-op opened. Further along the Sound the channel widened and there was a large edifice, standing four-square by the water with another little jetty in front of it - Carrick House. Turning right, the Sound continues, the high land on both sides crowds in and turns to cliffs as The Calf Sound debouches through the Heads into the grey waters of the North Sound beyond. But in all, there was little of the modern world to mentally remove from the landscape so as to be able to look back and see Neolithic man in his time. Why, there they were, over on the Calf. They were digging and putting large flat stones into place to make a rough edifice. Now others were carrying a heavy shape and placing it inside. It was another burial, all those centuries ago. The body of an earlier island dweller was going to their final resting place in a chambered cairn.

Now the Picts are passing through the hazy scene of history, leaving fewer footprints on the land of Calf Sound. They work with iron and have tools to till the land. Was there no broch or keep here? Have its remains disappeared, yet to be refound? Did the wild raiders from Scandinavia fall on them and wipe them out, or did there follow more peaceful men, farmers and traders, to mix and assimilate?

Then I moved forwards in time. Across the water came guttural shouts from a craft. Its sail pulled in the breeze, but not enough to drive the wooden ship against the tide. The oar at the stern was being used to steer close along the shore where the tide flowed the

least, and men sat at thwarts and pulled large sweeps to help pro-
pel their craft. It is a cargo ship, but of elegant lines, decked fore
and aft, but open amidships where bales and barrels are stowed,
These were not the *vikingr*, the raiders, in a sleek, fast longship, but
merchants trading where their compatriots might grab, steal and
lay waste. Their ship is deeper and broader. Where is she from?
Has she loaded in Westray. Has she come south from Hjaltland,
(Shetland) or even from Norway or Færeyjar (the Faeroes)? There
is rich land and good crops here in Orkneyjar, and fruitful work
for the merchants and traders, and this is a vessel that will carry
cargoes across the wastes of sea that separate the lands in the North
Atlantic. Where will she be in the months to come? Will she trade
south to the Viking towns in Normandy, or even go as far as the
Mediterranean? Or perhaps her route will lead her north again,
and to those other Viking lands of Faeroe, Iceland, Greenland or
Labrador?

Time moves onwards again. It is the 1630s, and there is now
much activity on the shore of Carrick Bay. Men scurry about
around stacks of cut, grey stones. A vessel is tied up at the small jetty
discharging more. A building is starting to take shape. There are
already rude crofts on the canvass that passes before my eyes, but
this new building is set to dwarf all others. There is a man who is
more smartly dressed. Is that the architect, or is it a member of the
Fea family, Lairds of Eday, for whom this imposing place is being
built?

Now it is less than one hundred years later; February 1725 to
be precise. Earlier where the Viking trading ship had been there
is a new ship, a sailing ship. She is deeper drafted than her Viking
ancestor, and the tides have left her aground on the Calf. On her
bows and stern we can read her name. She is the "Revenge", captain
Gow, on a voyage from Stromness. There is frantic activity as the
crew endeavour to work her off, but she has grounded on a high
tide and their endeavours prove fruitless. Now the captain takes to
a dinghy and, with some of his men, he rows for the Carrick House
to visit James Fea. But James Fea has had news of his visitor and

knows him for what he is, for the visit is not to seek succour, but to rob him of all he possesses. This man who he once knew as John Gow before he ran away to sea from Stromness has returned as the infamous pirate Gow, wanted for many an act of piracy against the vessels of the King. The "Revenge" had been in Stromness, where Gow had at first been welcomed as a returning son. How well he had done since running away to sea, thought the Stromness folk, but they didn't know that Gow had led a mutiny and murdered the ship's officers. Raised in the Orkney traditions of seafaring, he had made a fine seaman, and used his skills to lead his ship into numerous acts of piracy. Eventually the outrageous behaviour of the crew had caused suspicions, and then a prisoner escaped from the "Revenge" and raised the alarm. Keeping one step ahead, Gow vowed to go to Carrick and rob James Fea, who he had once known, but the vicious tides that run through the Sound have got the better of him. Now we see Gow and his men approaching Carrick House, but secreted about the place are other Eday men, armed and waiting. A fight breaks out, short and fierce and Gow, taken by surprise, is overcome. Struggling, he is taken up the stairs and is locked in an upper room. He struggles to free himself and escape, and in his frantic efforts spills his own blood on the wooden floor where it makes a stain that will last down through the years and was still there in our day. Later Gow and his men are being marched away and are sent to the Mainland. They will end up in London. At their trial they would be found guilty, and in Wapping, on the 11th. June 1725, they would end their lives dancing from a rope.

The years slip past. Is that Sir Walter Scott sailing by in 1814 in the armed yacht "Pharos" of the Commissioners for the Northern Lighthouse Service prior to hearing of the story of Gow from an old Stromness woman who was a seller of winds? (The ship's master would wend his way up the steep streets to her house before sailing and for sixpence she would sell him a favourable wind.) Whether he had sailed through the Sound or not, he went on to write about Gow in his book *The Pirate*. By the 19th. Century the island that swims across the tide of history is now much more populous. Rude crofts are sewn with profusion across the landscape. Many of these folks work at the peats. They cut the peat from the extensive workings in the southern half of the island and ship it away on vessels from a pier in the Bay of Fersness on the far side of the island.

On goes the voyage down the years. It is the 20th. century, warships steam by, war planes fly overhead, and then it is the year of 1953. Calf Sound is not the calm, beautiful and romantic place that the funeral cortege was passing through. There is a gale of wind blowing straight from the Arctic. The sheltered waters of the Sound have been whipped up to a fury. Spray from the waves is blown into the air and travels horizontally down wind, making track after track of white spume on the surface of the water. Even strong men must struggle to stand against the power of this monstrous storm. Higher and higher gust the winds. Up between the Heads the seas are building and building. This is a once in a lifetime gale. Everything loose blows headlong down the wind. Chicken coops fly like birds, barns collapse, roofing stones and tiles are picked up like leaves and hurled into oblivion. The seas become ferocious; the waves battering on the Heads have a violence and strength that is awe-inspiring, and they are funnelled in between Eday and the Calf, getting higher as they are pushed onwards by the seas behind them. Ahead of them lies Carrick Bay and the sea wall in front of Carrick House. Waves fall on the wall like a battering ram, blow after mighty blow, and the water and spume are driven inland up the road as far as the farm beyond. The House itself is surrounded by lashing spray, and disappears from view from time to time in the violence of the scene. One mighty sea rears upwards and upwards, and crashes on the shore with a deafening thunderous noise. This 100 year wave rises so high that when it breaks, its water goes down the chimney of Carrick House, over 100 feet above sea level. Other waves, just as mighty, are streaming down the west side of the island, and the old jetty in the Bay of Fersness receives a mighty hammering. First the waves get a hold of one weak stone, and that reveals another. By the time the gale abates, the pier has disappeared for ever.

That morning, the 31st. January 1953, the old steamer the "Earl Thorfinn", had left the pier at Backaland on the South end of the island. The weather was still fine and she expected to finish her run to Sanday and Stronsay. With no radio, there had been no weather forecast to indicate what a terrible gale was to come. Willy Meil had left Aberdeen the day before where he had been at the hospital. He could see his house when the hurricane force winds struck. Healed over in the sudden onslaught of the wind, the steering gear carried away. In the nick of time they manned the emergency gear and managed to clear the land. As the waves crashed on Carrick Bay, news came through on the radio of the demise of the ferry "Princess Victoria" between Stranraer and Larne with the loss of one hundred and thirty-three lives. In the crofts, as people cowered by their hearths and listened fearfully to the screaming wind, these island folk mourned the loss of those souls with more feeling than most, and pondered with heavy hearts the disappearance of the old 'Thorfinn', with so many familiar faces on board.

On that wild and fateful day, with hearts full of worry, the folk who lived by the side of the Calf Sound could not have seen the old steamship, her decks swept by sea after sea, as she heaved and wallowed before the wind. Towering waves bore down on her from astern. Every loose fitting was washed from her decks, seats and lockers were ripped up and flung away like so many specks of dust. The crew feared for their lives. In all the years of travelling around the islands in bad weather, nothing approached this storm for ferocity. It was not until late in the evening that news of the old girl arrived by phone. She was safe - in Aberdeen. The gale had driven her onwards to the south for league upon league until eventually she ran into the approaches to Aberdeen harbour and found shelter at last. Having seen his house William Meile was back where he had started.

The "Golden Mariana" steamed onwards past Carrick House, and turned to starboard. On both sides the high land closed in on the sea, and ended in cliffs that rose ever higher as we reached the Heads. Now we were dwarfed by the majesty of the scene and humbled by the sweep of history that came so easily to my mind as we carried the coffin onwards to its final resting place. And there was a strange thing - the headland on the Calf was grey, and on Eday it was red. The channel was the dividing line between granite on one side and sandstone on the other. This passage was a timeless one. One life had ended, but the cycle carried on. Births and deaths, seedtime and harvest, summer and winter, storm and calm, the life of Calf Sound went on generation by generation with scarcely a change to the rocks and land around us. The doings of man, his comings and goings, our passage on that final voyage, were as the scurrying of an ant. Through it all the magnificence of Calf Sound remained the same, a constant down through the centuries and the generations.

We passed close under the Red Head, just far enough off to avoid the rocks that lay at its base, and then turned away to port and crossed the entrance to the Sound of Faray, made our way through Weatherness, between the point of Weatherness and the Faray Holm, and came at last into the Sound of Rapness. Making fast to the jetty, the funeral party made their dignified way up to waiting cars. We took the coffin out through the stern door again and handed it over to the undertaker. As we cast our lines off and headed homewards across the Firth, the funeral procession wound its way along the shore road towards the cemetery in the north of the island.

The sombre passage that we had made that day had created memories that would stay with me for the remainder of my own ephemeral existence.

# Up Helly Aa - Shetland Ahoy

On the last Tuesday in January Shetland celebrates its Viking ancestry at Up Helly Aa. You would think it was a festival that has come down from the days of Viking supremacy, but it's current format stems from an earlier event of tar barreling - dragging barrels of burning tar through the streets. That was banned in the 19th century, but later was replaced by the more modern format of carrying flaming torches. Those taking part are called guizers and they dress the part as Viking warriors, carry the flaming torches through the streets and sing traditional songs. A Viking galley is built specially for the occasion and, led by the head guizer or Jarl, they parade to the galley and throw the torches into it. It is soon turned into a massive conflagration. Needless to say, the proceedings are accompanied by the consumption of a great deal of booze.

Orkney has no such festival, despite its historic connection to Shetland, but for years Orcadians could travel up to Shetland by ferry and join in the uproarious fun. Then, inexplicably, the ferry connection between the two island groups ceased and only the wealthy could afford to fly. It was time to put that right. Having played my role in modernising ferry services in the North Isles, I decided to try to rectify this other failure.

I travelled around the UK looking at ferries for sale and finally came across the Devoniun in Torquay. She had been running from there to Alderney. She had a good pedigree as she had previously been the old Scillonian, regularly crossing that other rough stretch of water between Penzance and the Scilly Isles. It was also fitting because of the historic connections between the two island groups.

She had a good reputation as a fine sea boat. In due course we bought her and I put together a crew and we sailed her around the coast to Kirkwall. On the way she had proved her seaworthiness in some quite poor conditions

This was to be a year-round service. and we arranged to start at once to have time to work up the crew and the booking system. After an enormously popular maiden voyage we were ready for that year's 'Up Helly Aa?

What a privilege to have witnessed such a scene, but first came the maiden voyage. We invited key people from Orkney, including members of Orkney Islands Council, but especially musicians. We had already encouraged musicians to travel free of charge on the Mariana as long as they played en route to work their passage. Also we had laid on extra trips to take them between gigs on different isles.

The ancient capital of Shetland was not Lerwick, but Scalloway, which is almost joined to Lerwick, but is on a natural harbour on the west side of Mainland right next to Lerwick which is on the east side. I chose Scalloway as our Shetland port. It was a marginally shorter passage, but most importantly it avoided passing around Sumbergh Head. The tide rushes around the head with force and is open to winds from many directions. The result is known as the Sumbergh Roust. You will have learnt that a roust is a tide race and the Sumbergh one is a particularly bad one and covers an extensive area. By using Scalloway we would be able to avoid it.

I had already employed a crew for the new ship and the trip around from Torquay was a shakedown cruise for them. Second engineer was the aforementioned Erik. He was an excellent engineer, but had no talent for passing exams, meaning that he couldn't be in charge of an engine room, but his island honed skills were of inestimable use at sea. In common with many people in remote communities, he had had all his teeth removed and replaced them with false ones. This practice stemmed from being far from dental care and it was deemed wise to avoid further reliance on treatment. Erik's false teeth didn't fit all that well. He would come into the crew mess on the Syllingar for a meal, where he would sit at the mess room table, remove the teeth and lay them on one side by his plate. He would then proceed to gum his meal, but if he found something that was a bit too tough, he would hold it on his fork and pick up the teeth in the other hand and mash the offending food around with them first.

On our way to Scalloway we stopped at Pierowall and half the island of Westray came out to see us.

Music was still very much of a feature for our first voyage. The passenger lounge on the main deck had a bar and plenty of seating and many musicians sat around some tables, got out their fiddles and an accordion and accompanied much of the voyage north. One of the fiddle players was none other than Mansy Flaws who ran the little ferry to Rousay from Tingwall, which is to the west of Kirkwall. Mansy was a great character and was known to entertain passengers on his boat by playing on the Jew's harp, which is a small instrument that can be held against the lips and teeth and made to resonate.

There was a big crowd on the quay at Scalloway to greet us and there was universal pleasure at the reopening of the traditional route. Then that evening an Orkney meets Shetland concert was held in the hall and a large crowd foregathered again. Shetland fiddlers are amazing, but Orkney has its share of great performers as well. One of the best known from Shetland is Aly Bain who has opened the parliament in Edinburgh and played at the Carnegie Hall. That evening in Scalloway and the following night in Lerwick we were privileged to hear some of the best fiddle playing in the world. In the Scalloway event the Orkney fiddlers and the Shetland fiddlers tried to outshine each other and the result was world class music.

It was soon time for the return voyage. Among the invited guests who were going back to Orkney there appeared the face of someone you have already met in these pages – Ian, the youngest of the four brothers mentioned earlier. He came aboard in Scalloway and approached me with a request. After a disagreement in Lerwick with the skipper of the Orkney trawler he was then sailing on he had been summarily dismissed and told to get off the ship. Could he travel back to Orkney with us? he asked. He had no money, but would pay me back when he was back home in Orkney. I agreed. It was good PR and I believed his promise to pay later, (and he did).

As a result, the bar on the way home was filled with happy imbibers plus one. He had no money, but there was no shortage of people willing to shout him a drink. The trip between the island groups is sufficiently long to allow time for a very convivial party atmosphere to develop. I walked among the guests and travellers making polite talk and as a result was privileged to overhear a classic snatch of conversation between Ian and David Lee, who was the Orkney representative for the Royal Society for the Protection of Birds (RSPB). Others might have bought Ian a fair few drams, but his quick wit was still working.

Such was the bird life in the islands that having a resident representative was entirely sensible. Birds that are extraordinarily rare can sometimes be seen. I have already mentioned the fish eagle and rarely snowy owls can be seen and they have been known to breed. Puffins, guillemots, razorbills, eider and other ducks, divers, all seem exotic for those in the home counties, but are part of everyday life in the islands. However, a fish eagle or a snowy owl will create excitement anywhere.

"Thoo kens," said Ian to David. "I'll no be at the fishin' fer much longer. Ah've got a grant frae the Highlands and Islands Board to start me ain business."

"Oh, yes," replied David. "What sort of business is it?"

"Hid's makkin' ladies' knickers oot o' snowy owl feathers!"

I actually thought that was pretty quick-witted for someone who was already inebriated.

The required skills of an island ferry operator are multifarious, and this was displayed perfectly on that voyage. One item of cargo was a female goat that we had in a quiet corner of a tween deck with adequate food and water. I was approached by one of the crew who told me that, as a result of the many hours travel between the two island groups, the goat was becoming very distressed because her udders had become extremely swollen and distended. Milking goats is not a skill required by any marine examiner and it is not on the curriculum of seamen, deck officers or engineers. The crew were at a loss to know what to do to help the poor animal. However, back at Horries we had a goat as it acted as an ideal lawn mower as well as providing us with a great supply of milk. As a result I have a photo of the owner of the ship milking the cargo. Multifarious or what?

Soon after we did a run for Up Helly Aa. What a privilege to see the ceremony, to watch the parade through the streets, to hear the traditional songs and to watch as the torches were thrown into the Viking longship causing this amazing conflagration. Once again the concerts had world class music.

I was also able to hire a car and drive right up to Baltasound and Haroldswick, which is as close as you can get to the Arctic Circle within the U.K.. That involves two ferry crossings; the first one to get to Yell from the Mainland and another to go from Yell to Unst. Haroldswick is effectively the end of the road, though we followed on beyond the town to get to Saxa Vord which is about as far as you can go. However, there was snow on the ground and we couldn't quite get there, even though we could see it ahead. It was indeed very cold and even the edges of the sea were frozen.

This time Rosemary could come with me. For her the maiden voyage had coincided with a spell of ill health and she had ended up in hospital and I had been split in two between the vital maiden voyage and the Balfour Hospital in Kirkwall. Friends and neighbours rallied round and there was no shortage of help and support at what was a critical time.

# NE'ER SPAKE

O r, to translate into English - Don't talk about it.

There was to be a big wedding on Eday. An Eday lass was going to marry a lad from Westray and there was to be a big reception at the island hall in the middle of Eday. There were numerous friends and family on Westray who wanted to attend, as well as a good few from Kirkwall. To add to the logistics problems the band was to be the Lamb's Tales from Rousay. The Lambs Tales were a three-piece band formed by none other than Robbie Hanson, the harbour master from Rousay. Robbie was widely known by his CB handle which was Mister Spok.

In common with so many other islanders he had had all his teeth removed and the false ones didn't fit that well. Also he was inclined to take them out when he had had a few. On one occasion we had done a special trip from Rousay to Westray. They were royally welcomed on Westray and Robbie had had a fair few drams by the time we were on the way back. One of his less endearing practices at such times was to take out the teeth and use them to walk up behind women and pinch their bums with them. The Free Kirk minister was also on board as we went back across the Westray Firth. I overheard him comment, "If he teks oot them teeth one more time they're goin' o'er the wall."

Anyway, the Syllingar was the answer to the logistics problem for the wedding. Kirkwall guests would join the ship when she left her home port. Then we paused at the entrance to the Sound of Rousay and the Lambs Tails came out on one of Mansy Flaws' boats and boarded us. There were doors in the side of the Syllingar which made this quite straightforward. The Syllingar was far too big for Rapness so we went on to Pierowall where all the Westray guests boarded, and in due course she went down through Calf Sound and berthed at the Eday jetty. A fleet of vehicles then took everyone up to the hall.

With the ceremony over, the dancing began. Scottish dancing is frenetic and everyone enjoyed themselves enormously. The Lambs Tails played non-stop for some while, but needed a break and an Eday country and western singer took over and performed while the three band members retired to the bar. There was time for them to rest and also time for them to sink a goodly quantity of booze. After their break they returned to the small dais in the corner and Robbie went to the microphone and said, "Tek thee partners fer a military two-step." The guests got to their feet and stood ready to trip the light fantastic. Nothing happened. Slowly people returned to their tables and started chatting again.

A few more minutes passed and then once again Robbie pronounced, "Tek thee partners fer a military two-step" and everyone stood up ready again. The same thing happened.

It so happened that the groom's family had wanted some film of the event and I happened to have a video camera. The days of taking video with your phone were still far in the future and a simple VHS video recorder was the size of a present-day state-of-the-art TV camera. I sat at a table in the corner and my son Andy and I filmed without paying too much attention. Thus, I wasn't aware of what had gone wrong, but later played back the recordings and it became clear. The accordionist had returned from the break the worse for wear. His accordion was a full sized 120 button version and you hold it onto your chest by way of leather straps that go over your shoulders. Putting it on is straight forward enough, despite its weight - as long as you're sober; and he wasn't. On the video I watched later as he struggled with the straps while standing uncertainly on the dais. As hard as he tried, the accordion fought back. With his arms flailing and him staggering from side to side, I watched his antics. Meanwhile, as Robbie twice prepared people for the next dance on the floor, the drunken dance on the dais continued unabated. Eventually as I watched the video the aspiring musician tipped himself right off the dais, landing accordion and all on the table of the nearest guests. The Lambs' tails had been well and truly docked! Robbie's next announcement on the loudspeaker said it all.

"Is there a body here thit kens hoo tae play the accordion?"

There would be few places in the land where such a request would bring a positive response, but nonetheless a Westray woman stepped forward. They had a quick consultation and found about five pieces of music that they had in common and so they went round and round those five pieces for the rest of the evening.

On the way home afterwards and before I had seen the video I spoke to Robbie. "Whatever went wrong, Robbie?"

"N'er spake, boy. He's sacked!"

Earlier you met he on Eday who wanted to marry me. His proposal was doomed to failure as same sex marriage was only legalised in Scotland in 2014, and in any case, Rosemary might justifiably have been very cross with me. At the time of the Eday wedding recounted above I had taken on an admin assistant. She was not the friendliest of women and rather seemed to try and lord it over Rosemary. She came on the wedding trip and attended the dance at the hall.

Meanwhile our alcoholic friend went on board the Syllingar, knowing that there would be booze there. He was a great believer in having his first drink when the sun was over the yardarm, this being the old tradition. Unfortunately, Jimmy's yardarm seemed to be under his table so the sun was over it when he first got up in the morning. He spent the day of the wedding working on a tractor. Already in his cups, he appeared on the Syllingar in a filthy boiler suit with his hands covered in black grease and oil. Suitably topped up by a couple of drinks he had purloined on the ship, he made his way to the hall. With another drink in his hand, he spotted a young woman he didn't know. It was my PA. He went unsteadily up to her and asked her to dance. To her credit, she didn't feel able to refuse for fear of giving offence. He took her unsteadily onto the floor and shuffled about, using his partner for support. This involved holding her firmly by the bum, so for the rest of the evening she could be seen with a very obvious black oily handprint on each cheek.

# THE VOYAGES FROM HELL:

W e only operated the Golden Mariana in the spring and summer months. The weather was just too bad for the rest of the year and passenger numbers would have been insufficient to make the service viable anyway. It was always said that summer ended with the Kirkwall Show, which takes place every year on the second Saturday of August. After that equinoctial gales were a constant risk with the violent weather that they engendered. That all meant that my income dried up in the winter, even though there remained plenty of work - annual refit and passenger licence renewal, marketing.

One winter I chartered a small cargo vessel called the Kilmany. She had been built as a middle water trawler and had fished as far away as Iceland, but had been converted to a small cargo vessel with its own derrick and carried some forty tons. She was very heavily constructed of wood. One of the main cargoes that I carried was something that was in very short supply on the islands - timber. To this day I could still tell you the whereabouts of most of the trees in Orkney and there certainly wasn't enough to supply the building trade, or even to satisfy the demand for kindling wood for fires. I could buy offcuts of wood from builders' merchants down in the northeast of Scotland, carry it back to Orkney and resell it where it was at a premium. I even had a chain saw and cut up anything that was left to sell as firewood. Given that most of the crofts had Rayburn stoves, there was no shortage of demand. The timber supplemented any other cargos that were needed around the islands.

There is a one word explanation for the lack of trees - wind. Fierce winter winds swept the islands and prevented any saplings from taking root. The oil company Occidental once handed out saplings to all the children at Toab school. Half of them were destroyed on the way home in sword fights, but those that were carefully planted fared no better. The wind destroyed them.

The January that I chartered and operated the Kilmany illustrates the problem of wind, and it was a malady that couldn't be tackled with bicarbonate of soda. That month there were twenty-one days when the wind blew at Gale Force 8 or over and there were three days in one week when it reached Hurricane Force 12. That's over 65 knots, which is 72 mph or 118 kph. With weather like that I was constantly looking over my shoulder. I would lie in bed waiting for the midnight news to be followed by the shipping forecast.

We had a commission to take a heavy-duty forklift to Papa Westray. It weighed nine tons, which was too heavy for any of the derricks on the Orkney Islands Shipping Company boats. It was clearly too heavy for the Kilmany's derrick as well, but I had concocted a method to land it. I would load a base of timber for the island of Eday and then use it to construct a ramp so that I could drive the forklift up and over the bulwarks of the vessel at the very moment when the tide height was such that it could be driven straight onto the pier. The main pier was completely unsuitable for that as it was far too high, but on the east side of the island was an old jetty opposite the small Holm of Papay, which is principally known for its prehistoric remains.

Loading at Lossiemouth on the Moray Firth passed off without incident. Oh that the rest of the trip could have been as trouble free. Prior to setting out I called up for a weather forecast and was told it would be south-easterly, Force 4 to 6. "Phew," I thought. It was a good enough direction on the quarter and it is officially described as being a strong breeze. Lumpy, but passable. We set out expecting a pleasant enough trip to Kirkwall, where we would get a night's sleep and then time our arrival at Papay to suit the tide.

For a while all seemed normal, but as we headed north the wind freshened and I started to question the forecast. It was nothing like south-easterly 4 to 6. I started to be concerned about the lashings on the forklift. I had put wooden chocks under the wheels, jammed it in gear and lashed it down with a heavy wire tightened up with a bottle screw, (which is a device for tightening wires). By now the motion of the vessel was starting to get quite bad, so I called up Wick Coastguard to update the forecast. (That Coastguard station has long since closed.)

"Wick Coastguard. Wick Coastguard. This is Kilamany. Forecast please. Over!"

"Kilmany. This is Wick Coastguard. Go Channel 67!"

I changed channels.

"Kilmany. Kilmany. This is Wick Coastguard. Forecast for you. Wind northwest Force 10 imminent!"

That's Storm Force - and we were just about to cross the Pentland Firth. Gulp!

The bulwarks on the Kilmany were low, as befits a fishing vessel, though there was a wire set somewhat higher. However, by now the motion was becoming so violent that I had to crawl up the deck on my hands and knees to examine the forklift. It was flexing backwards and forwards and if it broke loose it could have us over. I took mooring ropes, fixed them to any handy strong point and festooned the forklift with them. In order to tighten them sufficiently I used a Spanish windlass. That involved me putting a balk of timber between two parallel ropes and then twisting it round and round until the ropes were bar tight. I then had to lash the timber in place as well.

We were now in the tidal flow of the Pentland Firth and the seas were very sharp and unpleasant. I had no choice but to steer straight into the sea. Turning beam on would have created such heavy rolling as to be dangerous, especially as the forklift continued to flex backwards and forwards. However, it was at this very moment that we were beset by pair trawlers. These are trawlers that stretch the nets between them and are distinguishable by having to display particular shapes by day and an array of lights by night. It means that other vessels must keep out of their way and you can't go between them. That was all very well, but I couldn't alter course because of the state of the seas. My only course of action was to sneak away metre by metre, awaiting a slightly smaller wave to ease the Kilmany out of harm's way bit by bit. That was bad enough, but exactly the same thing happened a second time during the night. It was with the utmost relief that we eventually tied up in Kirkwall and could get some sleep.

The following day we had timed our departure so as to arrive at the old Papay pier at the time when the tide height would be suitable. The weather forecast meanwhile had deteriorated still further and was due to be Force 12 the following night, by which time we needed to be safely tied up at the pier in Eday to unload the timber. Things went wrong from the start. There were already some very strong gusts of wind, and as we left the basin in Kirkwall a creel (or lobster pot) on the pier by the entrance to the basin blew off the jetty and flew straight as a dye into our propellor. If you saw it in a film you would have thought how unlikely it was. The rope that was attached to the creel was immediately wrapped round and round the propellor.

Fortunately in the harbour there were boats that went diving for clams and in no time one of the crewmen had donned his wet suit and gone down and cleared the rope away from the prop. Off we went again, but as soon as we left the harbour and I increased the revs I could tell at once that we had bent the prop. That severely limited our speed because otherwise there was far too much vibration. Nonetheless, we limped out to Papay in time. I created the ramp from the timber, tied the Kilmany in tightly to the pier and drove the forklift up it. By then it was dark. I assumed that the weight of the forklift would cause the vessel to heel somewhat as we reached the bulwark, but the old vessel didn't budge. As I reached the bulwark I thought, "In for a penny; in for a pound," and carried on over the side, but I was still four or five inches about the level of the jetty so I was catapulted forwards. Fortunately no harm was done, either to me or to the forklift and the operation was a success.

We sailed at once for Eday and got tied up in the nick of time before the worst of the storm hit. I moored on the sheltered side of the pier. In the morning I needed to phone Rosemary to tell her that all was well, but the wind was blowing us to the very limit of our bar tight mooring lines and there was no way I could get ashore. There were no mobile phones in those days and there was no CB on the Kilmany. The phone box was at the head of the pier.

There is a method for bringing a vessel alongside under such circumstances called springing. A spring line is one that is led from the bow back towards the stern or from the stern towards the bow and they prevent surging backwards and forwards. If you run the engine ahead the vessel is prevented from moving by the spring, but instead the vessel can be made to nestle against the quay. I started up the big Gardner engine and ran it ahead, but the wind was too strong and nothing happened. I increased the revs - still nothing. Eventually I put the engine ahead with as many revs as the bent propellor would allow. Inch by inch we got closer to the quay until eventually I was able to leap across. However, the wind was by now so unremittingly fierce that the simple act of walking up the jetty to the phone became really quite dangerous and at some moments I found myself on my hands and knees. I no longer recall who was crewing, but after I had phoned we had to reverse the process. Eventually the wind abated and we discharged. Later we limped to Wick and slipped the vessel so the prop could be changed. The voyage from hell was over, though there would be another to come in the 'Mariana'.

The Kilmany wasn't a lucky ship for me. On another occasion we sailed from St. Margaret's Hope and south into the Pentland Firth. One fuel tank leaked its contents into the bilge without us noticing until the engine suddenly stopped. I raced down to the engine room, diagnosed the problem and tried to transfer to another tank, but the fuel line was now full of air and the lift pump needed to be bled. By then we were in rough waters and any job was hard. It was the only time that I have sent out a Mayday, (which comes from the French m'aidez or 'help me'.) The Longhope lifeboat launched and seemed to reach us quite quickly and took us in tow back to Longhope where we soon fixed the problem.

Back home a coastguard knocked on the door at home and frightened Rose to death when he told her that we needed assistance. If that wasn't bad enough, my father-in-law then phoned from Somerset to find out what was happening. He had heard it on the national news.

The 'Mariana's' voyage from hell was a very poignant one. It was to be our very last commercial run, though we didn't know it at the time. We had finished our programme of summer sailings as the weather and the nights were closing in. However, it was still within our seasonal limitations when the autumn half term came round. Those children at the Westray secondary school who wanted to continue their education had to come into Kirkwall where they stayed in a hostel. At the start and end of each term and half term their voyages to and fro were provided on the state subsidised Orcadia. That meant that they finished school on the Friday, went on board at the crack of dawn on the Saturday and finally got home at tea-time. Instead they clubbed together and chartered the Mariana to take them home on the Friday night, thereby gaining an extra day of holiday.

The news soon got round and I had a phone call from the skipper of a Westray fishing boat. He and his crew had taken their vessel to a shipyard down south for annual refit and were returning home on the afternoon flight into Kirkwall airport. "If we cums doon straight tae the Mariana, cans't thoo be waitin' fer us to cum oot wi' the bairns?" I had already phoned for a weather forecast and it was time critical. Later there was to be a violent gale. "Come straight away," I said, "but any delay and we'll have to go without you."

The students all came down to the harbour straight after school and shortly after a taxi screeched to a halt by the boarding steps and the fishing boat crew arrived. The engine was running, we cast off and were on our way. It was a beautiful evening, but did it flatter to deceive? The sky was a beautiful pale blue, and the sea was an even paler shade of blue and there was never a ripple on its surface. Could the forecast be wrong? However, as we left Kirkwall Bay the first zephyrs blew and the first ripples on the sea appeared. By the time we reached the Galt and the Westray Firth was ahead of us it was starting to get choppy. Crossing the Firth it got fresher and fresher and as we reached Rapness jetty it was nearly a full gale from the southeast.

In all the hundreds of times that I had been to Rapness I had never failed to get alongside - until then. The wind was blowing straight across the jetty. We could get a line ashore and could use it to perform the springing technique I describer earlier. However, by the time the line was made fast we had already been blown so far off the jetty that steaming ahead brought us frighteningly close to the small cliff face at the jetty head. I tried over and over, but meanwhile the weather was getting worse. All the parents were foregathered in their cars in the field and it all took place with an audience. I told the crew to let go of the line and shouted to those ashore that I would carry on up to the main harbour in Pierowall, and could they bring our mooring rope up with them?

The rest of the outward voyage was uneventful. We reached the main harbour and put our charges into the hands of their parents and the fishermen to their families. Returning to Kirkwall that evening was out of the question - or so I thought! I intended to tie up in the harbour and wait for the gale to subside. However, then two people came on board.

One was Billy Stout. In common with many islanders he had several jobs. He was one of the minibus drivers and also ran the doctor's boat if the doctor was needed on Papay. Like most islanders he had been brought up around boats. Billy had a PSV driving test on the mainland the next day and there was a job waiting for him in Shetland if he passed.

The other person was none other than Davy Hulme, the Westray harbour master. He was off on holiday on the ferry St. Ola the following day and his wife had flown to Kirkwall earlier on. That presented a quandary - to sail or not to sail. We sailed. After all, they were both experienced seafarers and knew what they were letting themselves in for.

We set out into the unknown and I informed Pentland Coastguard that we were at sea. With the wind veering to the southwest, the passage through the North Sound was passable and the Sound of Faray was also sheltered, but then we had to negotiate the way past Seal Skerry and into the Falls of Warness, behind the Green Holms and across to The Galt at the northwest point of Shapinsay. The whole trip back was in the pitch dark so we couldn't even see the holes in the sea before we fell into them. Everyone was in the wheelhouse while hanging on to something to keep their balance. There was little conversation as we all concentrated - especially me.

Eventually we made it into Kirkwall Bay and the lights of Kirkwall could just be seen through the spray. I called the Coastguard:

"Pentland Coastguard. Pentland Coastguard. This is Golden Mariana."

"This is Pentland Coastguard. Go ahead Golden Mariana. Over"

"Pentland Coastguard. Just to inform you that we have made a safe passage and are entering Kirkwall Bay. Over."

"For your information, Golden Mariana; according to our instruments here the wind is about to go Force 12."

However, the Coastguard station was somewhat sheltered, and I looked out at the sea state. I was very familiar with the description of the sea state at hurricane Force 12. It reads: 'The air is filled with foam and spray; sea is completely white with driving spray; visibility very seriously affected.' That was exactly what I saw.

"Thank you for that Pentland Coastguard," I replied. "For your information it has been Force 12 out here for the last half hour."

Billy Stout couldn't get across the Barriers to where he was due to stay so he slept on our settee at Horries. In the night I had to take a hammer and nails outside because the side of a residential caravan that we used for added accommodation was starting to peel off in the wind. Then dawn brought an extraordinary sight. Where yesterday there had been green fields, in the morning everything had turned monochrome, with the vegetation burnt black by the salt laden wind. It was a sight I had never seen before and never since. And the ferry to the mainland was cancelled so the harbour master's holiday was delayed anyway, but at least Billy got his job in Shetland.

It was portentous. We didn't carry another fare paying passenger. Nature had given us a dramatic send-off. Was it wishing us farewell or good riddance?

# VICTIMS OF OUR SUCCESS

We took the Syllingar down to Aberdeen where she was slipped and undertook the annual survey that is required for a passenger licence. However, soon after disaster struck. The Syllingar ran a bearing just as the main tourist season was starting. We were immobilised for a week or two and had to let people down. A specialist Norwegian team flew in and was able to refurbish the bearing in situ, thereby avoiding an expensive dry-docking. Meanwhile, though, we became the victim of our own success.

The next County Show day we covered the North Isles with the two vessels to bring the North Isles folk into Kirkwall for the day. This was traditional and the Orcadia also did special trips, but in the usual cumbersome manner. On that day the deficiency of the traditional service was highlighted in dramatic fashion. We carried over 90% of the passengers. What seemed exciting at the time actually ended up counting against us. The Orkney Islands Shipping Company had 100% of the subsidy, but we had the great bulk of the traffic. Something had to give!

We provided the opportunity. The Mariana had run many, many miles, and when it came time for her refit it was recommended that, rather than overhaul the old Gardner engine, it would be cheaper and easier to replace it. That was exactly the sort of circumstance that justified a grant, and we applied to the HIDB. (Highlands and Islands Development Board). The HIDB worked in conjunction with the local councils - and Orkney Islands Council were running the opposition. On the other hand, we had tremendous public support, so turning down the application would have been criticised by many. Their solution was to agree to support the application - but on the understanding that we passed the service over to them. With a great deal of reluctance I agreed - and that was that.

The Syllingar was sold to a Greek company who changed her name to Remvi and ran her from Corfu to Brindisi for some years. From there she was sold to West Africa and ran along the coast there for a good while. Finally she was bought by a Greek Cypriot company and an African crew sailed her back to the Mediterranean. Bypassing Cyprus, she berthed in Haifa to get fuel, but was detained because of non-payment. They left in the dead of night to make their escape and made their way to a port in the Black Sea where she was abandoned. The navigation equipment was sold to the police, but the African crew had no money and stayed on board living from handouts from other ships. Eventually a French charity paid for them to return home. Left to rot, a stern gland eventually gave way and she sank alongside her jetty. It was a sad end to an interesting vessel. She had made her mark, as had we. The Scottish Office did another survey and this time decreed that the islands should have ro-ro services, which was clearly what they should have proposed all along. Recently I was featured in an article in The Orcadian, Orkney's weekly newspaper. The headline described me as a ferry pioneer. I am happy with that.

# MEMORIES

Time has moved on, and many years have now passed since the episodes that I have recounted. That I have remembered them I owe to having had the foresight to write them all down when they were fresh in my memory. Rewriting the tales has been a nostalgic experience, and has brought to mind many people, many places and many events and my recent return to visit after thirty-five years has served to accentuate that nostalgia. At the time of the recent visit there were articles in Auk Talk, the magazine for the island of Westray, and my old friend Tommy Rendall wrote, "I personally will be forever grateful for what he did and to this day Chris Marrow will always be remembered as the man who changed the North Isles sea travel for the better, single handed." What a nice thing to say. Nonetheless, despite the passage of years, there are some things that have never left my memory; some scenes that are indelibly imprinted on my brain. I recount these in no particular order.

It was winter. For some reason we were heading for Pierowall. The reason is beyond recall, and it matters not. Clearly at that time of the year it was not a passenger run. We had reached the North Sound and there was a good deal of westerly sea running. As a result, many trawlers had come in to the comparative shelter of Westray to fish. The night was dark, the sea was darker and it slopped up and down around us in a formless sort of movement, sometimes splashing on board with a rush of spray. The working lights of the trawlers shone out bright and clear. Our engine was running steadily, and there was something peaceful about the scene that I cannot describe. It was somehow timeless - the sea, men earning their living from the deep, no noise other than our engine and the natural sounds of the sea and the wind, stars blinking briefly as scudding clouds left small holes through which the twinkling light briefly appeared. It was mid-evening; that much I remember, because my thoughts turned to the big cities of the South. In London all would be hustle and bustle. Traffic would be thronging the streets; pubs and clubs, cinemas and theatres, would all be in full swing; suburbia contained all the myriad scenes that go on every night. I would have swapped none of it. We were snug enough in our wheelhouse, a coffee to hand, and yet we could have been from any one of the generations of seafarers who had plied these waters. Apart from the bright deck lights and navigation lights, the scene would have been the same for the skipper of the Viking cargo vessel, and Westray men through the ages had passed this way on their journeys homewards from the other isles. Pict or Norseman, Gael or English, Scot or even me, a Cornishman, all had navigated these waters down through the years; and we were united in our recognition of the magic of the sea and of the wild, yet hospitable shores of Orkney. We were seamen, one and all.

My next memory is of sunsets. How often have I sat, the world over, and watched the sun go down while people around me have "ooohed" and "aaahed" at the wonderful sight. I have seen the sun sink over Africa and smelled the hot smell of the land. I have supped sundowners in the tropics and luxuriated in that brief moment between day and night when the coolness washes over one and refreshes the very core of one's body. I have watched the sun sink over the Tasman Sea, the Caribbean and the Pacific. It has all left me relatively unmoved, for I have seen an Orkney sunset. An Orkney sunset is not just a pinkness on the western horizon, it is not just beautiful rose-coloured strata of sky. An Orkney sunset is a deepest orange, almost a gold, that infuses everything. It spreads out from the last of the setting sun until the whole of the sky is a deep orange glow, and every other thing is also imbued with a golden hue. The sea turns a vivid orange as well, with silver bars that show each ripple. I have seen an Orkney sunset from our croft, and the dark, gold-tinged outline of the western hills and the shapes of the islands served to highlight the orange sea and the orange sky. I have seen an Orkney sunset as we crossed the Westray Firth, and Rousay and Rapness and the little island of Wart Holm were all that stood between a sea and a sky of an unrelieved deep orange golden colour. My words do not suffice to describe such scenes to those who have not seen them. It must suffice for me to say that all other sunsets that I have seen, and I have seen many, are but pale and inferior happenings compared to the brilliance and intensity of the sun sinking in the Atlantic to the West of the Orcades.

Glorious sunsets might occur in Orkney in winter, as well as in summer. The orange might reflect from snow, as well as from the sea and the sky; but the sight that I recall from the winter sky comes not from the sun, but from the aurora. As the winter nights draw in and the cold crisp air of frosts nips at the skin, one's eyes might be drawn to the North, to be greeted by a scene I described earlier; a scene of ever-changing colour and beauty, a curtain that ripples and shimmers and changes colour as it opens and closes across the firmament. Thus are the Northern Lights, the Aurora Borealis, the Merry Dancers. I make no claim for any world beating qualities of the Orkney version. Displays will improve the further north (or south) is the observer. There was that time while sitting in the New Zealand port of Timaru when I had seen an even bigger display in the shape of the Southern Lights or Aurora Australis. That had been an awesome sight, for all the world like some gigantic *son et lumière*, as curtains of light flowed and shimmered for hours across the Southern skies. There was one prime difference between the two aurorae – the one that I saw in New Zealand was pure silver, while the Orkney displays changed colours from reds to greens and only incorporates silver as part of a pattern of changing hues. However, I have no doubt that natives of the Northern Isles can be very nostalgic about their Merry Dancers, and they lit up many a night-time walk home and dragged us as a family from our hearth to watch on many an occasion.

There is another rather different memory that comes back to me. It was a day when the West wind had gone to bed at night, to use the Orkney seaman's saying. When a West wind blows all day, it can very often be seen to drop away at dusk as the land cools more quickly than the ocean. With the sea now warmer than the land, the air rises, tending to suck more air back from the area over the land where it is cooler. This does not create a breeze, since the flow of air is already going in the opposite direction, but it seems to counteract the flow of wind perfectly, leaving many an evening of complete calm. I have argued about this phenomenon with meteorologists, who have wanted to deny its existence, but observation alone is a strong proof that the old saying is true. On this occasion the sea had fallen away until the surface of the water was a perfect pale, mirrorlike blue. We were sailing down through Howie Sound, and the tourists were bowled over by the scenes of the St. Magnus Kirk on Egilsay, the hills of Rousay set in a beautiful pale blue sky. Every bird, every seal could instantly be seen against the uniformly flat surface of the sea. There was not a ripple to disturb the scene. For me, though, unlike the visitors, there was nothing new in the beautiful panoply of islands, the glorious and delicate colours. Like an arrow through the heart, it suddenly came to me. I had seen it all before. I had been there, I had done it, I had bought the t-shirt. The breath-taking beauty no longer took away my breath. The human capacity to be accustomed to almost any circumstance, however good, however bad, had caught up with me, and my days of glorying in my good fortune at being able to navigate these lovely islands were gone, perhaps for ever.

There is one more arbitrary memory that has used my brain like light sensitive paper and implanted a snapshot thereon that refuses to fade with the years. By chance, it is a picture from the final voyage that we made around the Isles as we took the "Mariana" to Scapa Flow for sale to the Council. There had been weather from the Southeast for some days, and conditions out around Copinsay looked very poor as grey topped seas poured in in constant succession from the North Sea. Instead of risking the eastern passage, we set out early one morning in the winter of 1985/86, steamed sadly out towards the West, past Eynhallow, scene of a lovely day out in the past, round Costa Head, Brough Head and Marwick Head, carried on by the Bay of Skaill with its Neolithic village almost intact, and came at last to the Hoy Sound entrance to Scapa Flow. It was at some point there as we approached the Sound that the photo was taken in my mind. Hoy lay ahead, snow-flecked on the winter's day. The Atlantic was a battleship grey, matching the steel grey of the sky. The cliffs of St John's towered from the sea, almost black in the poor light, and the land beyond was flecked with white on grey. It was a scene of almost unrelieved dullness, as if all colour had been leached from the world, leaving us to a monochrome existence. I knew I was looking at Orkney, but I felt that it was a scene that had been repeated over and over through the islands and coasts of the North Atlantic. At that moment we could have been Leif the Lucky, son of Eirik, approaching the coast of Labrador, or perhaps we were St. Brendan with his crew of monks sailing towards a landfall on Iceland. Or we could have been any one of myriad nameless navigators, most of them Norse, as we approached shelter somewhere in the Faeroes or Iceland, Newfoundland or Greenland. But we weren't. It was to be almost our last trip on the "Golden Mariana", and the northern land was Orkney, and that phase of my life was coming to an end.

# Saying Goodbye

When we finally left Orkney, I told Sandy and Belle what fine neighbours they had been. We were genuinely very sad to leave them, and I think they were sad to see us go as well. "Ah cuildn'a believe thee cuild get sae attached to thee neighbours in jist six year," were among their last words to us, and put it down to the fact that Orkney neighbours would have been inquisitive as to what they were up to whereas, "thoo're nae carin' whit we're doin'." This was said with the Orkney intonation. "THOO're nae carin' WHIT we're doin'."

The elderly housebound lady who lived with her rotund nephew, expressed the same sentiment, but in a slightly different manner when we eventually went to say cheerio to her. In response to our farewell, she observed, "We dinna want thee tae go fer we wis ne'er once molested by any o' the Marrows!" "I should hope not," was my response. She lived on for a number of years, but had something to say about things right up till the last. Her last words on leaving her small croft were worthy of her, and, though less succinct, are nonetheless of the same order as "Bugger Bognor!", which are the last words perhaps falsely attributed to King George V. By then we had left the islands, but the incident was reported to us. She had been persuaded to go into hospital for a couple of days to get herself back to health. As the two young ambulance-men wheeled her from the croft to the waiting ambulance, she proclaimed in her usual stentorian and authoritative manner, "Pull doon me shift, fer these nice young men dinna want tae see me auld wrinkled bum!" Within a day she was gone. Oh that my own last words are of the same memorable ilk.

It was a sad time, saying goodbye. I had been part of the pageant for a while, and now I was going to move on, and it would continue without me. Every now and then I pick up the phone and call an old friend. Kenny and Mary always sound genuinely pleased to hear from me. One crew member who did sterling work as purser, came to a sad end. Unable to control his drinking, he committed suicide. Stuart Ryrie is now coxswain of Kirkwall lifeboat with an RNLI award for rescuing a Norwegian yacht off Stronsay. He became one of the top captains of stand-by vessels in the north of Scotland and has now gone on to serve as Chief Officer on the Nothlink ferries. Good for him. He deserves it. And by chance the old "Mariana" was then operated for some years by none other than my old friend Tommy Rendall from Pierowall on behalf of the OIC. She no longer ploughed a furrow between Kirkwall and the isles, but took over the school run to Pierowall for the Papay children for many years. She was in good hands. When we went back all those years later, I heard that she was at the shipyard on Burray. We drove there at a weekend. Everything was locked up, but inside the covered yard I was able to clean the filthy window in the door just enough to see her pulled up out of the water. How nostalgic! How many miles had we ploughed together?

As we had left with a great deal of sadness those years ago our eyes were turned towards the South Pacific. I was working on a project to provide a regular service for Pitcairn; home of the descendants of the Bounty mutineers. It was fascinating, but in the end it was to be Africa, the mother continent, that formed the backdrop to our lives for many years. The family would live in a war zone. I explored forgotten waterways; went to places where people had never seen a white face. One day years later I was standing on a dais next to a band leader translating between English and Portuguese at a town twinning event. The band leader asked how come I spoke Portuguese, and I explained how I had ceased to run the ferries in Orkney and ended up in war-torn Mozambique. He replied, "This is not a normal career progression." I did consider using that as a title for the series before I opted for The Cornish Viking. If you want to come and explore more little-known places with me; meet more interesting people, then you will just have to read the sequels. They will be very different; no eccentricities, few humorous incidents. Instead there will be tales of a famous mutiny, crowds of starving people, rampant malaria, inflictions you may have never heard of, snakes and hippos and gunfire. Hold on tight. It's going to be a bumpy ride.

Meanwhile, I always felt that the islands were infused with history. If your interests also turn in that direction, I have added a bit of history from the far-off Viking days of the islands by way of an addendum.

# Addendum: Orkneyjar and Hjaltland – Some History of the Islands

History pervades the islands and you will have seen references to the distant past throughout this book. For the recording of those far off times we must thank an unknown Icelander who was probably associated with an Icelandic centre of learning at Oddi and wrote the Orkneyinga Saga at some time around the year 1200. The saga covers the period between the ninth and thirteenth centuries and it provides a fascinating insight into those far off times, but nonetheless times which formed the people of the isles as we knew them during our brief sojourn.

### *About Saint Magnus:*

On the days when we were heading towards Egilsay, we were linking the two main places in the tale behind the construction of the St. Magnus Cathedral. St. Magnus was known in his lifetime as Magnus Erlendsson and he was an Earl or Yarl of Orkney. (He is not to be confused with Magnus Olafsson Bare-Legs, nor yet Magnus Olafsson the Good.) Magnus came to share the rule of Orkney with Hakon, his kinsman. He was a man who was very highly thought of by all; just, magnanimous, generous. What is more, he had a look of great distinction. It all made him highly popular with his people. This grated somewhat on Hakon, so although the two were friends, eventually Hakon schemed to murder his cousin. He called

Magnus to a meeting on Egilsay. When it became clear to Magnus that he was to be killed, he exonerated the poor fellow who had been instructed to do it, and prayed for everybody, friend and foe alike, before stooping to receive the blow that was to kill him. It is told in the Norse sagas that the field where it happened turned green. Nowadays the exact spot has been lost. True, one might find a plaque marking where he fell, but it is said that a latter-day laird of the island, when asked his permission for the location to be marked, indicated a convenient place that would not interfere with the working of the land.

Magnus' body was removed to the Orkney Mainland where he was buried in the parish of Birsay, and his grave became a place of pilgrimage. People said they were cured of their ills after visiting the site, and many miracles were claimed in his name. Despite Hakon's evil deed, or perhaps because of it, he went on to become a fine ruler for the rest of his life. Believe it or not, from these far outposts of civilisation, he journeyed later in life to Rome and onwards to the Holy Land as a pilgrimage. After his death there were some years of fighting and confusion among Hakon's descendants. Eventually his nephew Rognvald (pr. Ronald) grabbed power, and incited the name and memory of his holy uncle in his support. When he came to power, he maintained his connection with the name of Saint Magnus by building the great cathedral. The first stones were laid in the year of 1137. In due course the building was dedicated to Magnus and his bones were removed and reinterred in the cathedral.

Every rock of Orkney is steeped in history. As we sailed out of Kirkwall Bay, not only did the view take us back to those turbulent Viking times. The very rocks and Skerries owed their names to events from the far past. Passing the sites of the old herring curing stations, we soon came to a rock that sticks up right in the way of a direct route from Shapinsay to Kirkwall. It is called Iceland Skerry, a name which owes nothing to that other North Atlantic island, but which perhaps stems from the old Norse word *oyce* for a pond. It seems there was once a pond on the shore nearby.

Further on we passed between Thieves Holm, a rather feature-less little island, and the peninsula of Carness, before heading out across The String to Shapinsay. Carness also stems from old Norse. Perhaps it used to be Kalladar Ness, meaning calling point. It is opposite Shapinsay, so perhaps one called for a boat from there, though those Vikings must have had lungs like bellows to shout over The String. Smaller vessels like the "Mariana" heading towards The String from Kirkwall were able to bear away slightly to star-board, come close to the Carness shore and pass inside Thieves Holm. This little island seems to have nothing remarkable about it. It is low and flat, no more than 250 metres long. There are no dis-tinguishing features, other than the little cairn that so many islets have. As we passed it, a passenger would scarcely have given it a sec-ond glance. But who were the thieves? What were they doing there? As long ago as a charter granted by James III of Scotland in 1486, the islet was described as a place where thieves and malefactors were executed of old. I have heard it said that they were stripped and left naked to die of hunger and exposure, though one Orkney lady castigated me one day for making Orcadians sound like bar-barians. The other theory as to the origin of the name is that it derives from Tiev Holm, or Island of the Gods. This explanation suggests that the Holm was used for trial by combat, and the Gods would decide who was innocent and who guilty. However, we once had a passenger who turned out to be an archaeologist who spe-cialised in the Viking era. His first love, he told me, had been Old Norse and he took a degree in that rather esoteric subject. He then spent many months looking at job adverts seeking the one that said, "Knowledge of French and Old Norse an advantage." Eventually he gave up and became an archaeologist instead. This chap loved the Viking era and had the knack of making it come alive when he talked about it. Through his tales we envisaged young fit, but poor, freemen, challenging wealthy old landowners to a trial over some trumped up charge, and then making their living by defeating them in combat and winning their possessions. This practice was known as "holmganging", or going to a holm which was where the combat took place. However, he told us that Thieves Holm could not have been such a place. It was too far from Carness, and an essential ingredient was to have land close by for the spectators. So there we have it. Was Thieves Holm a place of execution, a court of law or a sports stadium?

## *Svein Asleifsson.*

As I mentioned in the main body of the book, this arch-Viking's name is spelled in two different ways. I tend to opt for the shorter version, but he was also referred to as Svein Asleifarson.

We have all seen pictures of Viking long ships being beached on English shores, the helmeted and fearsome warriors, swords in hand, leaping ashore for a bit of rape and pillage. Our coastal history is full of tales of attacks by these ravening northern hordes. Or we may have in our memories the sight of Kirk Douglas in the film *The Vikings*. Where did these Norsemen come from? Well, we know that their origin is Scandinavia, and we perhaps fondly believe that the long ship had been rowed across the North Sea from Denmark, or had left the far-off fjords of Norway. Perhaps they had; but not all Norsemen lived in the modern-day Scandinavia. By the year 1200 there was such a story to tell about the Vikings of the Northern Isles that the Icelander wrote Svein's treatise. He lived in the 12th. Century, and his exploits were fresh in the memory when they were written down by the unknown author, and there are more about his exploits than about any other. There is a good reason for that. He had done more to write about than any other! Next time you have cause to imagine the Viking long ship rowing up the coastline of the Bristol Channel or into the Scilly Isles, remember that its origin may have been closer to home than you thought. Remember that it may have come from what is now part of the United Kingdom. It may have come from Gairsay!

What a character Svein was. Just reading the index of the *Saga* leaves one breathless at the scope of his activities. One moment he is in Helmsdale on the East Coast burning someone's house. Then, of a sudden, he pops up in the Isle of Man, and later is at the rape and pillage in Wales. Later still he reaches as far as Scilly, and in between whiles he acts as a one-man execution squad, bumping off enemies with the regularity of cookery programs on the TV. Meanwhile, he made and broke alliances, and was in turn friend and enemy of the Earls of Orkney. There is no doubt that he was the most powerful Viking of the islands who was never Earl. Indeed, he was himself more powerful than all but a few of the Earls. This is not the place to write a historical treatise about the man, nor am I equipped to do so, but I would like to pass on to you a couple of the more notable tales of this extraordinary and little-known character.

At one point in his life Asleifsson was at odds with a great number of Orkney's more powerful men, necessitating a peace settlement between them all. Svein heard that Earl Harald was at Svein's home on Gairsay abusing the terms of the agreement, so he chased him there using nothing more than a skiff and even thought of burning him in one of Svein's own houses. He did capture some of Harald's men, but it transpired that Harald wasn't there. He had gone hunting for hares on an island called Hellis Isle, the location of which is now lost, and, releasing the men he had captured, Svein went after him. Unfortunately, Harald's men made their way directly to Harald and told him what had happened, so Harald launched his boat with a much superior force and set off in pursuit of Svein. Suddenly Svein was fleeing instead of chasing. He had to think quickly because Harald's boat was catching up. On the island were steep cliffs and a cave, which rose upwards inside into a large chamber. The tide was rising, so Svein and his men rowed into the cave and ensconced themselves safely in the cavern, while the tide rose and covered the entrance. Harald's men searched the island on foot - no sign. They rowed around the island - no sign. Eventually they gave up and rowed away, thinking that the other boat must have sneaked off somewhere when they hadn't been looking. Still hidden in the cave, Svein could actually hear the conversation of the Earl and his men as they pulled away from the island. He left his boat in the cave and took a cargo vessel belonging to some monks and sailed away to Sanday, thereby concluding his escape. After more contretemps, including another chase, this time near Stroma in the Pentland Firth, the two of them were at last reconciled.

Where is Hellis Isle? Historians of the era disagree. Indeed, at times the heat generated by the disagreement has bordered on that generated by the row between Harald and Asleifsson themselves! There are two candidates. One is Eynhallow, which is close to Gairsay, and the other is the Muckle Green Holm, over close to Eday. I have seen no cliffs on Eynhallow, let alone caves, so I don't know how it became a candidate. On the other hand, the Muckle Green Holm does have cliffs and caves, and it is on the way to Sanday, so I have always assumed that it was there that this extraordinary episode took place. Our route to Eday would often pass close along these cliffs.

Svein's lifestyle was of such note that even that far off author considered it to be worthy of a chapter in the Saga. In the spring his men planted the seed for the year's crops. Svein himself supervised the work. Then, when it was over, he set out on what he called his 'spring trip'. This consisted of plundering, probably in the Hebrides and Ireland. Just after mid-summer he would return to Gairsay where he would busy himself with gathering in the grain and crops. Then off he would set again, this time on his 'autumn trip'. He would be away then until winter had set in, ploughing through winter seas in his open long ship. At last he would row in through Eynhallow Sound and see Gairsay ahead and would retire to the Long Hall with his men. Some eighty of them would spend the worst months of weather carousing there and living off the products of their raids. Come the spring and the rotation would start all over again.

Eventually, Harald, who was now Svein's friend, suggested that he should give up this rumbustious lifestyle. In essence, what he said was that those who lived by the sword would die by the sword. Svein replied to the effect that Harald was not exactly the most peaceable of men either, but he did think he was getting rather old for all that rape and pillage, so he would take Harald's advice. He would just go on one last Viking trip that autumn and would make it a grand affair so that he could go out with a bang, as it were.

Off he set with no less than seven long ships and took Harald's son along to boot. The Hebrides proved a disappointment, so he carried on and fell on Dublin to such effect that the town fell to him almost before the Dubliners had realised he was there. A surrender was agreed and Svein appointed his own men to rule the town. They proceeded to extract vast amounts of plunder. That night they retired on board their ships, doubtless freely celebrating the victory. While they slept, the Dubliners got busy. They dug pits inside the gates and here and there around the streets and covered them with brushwood. Armed men then hid in nearby buildings. When Svein and some of his men walked into town the following morning, crowds gathered, apparently innocently, thereby leading the Vikings straight for the pits. In they fell, the gates closed behind them, and everyone who walked into town that morning was killed. So ended the days of a little-known character from the pages of history, but whose life was so extraordinary that it deserves a wider audience.

I hope you have enjoyed the tales of our unusual sojourn in those beautiful islands. I fear that the life I have described here will go the way of that of Svein and Magnus – footnotes from a forgotten past. If so, at least I have endeavoured to keep alive the wonderful character of the people of those islands and have done my best to record an interesting part of the life of myself and the family. Stand by for the next volume. This time it won't be bad weather that affected the vessels. It will be AK47s, bazookas and hordes of malaria-bearing mosquitoes as life takes me and the family into an African civil war.

Printed in Great Britain
by Amazon